Georgetown University Round Table
on Languages and Linguistics 1982

Contemporary Perceptions of Language: Interdisciplinary Dimensions

Heidi Byrnes
Editor

Georgetown University Press, Washington, D.C. 20057

BIBLIOGRAPHIC NOTICE

Since this series has been variously and confusingly cited as: *Georgetown University Monographic Series on Languages and Linguistics, Monograph Series on Languages and Linguistics, Reports of the Annual Round Table Meetings on Linguistics and Language Study*, etc., beginning with the 1973 volume, the title of the series was changed.

The new title of the series includes the year of a Round Table and omits both the monograph number and the meeting number, thus: *Georgetown University Round Table on Languages and Linguistics 1982*, with the regular abbreviation *GURT 1982*. Full bibliographic references should show the form:

Ross, Haj. 1982. Human linguistics. In: *Georgetown University Round Table on Languages and Linguistics 1982*. Edited by Heidi Byrnes. Washington, D.C.: Georgetown University Press. 1-30.

Library of Congress Catalog Number: 58-31607
ISBN 0-87840-117-2
ISSN 0196-7207

CONTENTS

WELCOMING REMARKS

James E. Alatis
Dean, School of Languages and Linguistics
Georgetown University

Good evening, ladies and gentlemen. It gives me a great pleasure indeed to welcome you on behalf of Georgetown University and its School of Languages and Linguistics to the *Georgetown University Round Table on Languages and Linguistics 1982*. This is the thirty-third of these annual meetings, a not unimpressive series.

The Chairman of this year's conference is Dr. Heidi Byrnes, who has chosen as the theme of *GURT 82:* 'Contemporary perceptions of language: Interdisciplinary dimensions' The program she has prepared is impressive, and the superb organization of all the conference details is her work and that of her able assistant, Joy Kreeft.

This year I find presenting my customary welcome a somewhat bittersweet experience. For in addition to the deep pleasure of welcoming you, I must also inform you that Mr. Eugène Ionesco, who was to have graced the program, has been prevented by a high fever, flu, and a severe attack of bronchitis from addressing you. Given his advanced age and the severity of his illness, his doctors have forbidden him to fly here from France. However disappointed you might be, I am sure you will accept this last moment cancellation sympathetically, and will, I hope, be gladdened to learn that Professor Haj Ross of the Massachusetts Institute of Technology has generously accepted the task of addressing us this evening in place of Mr. Ionesco.

In reading the program I was pleased to note that once again the preconference sessions present as wide and as interesting a range of topics as the conference itself. This is a tribute to the energy and enthusiasm of Dr. Byrnes as well as an indication of the widespread interest that the programs of *Georgetown University Round Tables on Languages and Linguistics* generate.

I was especially pleased to note today's preconference session
on testing oral proficiency because it marks a continuation of
the joint efforts of Georgetown University and of the Inter-
Agency Roundtable, a sign of further cooperation between
government and the academic community. For testing oral
proficiency is an activity which is a common interest of pro-
fessionals engaged in language teaching, whether they are
teaching foreign languages, English as a second language,
English as a standard language, or are engaged in various
bilingual programs. Moreover, the establishment of oral proficiency achievement goals was one of the recommendations of
the President's Commission on Foreign Language and International Studies.

With reference to the President's Commission, it may interest
you to learn that just today the National Council for Foreign
Language and International Studies, a group which was established as a consequence of some of the recommendations of the
President's Commission, sponsored in conjunction with the
Georgetown University Center for Strategic and International
Studies a one-day conference on the development and utiliza-
tion of international skills. This conference brought together
a small group of the country's leading academic specialists and
experienced senior federal officials with foreign policy responsi-
bilities in order to explore ways in which the international resources and skills of our universities can be more effectively
and systematically coordinated with the research needs of the
federal government.

Most of you will already have noted, I am sure, the pleasant
coincidence that the *Georgetown University Round Table on
Languages and Linguistics 1982* occurs this year during National
Foreign Language Week. President Reagan has even issued a
proclamation for National Foreign Language Week wherein he
extols our profession, repeats his commitment to this type of
scholarship, and wishes us all, both teachers and students,
success in the coming year.

Today it is important to know that the community of foreign
language teachers is united and is developing coalitions engaged in political and public awareness activities which will
eventually insure that the President's Commission report will
be implemented and not remain a document collecting dust on
a shelf.

For your encouragement, let me mention one more item. You
may not know that the Joint National Committee for Languages
(JNCL) meets here tomorrow and Saturday. This coalition of
twenty-one of the most prominent language associations in this
country is another instance of a lobby which works to make
the public aware, forms networks, and promotes legislation
and legislative activities to see to it that all the things that
you and I believe in get the kinds of support that we know
they deserve.

Again, thank you one and all for the honor and pleasure of your presence. Now let us turn our attention to contemporary perceptions of language and its interdisciplinary dimensions.

INTRODUCTION

Professional gatherings characteristically have as their objective the in-depth exploration of a clearly (and that usually means narrowly) defined topic of current interest in their respective fields. However, that does not exclude a concurrent, seemingly contradictory additional goal. Aside from providing a forum for presenting new, highly specific materials, they offer a meeting place where researchers, typically drawn into the limiting focus of specialization, can allow themselves to be opened up to other perspectives which lead to different tie-ins, support networks, and justifications and thus, ultimately, a deeper meaning for their limited endeavors.

Over the past 32 years of its existence, the Georgetown University Round Table on Languages and Linguistics, no matter what its topic, has always sought such fruitful expansion of each participant's professional base of operation by bringing together scholars from numerous disciplines. In that respect the theme for the 33rd annual Georgetown University Round Table gathering, 'Contemporary Perception of Language: Interdisciplinary Dimensions', only gives official recognition to what, for this series, has implicitly been a preferred mode of conducting the investigation of language.

While an interdisciplinary orientation for language study is thus certainly not original, upgrading that aspect to be the focal point of an entire gathering is not without special difficulties. Even in its planning stages it invites the potential danger of diffuseness and vagueness, perhaps even inconclusiveness, particularly when one considers the very real limitations of time. It must be expected from the outset that the formal plenary session papers and the more intimate interest sessions can at best address the matter at hand in a very modest fashion.

Such deliberations notwithstanding, in the end what won out was the conviction that spotlighting interdisciplinarity could also spotlight what I see to be the latent challenge and, fortunately, the distinct opportunity, in our field today, namely, the call to a humanistic study of language.

Given the premise that interdisciplinarity is the most likely methodological orientation under which a humanistic study of language can flourish, it is important to try to narrow down its meaning and point out its timeliness. To some extent the term 'interdisciplinary' itself is not ideal since it might bring to mind clearly delimited areas of inquiry for the various language-related disciplines between which some sort of interaction is advocated. By contrast, it is precisely the realization of the historical arbitrariness of a discipline's subject matter--the realization of fuzzy edges, as it were--that is causing us to take a critical look at our scientific premises and, by extension, our scientific conclusions. In the most immediate past this point has been exemplified strikingly by the natural sciences, where biology, chemistry, and physics often converge on the same phenomenon.

Fortunately for linguists, one logical correlate of the arbitrary nature of disciplinary lines, the concept that it is the direction of inquiry which creates the subject matter of the scientific investigation, accompanied the very beginning of our discipline as a respectable scientific endeavor. And, in fact, many individual scholars before and among us have established and investigated the nature of the many ties between language and our total reality irrespective of disciplinary compartmentalization. Their work, along with other events, has led us to the fortuitous current state of our field as a whole which favors a humanistic approach to language on a broad scale. Be it cause or effect, the safe structure and comfortable orderliness--but also the sometimes self-righteous belligerence--of a dominant school no longer seem to be with us, neither in syntactic nor semantic theory, nor in philology, neither in applied linguistic research nor in literary criticism, neither in the actuality of the foreign language classroom nor in the writings of contemporary poets, novelists, and playwrights.

To avoid misunderstanding, allowing our intellectual vision to be widened beyond its previous setting is not tantamount to advocacy of grand pronouncements arrived at without substantiation by detailed practical analysis. There continues to be no substitute for detailed empirical work and I am fully satisfied that the papers in this volume bear this out. But I believe they also show that we are ready to approach empirical work with more fertile questions which, under the stringent application of careful methodology, can provide us with more fertile answers.

If such questioning, such looking beyond a limited and thus limiting well-defined conceptual grid entails uncertainty, perhaps tensions, it also offers the possibility of being more creative, more real, more whole, and more human in the pursuit of our work, allowing us to celebrate the broad spectrum of human experience as it becomes available in language.

It is this humanistic concern, traditionally the province of great literature, that, it seems to me, should and can be

captured in current work in linguistics without the dreaded
loss of scientific rigor and identity. Whether that will eventually result in a redefinition of what the term 'linguistics' entails
remains to be seen.

As in previous years, this volume comprises the papers
offered during the plenary sessions of the conference in the
order of their presentation, with brief comments on each included in this introduction. Most unfortunately, two of the
invited speakers, Eugène Ionesco and Dell Hymes, were taken
ill at the last minute and were unable to attend. Their contributions were to have added the crucial perspective of the
deeply humanistic man of letters and the long-time strong commitment to interdisciplinary work of one of the foremost linguists
of our time.

The scope of the conference was significantly enlarged by the
numerous interest sessions which preceded it. It is here that
the 'Round Table' aspect of free exchange of ideas among participants is perhaps best preserved. The following is a list of
the Interest Session titles and the names of those responsible
for their organization.

(1) Curricular and Instructional Practice in U.S. Government
    Language Schools. Peter A. Eddy, CIA Language School.

(2) Testing Language Proficiency. James Child, Department
    of Defense.

(3) Acquisition of the Phonological System in Foreign Lan-
    guage Teaching. Cornelia Meder-Lenski, Washington, D.C.

(4) Cultural Factors, Subjective Meanings in International
    Communication. Sven Groennings, U.S. Department of
    Education.

(5) Trends in Portuguese Linguistics: An Interdisciplinary
    View. Clea Rameh, Georgetown University.

(6) Methods for Assessment of Speech and Language Function-
    ing in Head Injured Patients. Christy L. Ludlow,
    National Institutes of Health.

(7) Literary Criticism and Modern Linguistic Theory: Their
    Need for Autonomy and Interdependence. Kurt R.
    Jankowsky, Georgetown University.

(8) The Aesthetics of Conversation. Deborah Tannen,
    Georgetown University.

(9) Linguistics and Psychotherapy. Daniel P. Dato, George-
    town University.

(10) Analysis of Spoken Discourse: Second Language Research and Teaching Practice. Ulla Connor, Georgetown University.

(11) Cultural Factors that Influence How Writing Is Learned. Candace Miyamura, National Institute of Education.

(12) Lexical Reflections of Views of Linguistic Action. Jef Verschueren, University of Antwerp.

(13) Association to Cure Monolingualism. Joshua Fishman, Yeshiva University and Dorothy Goodman, Washington International School.

(14) Interpretation and Nonverbal Communication. Margareta Bowen, Georgetown University and Hildegund Bühler, University of Vienna.

Separate publication of the proceedings of some of these sessions is currently being planned (Kurt R. Jankowsky: Literary Criticism and Modern Linguistic Theory). Definite arrangements have already been made for the session on Interpretation and Nonverbal Communication which will be published through the National Resource Center for Translation and Interpretation in its outreach series.

Opening session. In the opening session, Ross speaks to the theme of the conference by advocating a 'human linguistics' which, more than to a body of knowledge or a methodology, refers to an attitude toward the data we encounter. This data is not language material in the narrow sense but comprises all aspects of human communication. More importantly, the questions to be directed at this human communication are not only about its formal principles, those necessary and sufficient to describe its elements, their distribution, and relationships among each other; they are also questions whose answers will tell us something about ourselves as human beings through language.

Ross relates his personal progression from rigorous, precise, and, in their own way, satisfying and beautiful formulations inspired by generative grammatical theory to a considerably more tenuous investigation of poetry, an investigation which has come to grips with the fact that language remains intractable and still elusive. On a different level, this theoretical progression has its parallel development in the growth of the investigator who now must be ready to admit answers still incomplete. Even so, such an investigator, from all available information which truly engenders human understanding, finds himself most certainly closer to the truth.

The social context. Irvine's paper examines the communication of affect and explores the extent to which cultural and linguistic systems enter into it. It does so by first addressing the analytical issue of the display of emotion in general, by subsequently comparing it cross-culturally, and finally analyzing some instances of communication of affect in the particular case of the Wolof, a tribe in Senegal. She finds the previous dichotomy of 'cognitive' and 'expressive' functions of language to be misleading in that it confuses form with function and an individual level of analysis with a social one. Instead she proposes a distinction of referential, affective, and social as three functional dimensions of language which interact in various ways. This would take into account the fact that social roles, identities, and situations contribute to the expectations about display of affect. Only against the background of these social categories can valid judgments be made about an individual instance of communication of affect.

The necessity for positing parameters of social structuring is also the backdrop for Cicourel's study of a female patient's response to the bureaucratic setting exemplified in the doctor-patient relationship. In order to be able to produce appropriate speech acts of their own, members of a group or society must possess an elaborate understanding of the rights and entitlements they can expect in a specific social setting. In addition, however, these information-based schemata must be refined by the inclusion of schematized knowledge which is based on beliefs, which in turn are driven by feelings and emotions. On the one hand, the patient in Cicourel's study acts in accordance with the Gricean notion of the cooperative principle, whereby the patient accepts and follows the tacitly agreed upon aims of the conversation, implying belief of these notions. On the other hand, the strength and persistence of her own belief system totally contradict these propositional meanings. Decision-making processes like those required in all communicative situations are thus not simply based on the facts of the case but will vary depending on the interpretation of these facts by the participants against certain metapropositions, that is, their framing of the problem in one or the other fashion.

Social constraints in the broadest sense, interwoven with individual perceptions of facts, were also the focus of Szalay's paper. But this time cross-cultural implications of the issue were examined. To unlock the elusive domain of subjective culture--a system of perceptual-semantic representations as developed by a group of people sharing similar experiences and background--a methodology of free verbal association to selected stimulus themes by sample groups is employed. Various response analysis techniques lead to a determination of the most salient meaning components and meaning clusters which a given group associates with the stimulus concept. This information can be condensed pictorially in a 'semantograph' or summarized in a measurement of psychocultural similarity or distance between

subgroups within a culture or between entire cultures. Such
measurement promises to be of very practical importance in all
instances of cross-cultural communication where, very often,
what is considered common sense by one group is of no particular relevance to the other, an attitude which leads to deep
impasses precisely since neither side is aware of these hidden
yet pervasive frames of reference.

   The artistic context. Since the incisive work of the Prague
School it has been the received understanding that the essential quality of verbal art, the poetic function of language, is
its self-reflexivity. Relying in large part on Peirce's rich insights concerning semeiotic systems, Shapiro argues for an
alteration of this predominantly autotelic conception. While the
Jakobsonian tradition relies nearly exclusively on parallelism,
patterned juxtapositions, and recurrences for its understanding
of verbal art and thus characterizes a poem as a verbal icon,
the significant degree of asymmetry between encoder and decoder in poetic discourse seems to call for a different assessment. In a progression from ordinary language toward ever
more artistic usage, it is the dynamic, teleological, and essentially symbolic function which, within the hierarchy of semeiotic
functions, gains more and more prominence over the referential
and self-reflexive aspects inherent in the sign relationship.
This finally leads to the necessity for hermeneutic intervention,
for interpretation. Symbolic relationships as a whole show
directionality, as can be seen in the development of poetic
canons throughout the history of literature. Within literary
tradition, style, 'a trope of meaning', establishes a hierarchy
of interpretants, a framework within which an attempt can be
made to match the interpretation of the decoder with the
intentionality of the encoder.
   In a rather different vein the matter of stylistics is also
addressed in Levin's study, here with a focus on the specific
devices known in the handbooks of rhetoric as figures of
thought and figures of speech. Employing the conceptual
apparatus of speech act theory, figures of thought can be
categorized as acts of speech incorporating a devious intent
which may be a function of either the illocutionary force of
the utterance, its propositional content, or some interplay between the two. This allows a distinction between 'masqueraders'
(among them the rhetorical question, antiphrasis, and irony),
where the speech act belies its purpose, and 'masks' (among
them apostrophe, personification, and suggestion), where a
propositional element belies its character. With both categories
the operative plane is the utterance's pragmatic aspect, the
performance of the speech act, and not its semantic aspect, the
expression itself. It is the relationship between the expression
and its context of use which makes for the deviousness and misdirection so characteristic of these devices.

The special qualities that make for art, be it in language usage or elsewhere, constitute what we refer to as its esthetic value. By pointing to the hierarchy of constraints under which we operate, Becker exposes the cultural presuppositions underlying our frames of reference which inform our judgments on esthetic value. But he also points to the individual voice of the artist, whose work arises from the intense emotion which accompanies the integration of a live being and its context, and establishes an equilibrium with his surroundings. It is this complex interaction which, for Becker, is at the heart of esthetics. He illustrates his observations with a passage by Emerson which exemplifies various levels of integration, such as integration between meaning and referring, or integration between syntactic shaping and referring. The extent of the integration of a sentence becomes eminently clear during an attempt to translate it into another language, here Javanese. Is it possible at all to understand esthetic values across languages and cultures? Clearly, translation is merely the beginning point and, of itself, a totally incomplete source for understanding another language. Only when it is followed by an attempt to understand the sentence in a situation where all its relations to context are alive can one recreate the form of life from which it arose. This act of retracing across language and cultures can thus become an esthetic experience very special to the philologist.

To capture the essence of artistic language, literature has traditionally resorted to different rubrics--fiction vs. nonfiction, truth vs. falsehood, literary vs. nonliterary--or to diverse genre distinctions. In her paper Pratt argues for an analysis using, instead, more generalized strategies of representation which cut across these established lines and deal simultaneously with esthetic, social, and ideological dimensions of discourse. Interaction between them is particularly conspicuous in travel accounts, with their frequent landscape descriptions. Beyond the estheticization of the landscape conventionally practiced throughout literature, a particular social and even ideological meaning is being articulated. Depending on the historical, social, and ideological background of the writer-observer, we find expressions of a relation of dominance, of complete interpretative authority even in an alien environment, of the landscape being in need of outside civilized intervention, of its lack of history and perceived deviance from established norms. Such claims are particularly prevalent in Western literary descriptions of non-Western landscapes from which Pratt draws a number of her examples. Since ideological stance deeply affects the method of representation, an altogether more powerful stylistics could result if not only esthetic and social dimensions but also ideological dimensions were applied to the discussion of literary discourse.

The personal context. The theory of transformational grammar and the subsequent questioning of some of its central assumptions provide a broad forum in American linguistics for inquiry into the relationship between language and cognition, a topic of long-standing interest in European language investigation but of somewhat sporadic concern in America. For such an investigation Gipper proposes the framework of Humboldt's conception of language supported by systematic crosslinguistic analysis of the process of language acquisition. His own extensive research with German children up to three years of age is directed at the acquisition of a linguistic view of the world-- the organization of the meanings of words in order to verbalize external and internal phenomena. This is best accomplished in a global description he terms 'evolutive grammar', which specifically considers neurophysiological processes alongside the customary phonetic, morphological, lexical, and syntactic parameters. It assumes the existence, a priori, of certain faculties; but their functioning form emerges only in the postnatal phase, which is marked by extraordinary brain growth and interaction with the outside world. Since, in the strict sense, we cannot think these innate concepts, categories and ideas outside of language, language itself has to be considered as another fundamental precondition for human knowledge and cognition, leading Gipper to propose the concept of a language apriori.

The relationship of language and cognition is the focus also of Ludlow's research which, through the study of aphasia due to penetrating head injuries sustained by Vietnam war veterans, hopes to gain insights into different dimensions of language functioning. Aided by CT scans it is now possible to compare behavior along the three dimensions of language modality, linguistic system, and the requisite information processing demands, and furthermore to investigate the degree of their interdependence, all in relation to their location in the brain. This allows differentiated observation on right and left hemisphere functioning, resulting in the preliminary finding that one may have to posit significant bilateral brain involvement and assume that the control areas containing lexical knowledge are based in the left hemisphere while the other brain regions provide the stimulus input, activation, and arousal functions required for language functioning. This would account for post-injury recovery of those functions which are bilaterally represented and continued generalized language disorder in those cases where highly discrete, low-frequency lexical-semantic knowledge contained only in the left hemisphere is affected by the brain damage.

The tendency to process new phenomena according to a certain existent perceptual grid referred to in a number of papers finds yet another expression in the work undertaken by Lobo and Yoshida. They investigated transfer errors and over-generalization errors in the areas of phonology during the acquisition of English by Japanese students. Specifically, they focused on the stages at which each type of error is most likely to occur, which sounds were involved, their presumed 'difficulty', and the extent to which perceived knowledge of vocabulary tended to influence phonological assessment until the student achieved the desired error-free analysis of foreign sounds strictly on the basis of the foreign language system.

The closing paper of the conference, by Ervin-Tripp, provides insights into the mechanisms involved in children's formulations of requests. Getting attention, clearly expressing one's wishes, gaining the cooperation of the addressee, being persuasive, and remedying failures are all tasks involved in making successful requests. Precisely how they are accomplished is an indicator of the skill a child has developed in mediating between two seemingly opposing demands, that of making his intentions unmistakably clear while at the same time leaving that amount of ambiguity, engaging in that degree of politeness ritual, expressing that level of sensitivity to status or possession rights of the other, and bringing to bear that amount of persuasiveness which will lead to the desired result. The common feature for the elaboration of these strategies is an ever increasing ability on the part of the child to take the perspective of the hearer and to phrase this shifted viewpoint by deliberately being less and less direct.

Conclusion. It is with an enormous debt of gratitude that I look back over the period of preparation for the conference and events themselves of the Georgetown University Round Table on Languages and Linguistics 1982. Too numerous for individual recognition are those who lent advice, offered suggestions, provided encouragement, and proffered very tangible helping hands. But I would like to single out Dean James E. Alatis of the School of Languages and Linguistics, who allowed me the luxury of working for him with much freedom and complete institutional support. I also thank the invited speakers, session leaders, and session participants who gave so generously of their time and knowledge; my family for personal support, and the many fine Georgetown students who cheerfully volunteered whenever help was needed. Last, and clearly not least, I wish to express an enormous gratitude to my assistant, Joy Kreeft, without whose spirited dedication, efficiency, and unlimited enthusiasm the myriad chores would never have been accomplished so smoothly.

Heidi Byrnes

human linguistics

Haj Ross
Massachusetts Institute of Technology

Editor's note. The typographical format requested, designed, and employed by the author to make his personal statement is intended by him to reflect the style of an oral paper. He states that some of his typographical conventions are derived from those developed by David Antin in *Talking at the Boundaries* (New York: New Directions Press, 1976).

it's hard to know how to begin   there's something which i've been wanting to do sometime in the course of this evening with you   and i haven't known exactly at what part of the   proceedings it would be appropriate   and i just realized listening to heidi introduce me   that no time is like the   present
     i want to show you   some of my most recent work   which is not in   any way   to   be viewed as an extension of genera-   tive grammar   however   possibly a way can be found to relate it to the broad and very important concerns which in-   volve us tonight   we need soon   i think   to have a round-   table on the subject of linguistics and juggling

> ¡THE LECTURER JUGGLES!
>
> Some balls stay up in the air!
>
> Some fall!

(Applause)

i will be happy to teach any of you   who would like to learn   during the course of this conference   how to juggle i know a way of teaching that is almost guaranteed to teach   anyone in 20 minutes   and the record time is 4 minutes

you can learn how to do the basic juggle   and it's lots of fun
        one of the important things   i think   at least i've used
    it as sort of a diagnostic in my own work   is if i'm not
having fun in what i'm doing   i think   there must be some-
        thing seriously wrong someplace   and i start to worry
about it (applause)
                i'd like to say thank you very much   to everybody here
    to the particular magical group of people who are here
lots of old friends   a lot of old friends who i haven't yet
had the chance to meet   and will remedy   that defect shortly
    particularly to jim alatis and the faculty here
        georgetown has a reputation in the world of being a
place with an extremely famous sociolinguistics program   but
what i cherish particularly about the many visits i've had
    to this campus   is the sense of space   of air   of freedom
a possibility to talk about stuff which in other areas of the
    world would be *verschwiegen* as we say in german   would
    be 'silenced'   one would not dare to talk   about them   i'm
gonna try and talk to you about something which has been on
        my heart for a long time   and i don't pretend to speak
with any special expertise or knowledge about this   i've been
    thinking about it for a long time   this is one person's
voice   and actually i'm gonna try and be as short   as
        possible because i really would like   insofar as it's
possible with such a large number of people   for us to talk
    to each other about these issues   so i   would like to
thank jim alatis   and especially joy kreeft and heidi byrnes
for this opportunity to start the ball rolling
            when heidi called up and told me the topic of the
roundtable this year   i was knocked out   because it seems
to me that this is a very important topic in any year   but
    maybe now in particular   when there are many many ex-
        tremely severe problems which confront us   the world
seems to be sending us a message   'shape up or goodbye'
    we don't have much time left   i may be wrong   but
there seem to be very grave problems that beset us
        if we could really understand communication   it seems
to me that's a field where we linguists should be involved
and haven't been enough   a real understanding of communi-
    cation would be a heck of a gift to the world
            i was very sad to hear that eugène ionesco was not go-
ing to be here   i have been a real fan of his ever since the
first play of his that i saw   it is a play which   if i ever
    see an amateur production of it anywhere within about 50
miles   i think i will come out of retirement   the last play
        i acted in was as a senior in yale   in the play called
'salad days'   which ran for years and years in london   i   was
a martian in that play
            how many of you know ionesco's play 'the lesson'?   (many
hands are raised)   a lot of people   i guess you know the
role that i would like in it   'the lesson' concerns a professor

of neo-spanish philology who   is sitting in his study one
afternoon   when there's a knock on the door   the housekeeper goes to the door and ushers in a student   the
    professor is very diffuse and vague and sort of out of
it and the student is there to get extra lessons to study
for the total doctorate
        at the beginning of the play these are the only charac-
ters   the housekeeper then leaves and we have an encounter
between the student and the professor   at the beginning
the student is very sure of herself   snippy   bossy
arrogant   and then   possibly the professor's expertise
        and his knowledge of neo-spanish philology   which is
one of the most magnificent send-ups of linguistics that i've
ever seen   maybe only seconded by Pnin   there's a great
    story by nabokov where modern structuralist linguistics
is characterized in painful terms   anyway the power relation-
    ship shifts radically so that the professor at the end is
being domineering   bossy   and the student shrivels together
    and finally   in a fit of rage at the obtuseness of the
student the professor stabs her   and he calls in his
        housekeeper and says   'ah now look what i've done'
the housekeeper says 'professor! another one'   and the professor says 'what will we do?'   and the housekeeper says
    'well   i guess we'll put her in the garden with all the
other ones'   and so   they drag her out   and put her in
        the garden and the play ends as the professor is
sitting at his desk   and there's a knock on the door
        that's the kind of existence which we professors are
really entitled to   if you know of a production of 'the lesson'
someplace within 50 miles of boston let me know okay?
        i want to tell you one other thing   the university of
the air is listed as one of my institutional affiliations   some
of you don't know about this estimable organization   the
    university of the air is a collection   a tightly linked
inter-network of scholars who in   a well-run universe
    would all be on the same campus   taking each other's
courses   talking to each other at lunch   playing ping-pong
  skating   and so on   however   due to the usual cosmic
    confusion   we're all over the continents and also all over
        the centuries   in fact   in the university of the air
however   which is not localized at any geographical point   we
are together on a conceptual campus
        the membership requirements for UA affiliation are
rather easily satisfied   if you think you are a member of the
  UA faculty   congratulations you are

        okay let's talk about human linguistics
        what's in a name?   this term   human linguistics
what is it?   well i think myself that names are pretty important   everything is   in a name   in fact if you're
interested in reading a book which talks about this in   very

interesting terms you might look at james hillman's book (1975)
're-visioning psychology' in which he talks about the
historical accident which led to our present view that names
are completely interchangeable and completely arbitrary
and worth nothing   paul friedrich (1979) also talks about
plain proper names like fritz   frank   fred   jim   james
and he points out   what's the difference between jim and
james?   large difference   large difference   there's a
great cartoon by jules feiffer about this sort of mousey-
looking man who's been called adam and a variety of things
and he says 'really what i want to be called is spike'
there is a historical event   it happened about 300
years ago   i   think connected with the council of trent   a
debate which went one way and as a result of that debate we
now think   names are empty and have no import   i think
in fact that names are extremely important   in particular
take human linguistics   a dreadful name   on the one
hand it has lots of good implications   human   but on the
other hand it sort of suggests that anybody who is not doing
human linguistics is doing--*inhuman* linguistics right?   so
it draws a very nasty line across the domain of linguistics
while i was talking to heidi over the phone i   said   'really
possibly a better name for this endeavor is "[gəíɫə] linguistics" which you can spell with either a ue or an o'
maybe a better term yet is '_____ linguistics'   fill
in the blank   preferably with nothing   because it's very
very hard for a term like '_____ linguistics' to exclude
anybody   but fill it in as you want
and actually human linguistics is not a body of knowledge or a methodology or something like that   i   went to
a conference   a very lovely conference in korea in august
and i   gave a talk on human linguistics there to a lot of
koreans   and afterwards there was general nonplussment
and bafflement and they said 'well what are your results?
what are your methodologies?   what kinds of axioms
derivations and things are there   how does it work?'   it's
not like that   it's sort of   i guess   it's a stance   it's
an attitude   i'm going to try and talk   about   some things
which seem to me to be--the word *counterproductive*
sounds very lousy--i don't like that word--they seem to have
been going against my heart   have been bad for me as
a person or as what i have   seen myself doing   and many
others of my friends who have been in the linguistics
profession   not only linguistics   but in other disciplines
too   because you can not only forget about human in the
definition here   you can also   forget about linguistics
if what i   am saying has any value   it would be true of
psychology and biology and physics also
okay let me talk a little bit about the term human linguistics   *vic yngve* of chicago used the term in a paper
which i didn't realize until i had found or refound the

term myself   he used it in a paper   i   think in 1975   in
the 'functionalism' volume of the chicago linguistic society
      and what he means that term to cover   in a nutshell
      although i urge you   to look at the paper yourselves
and assure yourselves that this is true   he suggests that
      the focus of that enterprise that he wants to address and
feels is not being looked at today   is the scientific study of
      how people communicate   which will of course include
not only words   it will include gesture   gaze   facial
      expressions   body language   and probably a lot of other
things   which we don't know about now   all of those things
can carry lots and lots of information   and can be extremely
      important
            i'll give you an example   there's an experiment that
was done   a woman is in a phone booth and she comes to
accost people in new york saying 'excuse me could you give
      me a dime please? i just lost my last dime in the phone   i
have to   call my son who's 10 at home   he's waiting for me
i'm gonna be a little bit late and i can't call him without a
      dime'   two conditions   one   she only asks for the dime
            the second condition   she also touches the person on
the sleeve   the results are unbelievable   essentially zero
contributions without the touch   and 100% contributions   with
      the touch   touch is a very effective way of communicating
we don't know much about it right?
            well the question that vic asks   and with a great
deal of justification   is 'who's supposed to do this?   who
should study a field like this   the science of communication?'
      i think it's not exaggerating to say that we haven't done it
that we haven't been doing it   we've been pretty parochial
      although less parochial than we might have been in
previous decades   but we haven't really tried to make such
      a large science of communication   so i'm very much in
favor of vic's term   i think what i   want to say goes   even
      a little bit further than that
            george lakoff   in another paper which i didn't know
about until this fall   here at georgetown in 1974   wrote a
paper called 'humanistic linguistics' in which he contrasted
      two kinds of linguistics   i've quoted from page 103 of the
volume that frank dinneen edited for us   he contrasts *nuts
and bolts linguistics* with *human linguistics*   so nuts
and bolts linguistics   george is somewhat irreverent   is
concerned with answering this question

> What formal principles, both language-particular and
> universal, are necessary and sufficient to character-
> ize the distribution of and relationships among lin-
> guistic elements in each of the languages of the
> world?

and many of us   many of you who i know in this room
and me too   have been engaged in questions exactly like
this   how does the passive work in german?   or how can we
account for the acquisition of negation universally in
first and second language acquisition?   and we can spend easily
a lifetime   lots of lifetimes   working on questions
like that   they're very very difficult questions   and
the answers that can be given to them and have been given
are extremely beautiful   compelling   rich marvelous kinds
of questions to study   that's a sort of nuts and
bolts kind of question
the other question which george cites is focal for
humanistic linguistics

what can the study of language tell us about human
beings?

it's a different question

human linguistics is much closer to this latter question
of   george's   as i conceive of it   so one way of thinking
about it may be to think of human linguistics as a verb
'to human linguistick'   or 'to linguistick humanly'   it's
a process   it's not a body of knowledge   it's a kind of
stance towards one's work and towards one's colleagues
i can give a thumbnail sketch of what human linguistics
is   maybe if you think for a minute what the difference is
between knowledge and   wisdom   it seems to me as i   think
about it   that knowledge is concerned with the obtaining
or discovery of things like facts and higher-order facts   patterns of facts   generalizations about them and   on the
highest level   theories about those which would have those
facts as consequences   that's the kind of stuff   which i
think knowledge is about
wisdom however seems to me to be a completely different enterprise   an orthogonal enterprise   it seems to me
to be characterized   and i'm really very happy to hear
about other proposals   i would like to hear how you
would characterize it   this may very well not be right   but
it seems to me to involve trying to find answers to   questions like   who am i?   and lots of people are involved in
finding the answer to questions like this   people who might
be very happy to help us
other people are just stuffed full of encyclopedic
knowledge   incredible people   there are people like this
and we've probably met them in our careers as students
and yet we would hesitate to call   them wise   and they
might not be able to help us much if we're interested in
the other questions

and conversely   there are people who have not even a
third-grade education   they may serve us tea   they may fix
our car   they may drive us to work in the bus or something
like that   and those are wise people   the enterprises
are orthogonal i think
now i have come to realize   and it's sort of a shock
i guess to me   that i've always been interested in the second
enterprise   i'm also hopelessly addicted to language and
to finding out about the german passive and about the acquisition of negation and all   that kind of stuff   hokusai the
great japanese painter was a man who wrote   he   made up
his own name   one of his names means 'an old man who's
crazy about drawing'   i'm a middle-aged man who's
crazy about language   but i   also would like to obtain
wisdom   i would like to get closer to wisdom   than i am
now   if my
if my perception of the world which we're in is correct
there are things that routinely go on in my job   (which
is finding out   making up   theories and looking for facts and
general relations and looking for knowledge about language)
which are opposed   which are antithetic to and get in the
way of acquiring wisdom   i think   so that's what i'm
gonna try and talk to you   about
so basically i guess human linguistics   as i see it is
concerned with looking at the relationship between
knowledge and wisdom as that pertains to the study of language   to ask   are they compatible   are they incompatible
and so on
i must say that i have been helped by many many
people merely people who have said to me 'i don't think
you're crazy haj'   and that helps a great deal   in particular
however   there's one person that i'd like to single out
oh i shouldn't   but i   guess her paper has meant so much to
me over the years and i have a few copies of it here
in case some of you would like it   i've made hundreds of
bootleg copies of it   and given them to students and
colleagues   it's charlotte linde's paper (1971)   it's called
'science and personal transformation'   it was never
published   it's a fantastic paper   in it what charlotte does
is to suggest the following thought experiment   suppose
we were to go and talk to newton or kepler
the present attitude toward newton and kepler is   they
are wonderful scientists   but unfortunately they believed   in
things like alchemy and numerology and their astrology and
they couldn't pull themselves loose from the muck of
their time   so we'll take their science   and the rest we'll
leave
charlotte says   suppose we were able to go back and
bring newton or one of those scientists up to the present
and show them what we're doing in science   she theorizes
that what they would say is   'well you guys sure can

build long bridges and you've got some great pills and fast
   planes   but you've missed the nature of the enterprise   we
      weren't interested in that'   alchemists were not interested
in making gold out of lead   they were interested in *personal*
   gold   they were interested in transmuting personal lead into
      personal gold   they were interested in using science   the
study of the acquisition of knowledge   as a vehicle for trans-
   forming themselves   for transcending themselves   i'm
      not a good historian of science   charlotte may   be wrong
on this claim   but it immediately struck a chord in me   and
   that's what started me thinking

         what are the consequences?   i think there's one basic
stance   if you have to say one thing that is the most important   it seems to me   it has to do with our relationship
      to two things   to our colleagues and to the facts that we
study   to the nature which presents itself to us   and the
      relationship to each is the same   you can call it listen-
ing   if you want   listening with great   great attention and
   alertness and empathy
      george miller said it beautifully (1976)

         in order to understand what another person is saying
         you must assume it is true, and try to imagine what
         it might be true of

now that's completely at variance   not only with what i was
   taught in the little bit of history of science or philosophy
of science which i studied   but also implicitly
      how is science really supposed to work?   there's person
A and person B   and they differ on some issue and there's
   a debate   how does our science   how does our culture
view debate?   here i think we're indebted to the work of
george lakoff and *mark johnson* on metaphoring (1980) on
   helping us to stand back from the conventional metaphors
that are embedded in our language and which we don't see
   we just use them

         there's a metaphor that time is money for instance   just
like you see behind the bank president and on the wall 'time is
   money'   english thinks that time is money   it speaks about
time   an abstract concept   to get a handle on this abstract
   concept it uses words from the financial realm
      so i *spent* six hours   he *budgets* his time wisely   she
invested ten years in the project   that detour *cost* me six
   weeks   it's not *worth* your argument?   we talk about it
      in terms of money
         now   how do we talk about argument?   we talk about
it in terms of war   i *attacked* x's position   x *defended* the
   position   *buttressed* the position   i *shot* x down

english seems to view debate as if it's a war between A and B   lakoff and johnson in their book   which is called 'metaphors we live by'   which i recommend to you   they suggest that   supposing we replace that with a metaphor that argument is a dance   then you   and whoever you're arguing with or debating with   are partners in a collaborative work of art   if you're trying to create something beautiful you have your steps and they have their steps   you're very grateful to them because they're taking their time to be with you to make this thing of beauty together   in fact there are cultural traditions   i don't understand it well   but i believe in tibet   in the tibetan buddhist tradition   the unification   or the seeing of debate as dance   is very much more obvious   in fact their arguments are typologized   like in recent linguistics we talk about the morris halle-type argument against the phoneme   the tibetans would have particular types of argument   and to each type of argument there was a mudra   a positioning of hands   so when you were running a particular kind of argument   you knew part of the job was to assume this particular position which looked like a dance step

there's no necessity for our arguments to be conducted as if they were wars   we don't have to buy into that   i think we have   and i have seen at learned scholarly meetings of the linguistic society of america   i've seen a person who was giving a plenary session   an address to 200 members of the society   get in a debate   who it was   what the debate concerned   doesn't have to interest us now   the speaker was attacked by one of the questioners in the audience   the debate got hotter and hotter   more and more intemperate   and finally it ended in the trading of the most forbidden of all of the seven words which you are not allowed to say on radio or tv between the two   it was beautiful turn-taking   the speaker said '**** you' and the questioner looked shocked and then answered 'well **** you too'   and that was the end of the exchange

there's got to be something the matter because either you can say that the whole thing was just an accident   or you can say there's a root cause   a fundamental cause which we have to work on

i think that what i would like to do is try to live by george miller's words   i would like to try to assume that what i hear is true and that if i can't hear it as true   if it seems to me to be off-the-wall   wrong   crazy   then i'm gonna try and take that as being a statement or information about the clarity of my own ears   i'm gonna try and work on myself to be more open so that i can see the elephant from another side

many of us know the elephant story   the story of the blind researchers and the elephant   there were a number of blind scholars trying to discover the nature of elephants   one

is holding onto the elephant's leg   one is holding onto the
elephant's tusk   another is holding onto the elephant's tail
    and a fourth one is holding onto the elephant's trunk   the
first one says elephants are round and columnar and wrinkled
and they come from below   the second one says they are
    round   but they're not wrinkled   they're sort of firm
    and they come to a tip   they come from above   and
the third one says   well yes they do come from above   but
    they're not hard   they end in a tuft   and the fourth one
says   well they do come from above and they are flexible   and
    they are wrinkled   but they emit hot air
    the reason this is a great story   the sufis didn't make
up silly stories just to get laughs   is   i think   if we
    could open our eyes when we're engaged in a debate
    maybe we could see the elephant which is between us
and chuang tzu   a chinese thinker and sage   said it very
well

disputation is proof of not seeing clearly

another person who said it very well   i'm not a student of
philosophy   this is written on the wall at the museum of
    science in boston   but it's a beautiful quote by aristotle

the search for truth is in one way hard and in
another easy--for it is evident that no one of us
can ever master it fully, nor miss it wholly. Each
one of us adds a little to our knowledge of nature
and from all the facts assembled arises a certain
grandeur.

supposing you believe that to be true   and supposing even
    more so   and this was an example suggested to me also by
charlotte   that we view the enterprise that we're in   the
    collective dance that we're in   we view ourselves as being
nodes in the jewel net of indra   which is a hindu image
    i heard about this from charlotte   but it's in the 'aquarian
conspiracy'   another book by marilyn ferguson which i would
recommend to you

In the heaven of Indra there is said to be a network
of pearls so arranged that if you look at one you see
all the others reflected in it. In the same way, each
object in the world is not merely itself but involves
every other object, and in fact *is* every other object

so if we're all connected   each of us to everyone else   then
if one of us increases in luminescence   in light and under-
    standing   then the whole network will increase
    competing is foolish and especially this kind of horrible
nasty competing   the story which i made into a funny story

for you about the lsa meeting   that is maybe the cream of a
very ghastly crop   and there are lots and lots of people
who suffered a lot because of nastiness   that debate continues   albeit at a lower level   the combat is smaller battles
i think we can all think of probably terrifically nasty
things that we have done   or things that have been done to
us   or we've seen colleagues do to each other   i think it's
time to stop   i want to try and follow what aristotle said
and what chuang tzu said   and what miller said   i want to
try and listen very very attentively to my colleagues
the other thing i think we haven't listened to very much
is our data   the word 'data' is a latin plural of the past
participle of 'dare'   to give   it means 'that which is given'
or 'those things which are given'   interesting who is giving
them to us?   we might encourage ourselves and our students
to ask what does the fact that i'm interested in the
development of the french past participle   or the acquisition of negation   or something like that   what does that tell
me about myself?
i'll tell you how i came to have these disrespectful
thoughts   i've been studying poetry for four years   and
here's the way the enterprise proceeds for me   i find some
poem which   for who knows what reason   comes into my
blood   it just knocks me over   and i want to find out why
because essentially that's magic   a poet can do magic
a poet does something to the words which you and i use in our
everyday interactions   and puts them there and they become
what they call in german an 'ohrwurm'   an ear worm   you
can't get it out of your head   what i do when i find a
poem like that is   i live with it   i look at the poem again
and again and again and again   i memorize it   maybe i say
it to friends   i say it out loud   that helps a lot   and i
do a number of things   but the deal is this   there is absolutely no guarantee that i'm going to learn a single thing
about it   i'll give you a poem which i learned in the fall
from my colleague at MIT irene taylor   i don't know anything
about this poem   in a way it's a famous poem   it's an
anonymous poem written by some 15th century author nobody
knows   it appears anthologized again and again   a stunning
poem

> Western wind, when wilt thou blow,
>   The small rain down can rain?
> Christ, if my love were in my arms
>   and I in my bed again!

marvelous poem   where is it coming from?   where is that power
coming from?   i don't know   what i'm going to do is not impose   and actually i'm going to say something tonight to
you which i haven't said in my talks previously about human
linguistics   i think it's possible for us to avoid being

wielded by our theories   i'm going to talk about that in connection with a couple of poems
    one thing i think we should be is   we should be
philologues   we should love--'philo'--'logos'   the words which
surround us   we should love whatever it is we happen to
    work on   as it is to love 'western wind'   and the same deal
goes for work in more usual kinds of linguistic research--in
phonology   in sociolinguistics   in syntax   you may not
    come up with anything that is   you may work on turkish
participles for 20 years   and not have a single thing worth
saying   i think that's the kind of field we're in   i think
that's what science is too   it's a very dangerous enterprise
    a very risky enterprise

    one other thing which i think is important in this
enterprise   is   not letting ourselves get walled in by any
    kind of wall   that's one of the reasons why i'm very happy
to be here at georgetown   because we should pay attention
    to the connectedness of things   of everything   in par-
ticular how can we really do linguistics?   i don't feel i can do
linguistics without trying to have some notion of what the
    physicists say
    the root of the word *physics* is 'physein'   which means
'to be'   what the physicists were trying to do   the early
physicists in greece   were trying to understand everything
    that is   and what do the physicists say?   i didn't know
this   maybe our kids in school are getting this   i didn't
have this when i grew up   basically my physics was newtonian
until about five years ago   i only knew about einstein in a
    vague way   but if you read books like 'the tao of physics'
by fritjof capra (1977)   or another very good book is 'the
    dancing wu-li masters' by gary zukav (1979)   another
one is by bob toben called   'space-time and beyond' (1975)
what do the visionary physicists have to say?
    they say the universe is one entity   that is   it's an
illusion that you and i   see each other as being separate
independent   this is what the guys who get the most money
  · of all scientists do   they build these huge stellatrons
their best guess is that the universe is one entity   there is
    no real separation between things
    we need to have a lot of flexibility in our thinking
essentially what capra does is compare the views of modern
20th century physics   with the views of buddhist taoist
    and hindu mystics from several thousands of years ago
    here's a quote from   a modern student   a tibetan
lama who comes from europe   but has been studying tibetan
buddhism for a long time   lama govinda (Capra 1977:140)

    The Eastern way of thinking rather consists in a
    circling around the object of contemplation . . .
    a many-sided, i.e. multidimensional impression

formed from the superimposition of single impressions
from different points of view

in the end of the book capra talks about a very far-out
kind of physics   which has been developed by a physicist
named geoffrey chew   it's called 'bootstrap' theory   chew
says (Capra 1977:285)

a physicist who is able to view any number of different partially successful models without favoritism is
automatically a bootstrapper

there has been an implicit assumption in our academic wars
in the idea that we can get someplace by having a war   that
    is   when A and B have a dispute   what we should do
is fight it out   get in the trenches and slug it out   the
    assumption   and i   don't see any reason   to   believe
that it's correct   is that there will emerge from all disputes
    a synthesis   that whatever is good in A's position can be
combined with whatever is   good in B's position by maybe a
third position C   maybe A is better than B   and without
    modification can include B   or conversely   or maybe a
third position
    but how about a radical pernicious eternal inconsistency?
what tells us in advance that the world has been   so made
that the insights into   the nature of whatever we're studying
    for example language   can be translated from one theory
into another?   that there is something which will unify
these insights?   this belief tells us that we don't need both
ways
    like two sets of goggles for viewing the world   when
we put on A goggles we'll see beauties and insights in one way
    and when we put on B goggles   we'll see other ones   and
we need both sets of insights   there is no way   no single
consistent way of having them both   i think it's certainly
    true we wouldn't like it   the physicists didn't like it when
exactly that happened to them about a hundred years ago
    with the wave and particle phenomena in light   briefly
i won't tell you a lot about it because i'm a terrible physics
informant   but there are a lot of physical experiments which
    are only compatible with the view that light is a wave
there are a lot of *other* experiments which are only compatible
with the view that light is a particle   but in copenhagen
    sometime around 1930   there was a big conclave of all the
physicists and as i understand it   quantum mechanics was
    born   if you ask a physicist 'is light really a particle or is
    it a wave?' she or he will say 'that question has no meaning
we can tell you a theory   a formal theory   quantum mechanics
which will give us the kind of results we have   it does not
    allow us a view of reality   there is no way to see what
quantum mechanics says   it doesn't allow us to see things as

being a wave or a particle'   the physicists in a sense have
       solved this dilemma which beset them   on the one hand
    they had lots of things which said that light is a wave
they haven't resolved the debate   they have a formal theory
which does not allow any visualizable picture of 'reality' which
    will do the work for them   it won't allow the insights to
be captured
           how something like that might happen to us   when we
can't even find a formal theory   where all we can say is
    yes you must learn   for instance maybe you've got to learn
relational grammar   you've got to be able to speak the idiom
    of relational grammar   to be able to put on relational
grammar goggles   and then you will see very important
    things   also you're going to have to learn the idiom   the
theoretical language of chomsky's revised extended standard
    theory   so that you can see other things which are invisible
with relational grammar goggles   also you're gonna have to
       learn montague semantics   because there are things which
are available   which are visible under that perspective   which
are denied otherwise   maybe what we have to be is sort of
    multilingual   if we treat linguistic theories as languages
as has been done in a brilliant dissertation at the university
    of michigan by anneliese kramer (1980) who teaches at
the university of british columbia   whose thinking has
    greatly shaped mine   it might very well be that that's the
kind of world we're in

           one of the things which has been conspicuously absent in
much of science is the study of consciousness   but the visionary physicists say the universe is an idea   james jeans   who
    is a great astronomer   says   and this is indirectly quoted
in marilyn ferguson's book   she writes (kramer 1980:182)

       Astronomer James Jeans said that the universe is
       more like a great thought than a great machine, and
       astronomer Arthur Eddington said, 'The stuff of the
       universe is mind-stuff.'

i won't try to explain to you now what the implicate order is
    it is explained in 'wholeness and implicate order' by the
       physicist *david bohm*   it's magnificent and i think it's
important for us to have at least some understanding of it   i
       don't have much myself   but some   i've got more than i
did have
           what do the sages say?   if you look   i'm terribly
illiterate in this   but as far as i understand   people who
    started the great religions of the world in whatever faith
       they said we speak the world   basically we speak the world
into being
           in the beginning was 'logos'   that's the way the bible
starts   that's a statement which is very close to our culture

in connection with this power of language to create
a world   i'd like to read a poem to you   which is a
magnificent poem which i learned while i was in holland a
    couple of years ago   ida gerhard (1979:10)   a woman
who is still alive   i believe   wrote it

Biografisch I	Biographical I
De taal slaapt in een syllabe en zoekt moedergrond om to aarden.	(The) language sleeps in a syllable and seeks mothergound in-order to earth [=take root].
Vijf jaren is oud genoeg. Toen mijn vader, die ik het vroeg,	Five years is old enough When my father, who I it asked [asked about it],
mij zeide: 'dat is een grondel', --en ik zag hem, zwart in de sloot--	me said [=said to me]: 'That is a grondel', [Archaic] [a small fish with dark patches--a rare word, not known to everyone]
legde hij het woord in mij te vondeling, open en bloot.	--and I saw him, black in the ditch--
Waarvoor ik moest zorgen, met mijn leven moest borgen:	laid he the word in me to foundling [=he laid the word as a foundling at my doorstep]
totaan mijn dood.	open and naked [=vulnerable].
	For which I had-to care, with my life had-to stand-bond:
	Up-to my death.

now let's look   at the poem from the beginning

| De taal slaapt in een syllabe en zoekt moedergrond om to aarden. | (The) language sleeps in a syllable and seeks motherground in order to earth |

there's something you have to know about dutch   what has
happened there is *moedergrond* is strange in dutch   i under-
    stand   as 'mother ground' would be to our ears   'mother
earth' is what they hear   *moeder aarde* is what they have in
dutch as we have it   as if 'ground' has come between 'mother'
    and 'earth'   this is a message which we will see happen
many times in this poem   it's sort of a similar pattern

i'll read the poem in this halting way now   and then go back over it later

mij zeide: 'dat is een
  grondel,'
--en ik zag hem, zwart in
  de sloot--

he said to me: 'That is a
  grondel,'
--and I <u>saw</u> him, black in the
  ditch--

what you have to know about *zeide* is that it is an old and
  archaic past tense of the verb 'to say'   *zeggen*   it's sort of
    biblical   so it's something like 'quoth' in the bible   it's
as if the father were one of the original namers   a *grondel*
is a small fresh-water fish   by the way   this information
  which i'm telling you   essentially no speaker of dutch
knows   that is the word *grondel* is a very very rare word
    dutch speakers don't know what it means   it's like
maybe   the difference between beeches and elms   which
hillary putnam talks about   we know that they're both trees
  but what's the difference between a beech and an elm?   we
know   probably somebody who knows   somebody who could
really tell us   or we could find a book that could tell us
  but we don't know   similarly maybe in dutch people might
know that *grondel* is some kind of fish   and they might not
    even know that   they know however   morphologically
that a grondel contains *grond* and a suffix   he said *dat is een
grondel*   so what's happening is a 5-year-old girl   ida
    gerhardt   is on a walk   with her father and she sees
swimming   in a ditch something for which there are no words
she says 'what's that?'   and her father 'quoth' or 'spake'
  dat is een grondel   and what happens?

--en ik zag hem, zwart in de
  sloot--

--and I <u>saw</u> him, black in the
  ditch--

so when my father said that

and i   saw him   black in the
  ditch

legde hij het woord in mij te
  vondeling,
open en bloot

he laid the word in me to
  foundling
open and naked

so he laid the word as an orphan on my doorstep *open en
bloot* 'open and naked'   which means   it's an idiom in dutch
  'vulnerable'   so he laid the word at my doorstep as a
foundling

Waarvoor ik moest zorgen
met mijn leven moest borgen:

For which I had to care,
with my life had to stand bond:

with my life had to stand bond for it   to guarantee it

totaan mijn dood   until my death

   what's this poem talking about?   it's talking about the
birth of a poetess   this is how she became a poet   in a way
   what happens in the content of the poem is   there are
two things that the father did   the father said something
and he gave her a responsibility   *toen mijn vader mij zeide*
 when my father said to me   *dat is een grondel*   he laid
this burden on me   what happens?   syntactically   it's very
interesting   because that's the middle of a subordinate clause
 the subordinate clause in dutch starts with the word *toen*
which means 'when'   so in the middle of a subordinate clause
which has a word order in dutch such that the verb comes at
the end of the subordinate clause   what do we find?
 en ik <u>zag</u> hem   'and I <u>saw</u> him'   the verb is in second
position   the position of   the verb in a main clause   we find
a subordinate clause ending with a main clause right in the
 middle   he said   my father said something   he gave me
this responsibility   in the middle was perception   this
word was the key   before there had been nothing in the
ditch   before there had been water rippling   and he gave me
 the word for this   and in his giving me that word
entrusting that word to me   he made me a poet   i'm a
poetess
   now i'd like to say just a little bit about the structure
of the poem   the poem is about birth   in a way   it's about
splitting open   about letting the seed out   look at the first
 three words   *de taal slaapt*   't'   long 'a'   'l'   *slaapt*
language sleeps   the word   *slaapt*   contains the letters of
taal 'language' in it   the relationship phonologically between
 slaapt and *taal* is that *taal* is inside *slaapt*   and a lot of it
is in *syllabe* too   's'   'l'   'a'   so it's as if language is a
seed inside this syllable
   which syllable?   the syllable at the end of *grond* --
grondel   that little syllable is the one which made her a poet
adding that syllable onto the end of *grond*   to make a new
 word   a special word   the correct word   the right name
for that blackness in the ditch   that was a special moment
  for her
   what's the structure of the poem?   i'd like to say that
these lines have a structure of 3 lines at the beginning   3
lines at the end   and 5 lines in the middle   two things
 argue for this 'sectioning' of the poem   first notice that
those 3 lines beginning and closing have the same formal
 structure   the first 2 lines of the poem constitute a
sentence with a conjoined verb phrase   and then there's a
 one-line sentence as line 3   similarly lines 9 and 10 constitute a sentence with a coordinate verb phrase   they end with
a colon   and then we find a phrase ending with a period

there's a certain   formal similarity between lines 1-3 and
   lines 9-11   we notice also if we look   at the quality of the
      rhymes   whether the rhyme words are masculines (i.e.
end in a stressed syllable) or feminines   we notice that each
of those 3-line segments   starts with a pair of feminine lines
      namely *syllabe* and *aarden*   that's the first pair followed
   by the masculine *genoeg*   and the last two from the end
      are *zorgen* and *borgen*   the poem ending with a mascu-
line   *dood*
         what happens in the middle?   there's that   long sen-
tence which starts with the subordinate 'when'-clause   in the
middle of which is a main clause   which is a symbol for
   her being born   so from line 4 to line 8   *open en bloot*
look how the rhyme schemes go   how the words are masculine
or feminine   ₄*vroeg* masculine   and the next one is feminine
   ₅*grondel*   the middle one ₆*sloot* is masculine   and the
next one ₇*vondeling* feminine   and the last one ₈*bloot* is
masculine: so we end up with an alternating pattern   masculine   feminine   masculine   feminine   masculine   just
as we have 3 lines at the beginning   3 lines at the end
embracing this event of birth in the middle   we have 2
      masculines   in four lines of the 5-line segment around
the middle focal, masculine   *en ik zag hem, zwart in de sloot*
         note also that the last masculine line of the first triad
₃*genoeg* rhymes with the first line of the long 5-line central
sentence   the last line of this long sentence ₈*bloot* rhymes
      with the last masculine line   of the final triad *dood*   so
the outer triads are tied to the central sentence in a parallel
fashion
         another thing which balances the middle off against the
outer triads is the number of finite verbs   there are 5 verbs
   in the 6 lines in the outside (*slaapt, zoekt, is; moest, moest*)
and 5 verbs in the 5 lines in the middle (*is, vroeg, is, zag,*
   legde) which also sets off the periphery against the
   center

line 1	*syllabe*	1
line 2	*moedergrond, aarden*	2
line 3	*jaren, genoeg*	2
line 4	*vader*	1
line 5	*zeide, grondel*	2
line 6		0
line 7	*legde, vandeling*	2
line 8	*open*	1
line 9	*waarvoor, zorgen*	2
line 10	*leven, borgen*	2
line 11	*totaan*	1

here we see a mirror asymmetry   the first and last line
have one poly-syllabic word   the next 2 lines have two apiece
then one and then two   and the crucial middle line has   none
   here's a formal structure which points to the moment of
birth of the poetess
   let me recapitulate a bit   i see this poem as being
concerned with being born   with coming into the world   with
the splitting open of the seedhusk   so that the young shoot
   within   can start its growth toward the sun

   one way of making a poem *be* a birth   for us readers
is to   fill it with many instances of one structure being
interrupted by another   which 'grows' out of its middle   we
   have already seen how this is the case with the central line
line 6   a main clause--set off by dashes--interrupting a subordinate clause   and also how the longest central sentence
in lines 4 through 8   is sandwiched between an opening and
   a closing triad of lines

   and in harmony with these interruptions on the level of
syntax   we saw that the phonemes in *taal* 'gave birth to' the
next word *s-laa-p-t*   which in turn provided the germ   for
   the next word with a long *a*   *s-y-ll-a-be*   and finally
i noted that the familiar collocation   *moder aarde*   'mother
earth'   had been split apart by the strange new syllable
   grond   which   itself becomes the root for the central
word in the poem   *grondel*
   i see this poem as an example of the connection between
existence and language   just as the poetess' father spoke
the grondel into existence   at the same time a poetess was
   spoken into existence

   let me talk now briefly about being wielded by one's
theory   my teacher and thesis supervisor   a man to whom i
owe many many things   and whose intelligence and clarity of
vision has been to me an incalculable gift   noam chomsky
   said in a very influential book that appeared in 1957
'syntactic structures'

The search for rigorous formulation in linguistics has
a much more serious motivation than mere concern for
logical niceties or the desire to purify well-established
methods of linguistic analysis. Precisely constructed
models for linguistic structure can play an important
role, both negative and positive, in the process of
discovery itself. By pushing a precise but inadequate
formulation to an unacceptable conclusion, we can often
expose the exact source of this inadequacy and, consequently, gain a deeper understanding of the linguistic
data. (Chomsky 1957:5)

this made a deep impression on me when i read it and i quoted it in my thesis   but since i wrote my thesis 15 years ago   i've noticed that what happens is   once one has a   precise formulation   one doesn't give it up very quickly   one makes decisions to preserve it   it sort of has its own autonomy   one makes decisions to preserve the theory   as j.r. ross in 1964 did in his master's thesis at the university of pennsylvania   which was called 'a partial grammar of english superlatives'   i have taken one rule of this thesis   you don't have to read it   it's immaterial

$$^T\text{Range Move} \quad \left\{\begin{matrix}\text{many}\\\text{much}\end{matrix}\right\}\overline{\left[\begin{matrix}+\ N & \left\{\begin{matrix}+\text{ count, }+\text{ pl.}\\-\text{ count}\end{matrix}\right\}\end{matrix}\right]}$$

$$\begin{matrix}1 & 1 & & 1 & & 1\end{matrix}$$

$$Q: \quad \# + X_1 - \text{Sup} - (D_R) - \left\{\begin{matrix}\text{Adj (N)}\\ D_{MAN}\\ D_{TM'}\\ D_{DEG'}\text{ (Adj (N))}\\ \text{often}\\ \text{long}\\ \text{short}\end{matrix}\right\} - X_2 + \#$$

$$\begin{matrix}Z_1 & - Z_2 & - Z_3 & - & Z_4 & & - Z_5\end{matrix}$$

$$\alpha \longleftrightarrow (\ I,I \mid I,I \mid I,I \mid \qquad I,3 \qquad \mid I,I)$$

$$\sigma \longleftrightarrow (\ 1\ ,\ 2\ ,\ 0\ ,\qquad 4 \qquad ,\ 5\ )$$

SC: $1...5 \rightarrow 1\text{-}2\text{-}4\text{-}3\text{-}5$ $\qquad t = \sigma(\alpha)$

Condition: $Z_2 - Z_3$ ISA D_{DEG}

it's pretty clear   isn't it?   there's not much insight in this rule   it goes something like   superlatives   have to do with the morpheme '-est' as in 'biggest'   and with a constituent that i called DR   that means adverb of range   like 'of all my friends'   so this unwieldy rule has converted a structure like 'the -est of all my friends big' into 'the bigg-est of all my friends'   that's what happens in that rule

that was the then current way of writing rules and i did it   i sort of spoke that dialect and i   did it   but looking back on it   i don't think it taught me anything   i don't think i or anybody else learned anything from that way   of doing it   i think it was something that i let be

imposed on me   because i was so swept away by the theory
that i was working within that   i didn't ask whether i had
   really seen anything important
      i'd like to say a very similar thing about the next poem
which i'm going to read to you but not say much about
it's a very complex wonderful poem by hopkins   apparently
   hopkins thought of it as one of his best poems   maybe
      his favorite   it's about a falcon   a kestrel   a small
english hawk

THE WINDHOVER: To Christ our Lord

I caught this morning morning's minion, king-
   dom of daylight's dauphin, dapple-dawn-drawn Falcon,
      in his riding
Of the rolling level underneath him steady air, and striding
High there, how he rung upon the rein of a wimpling wing
In his ecstasy! then off, off forth on swing,
   As a skate's heel sweeps smooth on a bow-bend:
            the hurl and gliding
   Rebuffed the big wind.   My heart in hiding
Stirred for a bird,--the achieve of, the mastery of the thing!

Brute beauty and valour and act, oh, air, pride, plume, here
   Buckle!   *And* the fire that breaks from thee then, a billion
Times told lovelier, more dangerous, O my chevalier!

No wonder of it: sheer plod makes plough down sillion
Shine, and blue-bleak embers, ah my dear,
   Fall, gall themselves, and gash gold-vermilion.

         what was the theory of poetry that i was working
on   when i started working on this three years ago?   the
major division in this poem is between the octet and the
sextet   it's indicated typographically   it's a sonnet
      and what i   wanted to show was the distribution of every
   linguistic element that i could think of which would sort
of underline or be in consonance with that boundary   my
thoughts on this are summarized in the table on page 22
         one of the things i focused on was the use of the sound
/ŋ/   it is not only in the rhyme of every line in the octet
but   also in several other places   like 'rolling' in line 4
   'wimpling' in line 5   that sound /ŋ/ does not occur in the
sextet whatsoever
         furthermore in the octet we have s-clusters   all the
s-clusters are in the octet   all the occurrences of the
phoneme /ŋ/ are also in the octet   i won't go on and go
   through the whole poem   but i think that you can see
this analysis which i   did three years ago bears the same
      kind of relationship to the poem it was used on as the
above rule about superlatives had to the superlative

The Windhover

Octet

Splitters	Balances	Echoes	Foretastes
s-clusters	air	[I]20/1(12)	Palatals achieve (8)/[5]
ŋ	then	h 10/1(a)	VlC │ Falcon/told themselves gold
Vf[4]	level-lovelier	the 7/1(10)	
		or 4/1(10)	
k+vowel[3](1)	Final obstruent	of 5/1/(12)	ClV̇ gliding/[5]
			plume plod
ō^rn[2](1)	clusters (4 each)	w 5/1/(12)	(6b) plough blue bleak
	ʒn# (3 each)	ōr 4/1(11)	(v...l) level (3)/ valour (9)
ə[2]	f...l		lovelier (11)
	f...r		(l...v) [4] chevalier (11)
	f...r	3rd person 4/1(12)	themselves (14)
vz[3]	f...r		
	f...r		
	f...l		
Past tense [3]	#f...L (3 each)	?ēr 2/1	Cz
			morning's (1)/[3] times (11)
			embers (13)
#r[4] 3,4,4,7	1st person		themselves (14)
	I my/my my	āyd 4/1(9)	
	əV mastery/dangerous	^ty 3/1/(9)	Present tense
	ə 5/6 [vermílion]		sweeps (6a)/[5]
	all others		breaks makes
	in the poem		fall gall gash
	are post-tonic		

Sextet

Splitters	Balances	Echoes	Foretastes
#t b {L G}[5]	Ʌ: underneath (3)		ōw#bow (6a)/[3] oh oh no
#-ōld	⌐rung (4)		ūw smooth (6a)/[4] brute beauty
oh oh ah	↑rebuffed (7)		(all follow labials) plume (9) blue (13)
#gV [2]	↓búckle (10)		p(L)V̇ upón (4)/[4] pride plume (9)
i yr [4]	lovelier (11)		plod plough (12)
ə# [4]	wonder (12)		Vk ecstasy (5)/[5] act (9) buckle breaks (10)
#V[2] valour (9)	V̇nd 5 each		[Falcon?] makes (11) bleak (13)
	V̇N] dawn̲ drawn̲ rung rein		
vermilion (14)	Lex plume times down̲ shine̲		
Plural NP[3]	?Vs (1)/(11)		
Bare V[5] (2 inf+3 pres pls)	OV order (3)/(12)		
āy[+son][3]	ēy not before r:		
	2a,4,6a/10,11,12		

Splitters: Elements which occur either all in the octet or all in the sextet.
Balances: Elements which occur the same number of times in both sections of the poem:
Echoes: Elements which are all in the octet except one.
Foretastes: Elements which are all in the sextet, except one in the octet.

construction   i think   i was wielded by a theory of poetry
some of the things in this table i would stick by   i think
    that's true what i   told you   about the / ŋ /   i   think
that the distribution of the / ŋ / does draw that boundary
    between   the halves of the poem   between the octet and
the sextet   but the other things   many of them   i think
don't   there's a place where i let my theory push me into
    making a whole lot of claims that i   wish i hadn't made
        pete becker   from whom i   always learn vast amounts
is of a different opinion   and he says i shouldn't castigate
myself or other people for having committed excesses   of
    youth   maybe it's necessary to let yourself be led   be
wielded by your theory   maybe if we want to have real in-
    sight as i want to try and demonstrate   there are stages
we have to put up with   we have to grit our teeth and go
through with it   it's like someone who is trying to stop
    smoking   maybe some of you have tried to stop smoking
maybe you've stopped a number of times   it's hard   when
the cigarette comes around another time and you take it   well
    maybe what you should do is not hate yourself   but say
'well i'm not quite ready to stop now   i should keep working
    on it'   something like that   anyway these are things that
you have to take as part of the bargain: that we're going to
    have unenlightening   uninsightful   cluttered   theory-laden
descriptions
        i'm not sure about that   i don't often disagree with
pete   maybe i'm not disagreeing with him now   i hope i'm
characterizing his view correctly
        but maybe another stance is possible--in syntax and
in poetry   let's look at these syntactic data

1.a.   on*(the)$\begin{Bmatrix} \text{top} \\ \text{tops} \end{Bmatrix}$*(of) the car [but cf. <u>atop</u> the car]

  b.   in (*the) $\begin{Bmatrix} \text{front} \\ \text{*fronts} \end{Bmatrix}$ *(of) the car

  c.i.   in (*the) side of the car
   ii.   inside (of) the car

  d.i.   *$\begin{Bmatrix} \text{by} \\ \text{be} \end{Bmatrix}$side of the car
   ii.   beside the car
  e.   behind (*of) the car [cf. <u>hindsight</u>, <u>hindquarters</u>]
  f.   between (**of) the car [cf. <u>Never the twain shall meet</u>]

    i'd like you to just sort of run your eyes over it
kind of hang out with it   just like i'm hanging out with
'western wind'   i may never learn anything about 'western
    wind'   i'm resigned to that
        these facts have to do with english locative prepositions
periphrastic and some one-word ones   a word about the
    notations: when you have a parenthesized element A(B)C

that means you can either have ABC or AC   the parenthesized
element doesn't have to be there   if you have A(*B)C   a
    star inside the parenthesis   that means don't add B   that
means AC is okay   but if you add B   it's no good   and if
    the star is outside the parenthesis as it is in the first line
if you have A*(B)C   that means it's starred to remove B
    that means that ABC is okay   but AC is no good   this means
        in the first line you can say *on top of the cars*   but you
can't say   *on tops of the cars*   you can say   on *the tops of
    the cars*   but you can't say   *on tops of the cars*   and it
says also you can't get rid of the *of*   so you can't say   *on
top the car*   (although there is an old preposition *atop*)   so
    in the first line 1.a. you can't get rid of the *of* and you
can get rid of the *the*   but only   if the noun is not
        pluralized
            on to the second line   1.b   *in the front of the car*
now *in the front of the car* does not mean 'in front of the car'
in the front of the car means like 'under the hood' or some-
    thing like that   what i mean is in the meaning of 'before
the car'   so the stars have to do with that meaning   here
also you can't get rid of the *of*   you can't say *in front the
    car*   nor can you say   *in the fronts of the cars*   except
when you mean inside the car   in the non-prepositional
meaning   so *front* and *top* are different   *top* allows under
    one circumstance pluralization   *front* doesn't   in 1.c.i.
you can't say *in the side of the car* in the prepositional sense
    you can when it means 'between the walls of the car'
        'hidden in the door'   or something like that   but not
when it means 'within the car'   you can't have the article
with *top* you could have it or not with the singular one
        in *front* you could not have it
        and in *side* you can't have it   with *side* we see for
the first time that the *of* can be there
        so we can say *inside of the car*
        it can also be gone   *inside the car* in (1.c.ii)
        notice when we have *inside* we must write it as one
word   *inside*   the *in* can even lose stress   we can't write
in side the car
        in (1.d.i.) *beside the car*   we can't have *of* now with
beside   we can't say *by side of the car*   or *be side of the
car*   all we have is what corresponds to *inside the car*   we
have *beside the car*
        in (1.e.) we have the same thing   we have here how-
ever a word 'hind' which only exists marginally in the rest of
english   not ever as a free noun   it used to mean the rear
    part   we have only things like *hindquarters*   *hindsight*
hind legs   and so on
        finally *between of the car* is unbelievably bad   a double
star for splendid ungrammaticality   maybe we don't know that
there is a word related to '-tween'   we're not even sure
    because the word *twain* we have only in one poetic

expression and maybe you haven't even in your high school
days ever had the line *east is east and west is west and never
the twain shall meet*   if you haven't   then that word *twain*
is an isolate
        now i ask you   how do you see those data?   i know
how i see them   and there's a nice expression in german
ich würde meine hand ins feuer legen   'i would put my hand
in the fire'   it seems to me these data that i've hung out
with have sort of imposed themselves on me   i don't have a
big formal story   i have the beginning of a formal story for
them   but what are your suggestions?   what can we say
about these data?
        it seems to me one thing to say is   they're losing
more and more of their nouniness   they lose it as we go down
the list   the element just ceases to be a noun
        top is still a noun   it has the possibility of being
pluralized   it can even be modified   you can say *on the
spacious top of the car*   notice we cannot say anything like
in spacious front of the car   or *in immediate front of the
car*   *front* can't be modified   it can't be pluralized   so the
difference between *top* and *front* is that *top* has degrees of
freedom   it is closer to a true noun   *front* has begun to
lose some of the options   *side* more so   *hind* even more so
and so on   one of the ways which we notice that is   there's
a rule in english that within a noun phrase you never find
two nouns in adjacent positions   so you don't have *a picture
jack*   there has to be an *of*   *a picture of jack*   well that's
what we have with *top*   *on top of jack*   or *on top of the
car*   *in front of the car*   *inside of the car*   but now we
notice that 'side' has lost so much of its connection to the
        true noun *side* that the *of* can go   and we get *inside the
car*
        beside is so frozen into a one-word thing that it has
no possibility of even an optional occurrence of *of* with 'hind'
its connection to the noun *hind* is completely lost   and
        twain is almost entirely out of the language
        it seems to me that what we're witnessing here is a
process of nominal decay   that's also historically corroborated
those things were nouns and they have lost their nominal-
ness   and we have come not to impose an analysis on
between anymore   maybe it's *be* plus something   but we
don't know what that *tween* is and we certainly don't call it
a noun anymore   i'm sure that's right
        i may be wrong of course   i may be wrong but i would
put my hand in the fire for that analysis   i wouldn't put even
my pinkie in for the analysis of the superlative   i don't
        know if you've had that feeling before   those of you who
have done syntax   times when you've felt uneasy   you say
well within this framework   i guess i'll *have* to say this   what
i'm suggesting is that you don't say anything in a case like
        that   say 'i don't know what the answer is'

       i'm willing to say only this much about these nouns
here: it seems to me that there's a gradual loss   decrease
in the nouniness of the second word   of the thing that
    follows the preposition in this case
       let me give you a poem which i have the same hand-
in-the-fire feelings about   i don't feel very good about what
i said about 'windhover'   let me suggest a stance toward
    the following poem by hilde domin   this poem was sent to
me by anneliese kramer   my friend from british columbia
it's a fantastic poem   an english translation is underneath

    Lied zur Ermutigung II
    --Hilde Domin

Lange wurdest du um die türelosen
Mauern der Stadt gejagt.

Du fliehst und streust
die verwirrten Namen der Dínge
hinter dich.

Vertrauen, dieses schwérste
ABC.

Ich mache ein kleines Zéichen
in die Luft,
únsichtbar,
wo die neue Stadt beginnt,
Jerúsalem,
die góldene,
aus Nichts.

    Song of Encouragement II

Long were you around the doorless [=For a long time you were
walls of-the city chased.   chased around the doorless
                                  walls of the city.]

You fell and strew
the confused names of-the things
behind you.

Trust, this most-difficult
ABC.

I make a small sign
in the air,
invisible,
where the new city begins,
Jerusalem
the golden,
out-of nothing.

this was taken from a book called 'doppel-interpretationen' which contains poems with a commentary by each
author   in this case hilde domin   who is an austrian poet
and then author commentary on each poem by a literary
critic   in this case hans georg gadamer   what domin herself
says about the poem is that it has 14 lines and is in 2 halves
    du 'you' is the subject of the first stanza   you are
chased around the doorless walls of the city   in the second
    stanza you flee and strew the names of the things
    behind you   and then trust   that's what's missing in
the third stanza
    she says that in the first half of the poem there are
three jagged breaths   the three sentences   that in the
second half there's one long sentence-breath   which she
    calls rising   it's one breath from line 8 to line 14   and
there's clearly a change from negative in the first half to
positive in the second half   what's the change?
    well what are the connotations of doorless?   'the door-
less walls of the city'   what kind of city has no door?   a
    city is supposed to provide its inhabitants with shelter
    from the people outside   but this is an un-city which
keeps people who seek shelter and haven out   this is the
wrong kind of city   it's the wrong world
    what else is the matter?   she says there is a crisis
in language   that something that is part of the very nature
    of language is wrong   namely words don't fit things
anymore   and so what do we do?   we throw away these
    confused names   because they don't help us   we have
things   we don't need the words anymore   we have un-cities
she calls our present language *verlogen*   *verlogen* is based
    on the root *lüge* which means 'lie'   somebody is *verlogen*
if they lie to you all the time   if it's part of their character
    a language is *verlogen* if   like newspeak in '1984'   it
doesn't tell you the   truth   if it is sort of constrained to
lie to you   so she says   the crisis of language in which
    we now are is such that our language lies to us
    what's the matter?   trust   'the hardest ABC'   we
don't have the trust   and then what happens?   there is change
    a polar change   'i make a small sign/in the air'   an
invisible sign   'where the new city begins/jerusalem'
    and what are the connotations of jerusalem?   it's a
city of many religions   a city incredibly rich in history   a
fabulous miracle city   'the golden one/out of nothing'
    it's a great poem   a wonderful poem
    my analysis is very similar to that of the dutch poem
my hand goes into the fire for this one too   look at the
rhyme words of the poem

Lied zur Ermutigung II
  --Hilde Domin

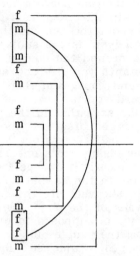

Lange wurdest du um die türelosen   f
Mauern der Stadt gejagt.   m

Du fliehst und streust   m
die verwirrten Namen der Dínge   f
hinter dich.   m

Vertrauen, dieses schwérste   f
ABC.   m

Ich mache ein kleines Zéichen   f
in die Luft,   m
únsichtbar,   f
wo die neue Stadt beginnt,   m
Jerúsalem,   f
die góldene,   f
aus Nichts.   m

stress is marked on the words that do not have stress on the
  last syllable   so they're feminine words   türelosen   dinge
    schwerste   those are feminines   the other words in the
  first half are masculines   so we have feminine türelosen and
two masculines gejagt and streust   then a feminine again and
then a masculine dich   and then a feminine schwerste   and
  then ABC stress on C   that's the masculine rhyme
      what do we have in the other side?   zeichen   unsichtbar
jerusalem and goldene all have stress away from the end   so
  those are all feminines   so we have feminine masculine feminine
    masculine   two feminines and a masculine   what does the
first half of the poem look like?   essentially an alternation
between masculine and feminine   however with one place where
    there are two masculines in a row   the second and third
  line from the upper edge   what do we find on the bottom?
the same alternation basically between masculine and feminine
but with two masculines together two lines from the bottom   in
  other words that invisible line between the first seven lines
  and the last seven lines is a polarity change   an interchanging
    of masculines and feminines   just as we change from this
mood of despair to a mood of encouragement   so we have this
formal structure on which the poem is based   as you can see
  i've drawn the lines   it's a sort of onionskin structure
like that
      that's all i can tell you about the poem right now   i
have had theories about the poem   and about other poetry but
  what i want to do is stop right there   not say anymore than i
  feel i could put my hand in the fire for

it seems to me you can divide thinkers about language
into two groups   there's one kind of thinker who thinks that
language is basically tractable   maybe incredibly complex and
intricate but not limitless   we don't have all the tools yet
but we'll get to the end sometime   the other kind of
thinker thinks that language is ineluctable and ineffable   it
will always slip out from our clutches   in a way like sapir's
famous quote about all grammars leaking   i think a lot of
us have behaved as if language were something rather trivial
maybe not everybody
take language 'acquisition'   what's the metaphor there?
it's like rug acquisition   what do you acquire?   you acquire
possessions   when i acquire german it's like i have a new
rug in the living room
we all know that it's very difficult to teach people
languages   why is that?   i think that any of you   and there
are probably lots of you who have learned a foreign language
you know it changes your soul   basically you *are* a new
language   it's not that you *have* a new language   you are a
new person in that language   and it's very scary to lose
that soul that you know and love which you've been living
with all your life   to go and get another one in german or
turkish or french or whatever it is
language acquisition is a wrong metaphor   i think that
we could use a little bit more balance   i think that language
is vast and unguessable and unpalpable
i'll end with a quote from archibald macleish which is
quoted in a h maslow's marvelous book 'the farther reaches of
human nature' (1975:165)   when macleish was dedicating the
lincoln center for the performing arts in new york he said

What is wrong is not the great discoveries of science.
Information is always better than ignorance, no matter
what information or what ignorance.   What is wrong is
the belief behind the information--the belief that information will change the world.   It won't.   Information
without human understanding is like an answer without
its question--meaningless.   And human understanding is
only possible through the arts.   It is the work of art
that creates the human perspective in which information turns to truth.

thank you very much for your patience

REFERENCES

Bohm, David.   1982.   Wholeness and the implicate order.
   London: Routledge and Kegan Paul.
Capra, Fritjof.   1977.   The Tao of physics: An exploration of
   the parallels between modern physics and Eastern mysticism.
   New York: Bantam Books.

Chomsky, Noam. 1957. Syntactic structures. The Hague: Mouton.

Domin, Hilde. (n.d.) Doppel-Interpretationen.

Ferguson, Marilyn. 1980. The aquarian conspiracy. Los Angeles: J. P. Tarcher.

Friedrich, Paul. 1979. Language, poetic language and the imagination. In: Language, context and the imagination. Edited by Anwar S. Dil. Stanford, Calif.: Stanford University Press. 441-512.

Gerhard, Ida. 1979. Vyf Vuurstenen. Amsterdam: Athenaeum-Polak and van Gennep.

Hillman, James. 1975. Re-visioning psychology. New York: Harper and Row.

Kramer, Anneliese. 1980. The languages of linguistic theory: Aesthetic perspectives on a scientific discipline. Unpublished Ph.D. thesis. University of Michigan, Ann Arbor.

Lakoff, George. 1974. Humanistic linguistics. In: Georgetown University Round Table on Languages and Linguistics 1974. Edited by Francis P. Dinneen, S.J. Washington, D.C.: Georgetown University Press. 103-117.

Lakoff, George, and Mark Johnson. 1980. Metaphors we live by. Chicago: University of Chicago Press.

Linde, Charlotte. 1971. Science and personal transformation. Unpublished MS. Structural Semantics Co., P.O. Box 707, Palo Alto, Calif. 94302.

Maslow, A. H. 1975. The farther reaches of human nature. Baltimore: Penguin Books.

Miller, George. 1976. Thirteen maxims for the mind. Unpublished MS.

The Norton anthology of poetry, revised. 1975. Edited by Alexander W. Allison et al. New York: W. W. Norton.

Toben, Bob. 1975. Space-time and beyond: Toward an explanation of the unexplainable. New York: E. P. Dutton.

Tzu, Chuang. In: Capra (1977:101).

Yngve, Vic. 1975. Human linguistics. In: Functionalism. Edited by Robin E. Grossman et al. Chicago: Chicago Linguistic Society.

Zukav, Gary. 1979. The dancing Wu-li masters: An overview of the new physics. New York: Bantam New Age Book, William Morrow.

LANGUAGE AND AFFECT:
SOME CROSS-CULTURAL ISSUES

Judith T. Irvine
Brandeis University

0. Introduction. This paper concerns the communication of affect, and the role therein of cultural and linguistic systems. It explores some analytical issues in cross-cultural comparison and the notion of 'expressive language' and it examines modes of affective expression in a particular ethnographic case.

The question of whether there are significant cross-cultural differences in the ways emotional states are displayed, and if so, what these differences might be, is of course an old problem. One aspect of it focuses on emotion itself, its biological basis, and the degree of its universality. A related matter is the degree of universality of certain ways of expressing emotion, especially in gesture and facial display. Since Darwin's *The Expression of the Emotions in Man and Animals* (1872), a work that continues to influence contemporary thinking on the subject, the literature on these questions has been voluminous.[1] Among anthropologists and psychologists, LaBarre (1947), Birdwhistell (1970), and Leach (1972) have made some of the best-known arguments for the cultural relativity of expressive behavior, while Eibl-Eibesfelt (1972) and Ekman and his colleagues (e.g. Ekman and Friesen 1971; Ekman, Sorenson, and Friesen 1969) have emphasized panhuman similarity and innateness, relegating cultural conventions to a more superficial role.

On the linguistic side, a classic examination of the problem is Sapir's 1927 paper, 'Speech as a personality trait', which--though focusing on personality much more than on affect per se--outlines the variety of aspects of speech that might reflect differences in personality and emotional state. Though acknowledging that innate biological factors play a part in the genesis of personality and the physiology of speech, Sapir points out that one cannot assess a speaker's personality from his or her speech until one knows something about the social norms of the

31

speech community in which that speaker lives. In other words, one must not confuse differences in norms of communication with differences in personality. This remains, I think, the heart of the problem for affect, too: not to confuse communicative norms with affective states, nor to confuse a community level of analysis with the individual--yet to be able to assess what relationships there may be among all of these.

I think it is fair to say that most work on the intersection of culture, affect, and semiotic systems falls into two types: (a) the study of kinesics and 'paralanguage' (prosodic systems and voice quality); and (b) the study of the vocabulary of emotion. As treated by anthropologists, the emotion lexicon represents a native analysis of the affective domain, which the anthropologist generally studies at some remove from behavioral display--that is, as labels for behavioral displays rather than as occurring in such displays--emotion recollected (and recounted) in tranquility. Although both these types of study address useful questions, I propose, following Sapir, to take a broader view, going beyond voice and lexicon to include a fuller range of communicative means, and focusing on communication itself as well as, or more than, on the reporting of it.

Some of these other means are examined in Stankiewicz (1964), which devotes much of its attention to phonological and morphological devices involved in an emotive function or dimension of language. A few other linguists have written, too, on 'ideophonic words' (e.g. Samarin 1970) and 'expressive vocabulary' (Fudge 1970; Diffloth 1972, 1976): 'plops, squeaks, croaks, sighs, and moans', as Mithun (1982) describes them. Although it is not clear that all these 'expressive' phenomena express affect--and I return to this point later on--I think it is useful to consider together those devices that do concern affective display. Such an expanded notion of an affective dimension of communication would take in all levels of linguistic organization as well as nonverbal phenomena and the organization of discourse and interaction. These behavioral forms must be seen not only in relation to each other, but also against a backdrop of social contexts, social identities, and culturally constituted expectations.

My discussion of these matters, which is more like an exploration than an argument, is divided into two main sections. The first considers some general issues involved in looking at the expression of affect cross-culturally: definitions (our own and other peoples') of the domain of emotion and affective expression; the problem of sincerity and the evidence one uses to impute particular affective states to others; and the role of situational context, as intervening between expressive form and communicative effect. The examples in this section, though anecdotal, derive mainly from a speech community for which I have some field experience: rural Wolof of Senegal. The second section presents a more systematic outline of the range of channels of affective expression that are available to Wolof speakers. I then discuss some of the differing properties of these channels and how they may affect each other when combined. Although these channels and devices provide a rich set of possibilities for affective expression, those possibilities are informed--one might even say constrained--by cultural stereotypes about behavioral styles and the kinds of persons who are likely to display them. These culturally constituted images, which crosscut and summarize the communicative devices, make an important connection between culture, communicative forms, and imputed affect.

1. General issues

1.1 Defining the domain of affect. Let us begin with some definitions. First of all, what do we mean by 'affect'? Are affects different from emotions and drives? How do they relate to cognition? Psychologists have disagreed on these matters but often for reasons that need not concern us here. As a useful starting point, therefore, we might consider a definition offered by Kagan (1978:16-17), who writes that

> at present many psychologists...regard the category *affective* as being characterized by the following dimensions:
> (a) a change in feeling state that is derivative of internal physiological events (b) produced by an immediate incentive event (c) that is short-lived in duration, (d) linked to cognitive structures, and (e) not related to physiological deprivation.

(That is, affects are not the same as drives.)

Note, first, that this statement defines affect as a subjective state distinct from its behavioral expression--'those potentially observable, surface features of change in face, body, voice, and activity that accompany affective states' (Lewis and Rosenblum 1978:5). From these observable features we ascribe affective states to other people. The 'we' here--the observer-- is not only the outside observer but also the native observer, a comember of the observed person's speech community. Of course, communities and their members may vary as to the extent to which they engage in such inferences, the detail with which they articulate them, and the extent to which they invoke other kinds of information as well. What must be distinguished, then, are: subjective feeling state; observable behavior; ways members of a community describe the feeling states; and the evidence they bring to bear upon their inference.

Now, among these matters Kagan points to three facets-- feeling state, internal physiological events, and incentive events--which might well not be accorded the same importance in other cultural articulations of the domain of emotion. Ifaluk emotion terms, for example, as described by Lutz (1982:

124), focus more on the situation eliciting emotion than on internal feeling states. Yet, some important connection with the internal is evident from the Ifaluk definition of the domain of emotion words as words 'about our insides' (ibid.:115). Wolof, too, employ an inner/outer metaphor, locating feeling states such as anger or contentment in the heart (xol), though the feeling states may also be linked with physiological antecedents located elsewhere in the body, especially the liver. Indeed, I believe Wolof discussions of emotion focus more on physiological aspects (agitated/tranquil, hot/cold, and inherited predispositions to such states) than do our own folk analyses. It is not clear, however, whether all cultural systems explicitly distinguish inner from outer states in defining emotion or describing its physiological dimension.

When we consider other peoples' descriptions of feeling states, and the rationales given for imputing a particular state to someone, we must bear in mind that the way people report or describe emotion is not necessarily the same as what they actually rely upon to impute that emotion, much as the two may inform each other. The folk analysis implied in such descriptions is part of the data, not equivalent to an anthropological analysis. Yet, the reports, labels, and descriptions are linked to cultural images and stereotypes that mediate between behavioral display and members' inferences about affective states. Some Wolof informants, for example, explain their expectations about how certain categories of people display emotion in very physiological terms: some people are (hereditarily) less physically solid than others, and so are more easily agitated.

1.2 The sincerity problem. Let us turn now to the problem of reliability or, from another point of view, sincerity. How sure can the observer be that some person X 'really' experiences the affective state attributed to him or her? Again, this is a member's problem as much as an outsider's problem. One thing it involves is masking and deception. For example, some Wolof villagers told me they found Europeans' hearts 'clearer' than Africans'; that is, they thought Europeans less likely to hide their true feelings and intentions, and more likely to display them openly in outward behavior. Now, I am not certain as to precisely what cues in the Europeans' behavior were considered the giveaways; and my informants' statement is as much a statement about intention (to deceive) as it is about behavior. But it would seem that Wolof identify certain nonverbal behaviors (such as types of gesture, stance, and degree of activity) as more involuntary and more likely to reveal true affective states than are verbal statements.

My informants are not alone in this opinion, of course, nor is the point new. It has been suggested by Darwin and many others, including (for a recent example) Ekman and Friesen (1969)--who, however, exclude posture from the list of nonverbal phenomena most likely to 'leak' affect and so provide

clues to deception.   But whether posture is to be included or
not, the point is that some communicative channels may be
privileged over others as more likely to convey 'true' information about affect; and actually, this does not have to do only
with deception, or even with a stoic maintenance of apparent
calm, but also with metacommunicative commentary on how information presented in another channel is to be 'taken'
(seriously, sarcastically, playfully, etc.; see Goffman 1961,
1974; Bateson 1972).   Perhaps the classic statement on such
commentary as regards affect is Bateson's discussion of the
'double bind' (Bateson et al. 1956), where affective information
presented in one channel is contradicted by information presented in another.   I return to this matter later, but for now
note that we are not dealing only with two communicative
avenues but with many.
   Whether deception is at issue or not, attributing a particular
affective state to someone depends not only on that someone's
behavior, but also on its context.   One needs to consider what
expectations members of a society hold about whether some particular social circumstance will give rise to some particular
feeling on the part of those who experience it.   At an extreme,
social circumstances might even be sufficient grounds in themselves for some emotion to be attributed to a person, that person's actual behavior being virtually irrelevant.   This suggests
that, at least in some circumstances, it does not matter how the
person (call this person P) behaves; any behavior might be
taken as 'the way P manifests emotion E' and not as indicating
'P has emotion F instead'.   Suppose that P's mother has just
died and P goes around smiling.   Under what conditions do
witnesses conclude that 'P is covering up his grief', rather
than 'P is glad his mother died'?   Perhaps the best way to
think of this is in terms of some range of variation for P's behavior, the interpretation of which will be influenced by what
the antecedent event is, how 'serious' the imputed emotion is
considered to be, witnesses' ideas about what causes particular
emotional states, and witnesses' knowledge of P's personal history.   These are all ethnographic matters and suggest the complexity of contextual factors intervening between behavioral
forms and the interpretations observers give them.
   Finally, it must be borne in mind that, depending on the
nature of the acts involved, it does not always matter whether
the speaker (or actor) really has the feeling attributed to him.
Sometimes what is much more important is simply the public expression of some feeling--so that the public social order can continue, despite what anyone may privately believe.   I suppose it
is partly for this reason that Austin (1962:40), discussing sincerity as a felicity condition of communicative acts, argued that
acts expressing feelings are not voided if the speaker does not
in fact have the feeling that is being expressed--if, for example,
someone expresses condolence without actually feeling sympathy.
Such insincere acts are not void, but merely infelicitous; they
still 'count', whether the feeling is present or not.   It is not

clear to me, however, what happens if sympathy, for example, is expressed only in one channel but not in others. If I giggle while expressing condolence, have I really condoled?

As another example, suppose one studied apologies in some other society. Under what circumstances would an apology have to be public, and what happens if the apologizer counters the public apology with private indications of not being 'really' sorry? What are the constraints on the apologizer's behavior during the public apology--must a 'sorry' display be maintained consistently over all communicative modalities and throughout the public occasion? What would be crucial to these questions would be ethnographic information about the boundary between public and private domains, the relation of both to the maintenance of face, and their link to personal histories and relationships.

1.3 Markedness and situational expectations. I mentioned earlier that the attribution of some particular affective state to someone depends partly on the social context. That is, communicative norms about the display of emotion vary according to social situations and the social identities of their personnel. Both the type of affect that might appropriately be displayed, and the intensity of display, are involved. Among rural Wolof, for example, low-ranking persons are more free to express affect, and express it unrestrainedly, than are high-ranking persons, who are more constrained to exercise self-control.

Of the Wolof low ranks, it is especially the griots--a bardic caste of professional speechmakers, musicians, historians, and message-bearers--who most appropriately display high affect. Actually, it might be more accurate to say not that the griots are most free to express feeling, but that they are expected to display it (whether they feel it or not) and to display it on behalf of others as well as themselves. This contrast between griots and higher-ranking persons was sharply illustrated for me on an occasion when a woman in the village where I worked attempted suicide by throwing herself down a well. Among the other women who happened to witness this act there were two griot women and several high-ranking (noble) women; but only the two griots screamed. Now, the fact that only they screamed does not mean that only they were shocked. The point is, rather, that the emotional level attributable to a person cannot be read directly off his or her affective display; there is no simple one-to-one correspondence between the behavioral form and its pragmatic effect (here, the attribution of emotion of some particular type and intensity). Instead, sundry situational variables must intervene.

In fact, many Wolof social occasions would involve a more complex set of situational factors than the suicide occasion did. It is not only the absolute rank (caste) of the persons present at the moment of talk, which would impinge upon their display of

affect, but also their relative rank.   (Thus even if everyone
present is noble, some people still rank higher than others--
because of age, for instance, or because of the seniority of a
lineage segment.)   Also relevant would be the location and tim-
ing of the occasion, and socially constituted definitions of it--
such as the purpose of talk, whether it is public or private,
etc.   Certain high-caste women who exhibit a rigidly decorous
demeanor and near-silence in the village plaza or in a public
shop may shift, at home, to loud laughter, angry shouting at
naughty children, and so forth, as long as no strangers, or
members of other castes, are present.   If they are, this seems
to be sufficient to define the situation as public, demanding
the more bland, laconic style of high-caste demeanor.

To assess affect, therefore, one must compare the speaker's
actual display with what kind of behavior is expectable and
appropriate from that kind of speaker in that kind of situation.
A single tear from speaker A in situation A could mean as much
(in terms of imputable emotion) as noisy weeping from speaker
B.[2]   So there is a need to distinguish two levels of analysis:
(a) the display itself, and the type and degree of affect en-
coded in it; and (b) the relation between the display and the
situationally defined expectations.   This distinction allows us to
see that a deadpan expression, for instance, may communicate
a great deal about affect, while a display of weeping might not
communicate much if it conforms to what was prescribed anyway.
Intensity of display, and situational markedness (with respect to
expectations) are different things, though they interact to
bring about the observer's overall impression.

2.   Modes of affective expression in Wolof.   As I have said
earlier, it is useful to inventory the communicative devices that
involve affective display, so that one can compare them with
each other and so that one can get a sense of the range of
devices available in a particular linguistic and cultural system.
Accordingly, I have sketched an outline of modes of affective
expression in Wolof, which appears as the appendix to this
paper.   What I have aimed at here is not, by any means, a
complete inventory of all possible expressions of affect; indeed,
any such inventory would be coterminous with the total set of
utterances in Wolof.   The communication of affect is not done
only by a finite set of linguistic elements present or absent in
a particular utterance, but, instead, represents a function or
dimension of any utterance, even the most bland (for blandness,
as I have already noted, may say something about affect).
This is true despite the fact that certain of the most intensely
expressive forms pattern somewhat differently from other aspects
of language.   Consider the interjections, for instance (Appendix,
Section A, 'Exclamations').   As Stankiewicz pointed out (1964:
253), interjections show various oddities: they often have
phonetic features or clusters not found elsewhere in the language; they are morphologically relatively unmarked; and they

are syntactically isolated. Similarly, the phonological devices expressing affect may differ from those used for referential communication, by using, for instance, grading rather than contrastive discreteness (Stankiewicz 1964:267; Diffloth 1976). For Wolof, we see this in the use of graded quantity for vowels and continuants; the same phenomenon is found in many other languages, including English.

Now, one might expect some differences in patterning between the affective system and the referential one, since we are dealing with two cooccurring linguistic functions: in effect, the same utterance can have two dimensions, the referential and the affective, and so one might expect these dimensions to involve at least partly different modes of communication. (Incidentally, I do not mean to suggest that language has only these two poles.) Yet, the affective devices are also part of the linguistic system and intersect or merge with other aspects of patterning in a number of ways. Take vowel length, for example. In Wolof, vowel length is phonemic, and widely used to convey differences in referential meaning; the affective use of vowel length, constrained by the referential use, applies only to vowels that are already long. In this case, the referential function has priority, as it were.

Consider, too, the exclamations and their syntactic isolation. In a way this isolation, this lack of integration into an overall syntactic structure, has its parallels in the syntactic affective devices themselves (see Appendix, Section C (4)). The process of left-dislocation, widely used for emphasis in Wolof, has the effect of producing a partly isolated item (the emphasized element) at the front of the sentence. Sometimes Wolof speakers apply this process several times in the same sentence, giving a series of stranded forms on the left, linked to a sentence structure only as antecedents of pronouns. For instance, the sentence, *Fatu Ture moomu loxo-ëm* 'Fatu Ture doesn't own her hand (i.e. she can't control herself)', might, with two left-dislocations, be rendered *Fatu Ture--loxo-ëm-- kii moomu ko* 'Fatu Ture--her hand--she doesn't own it'. Multiplying left-dislocations in this way leads to a sort of spluttering effect, with stranded items separated by pauses, which seems to occur in association with intense emotion. Actually, the connection between some sort of 'broken syntax' and strong affect is not limited to Wolof. My point was not to show that Wolof is special, but rather to note that affective expression blends in with the system of focus and topicalization; and I imagine this occurs in other languages as well.

I want to mention two other kinds of connection between the affective system and the system of referential communication. First, emotion itself can serve as referent. We see this most directly in the lexical devices (emotion words and words for affect-related speech acts; see Appendix D, Sections D (4) and (5)). But the boundary between this part of the lexicon and other parts is difficult to draw precisely, because of forms like those in sections D (2) and D (5): items with reference but heavy affective loading, and items with straightforward reference that are frequently used in evaluative statements.

As the Appendix shows, I have not tried to draw up as full an emotion lexicon for Wolof as has been attempted for some other languages by investigations of the kinds of emotion highlighted in particular cultural systems. Were one to draw up such a list, one could compare the content of a Wolof folk analysis of emotion with that of other cultural systems. But one would have to bear in mind that the list obtained would not represent all the ways Wolof have of expressing affect, or all the kinds of affect they might express and react to. It would still be interesting, though, to consider what difference it makes that certain affects are lexicalized (and thus explicitly expressible referentially) and others not.

The other connection with the referential system is one I have already touched upon earlier: the use of the affect system as metacommunicative commentary on a referential proposition. The part of the affect system that would have to be involved here is not the morphological, syntactic, or lexical part--these are too closely tied with the referential structure in the first place--but some separate avenue or channel, such as intonation or nonverbal devices. As Goffman and others have pointed out, the metacommunicative commentary frames the proposition, indicating (among other things) whether it is to be taken seriously or not. If not, of course, the effect of the commentary can invert or negate the meaning of the proposition (as in sarcasm).

This brings me to a consideration of the multiple channels of affective communication and what happens when these different types of devices cooccur. The cooccurring devices can be disjunctive (signalling radically different types of affect) or they can be reinforcing and cumulative (signalling the same type of affect consistently over many channels). Let us take disjunction first. There are three ways in which this could operate.

(a) The first is disjunction across channels. This is the metacommunicative process just mentioned, where opposite affective messages are signalled simultaneously (as in sarcasm). The channel that can express propositions involving truth-conditions is the one whose message gets commented upon (in effect, falsified); the falsifying channel must be something like intonation or nonverbal signals, some patterning distinct from the propositional, and occurring simultaneously with it.

(b) A second possibility for disjunction is disjunction over time, where the behavioral display switches rapidly from one type or level of affect to another. For instance, if one inserts five seconds of tragic display into an otherwise lighthhearted conversation, the tragedy might not be taken too seriously. This rapid switching has not been much written about as a matter of communication--rather, people seem to think of it as directly reflecting the quality of the feeling itself or the

switcher's personality (shallowness, for instance).[3] But perhaps this assumption is not fully justified.

Actually, there are many problems involving the duration and
scope of affective display. As an example, suppose Alice is
angry at Barbara, but Cynthia is present too. Does Alice's
display of anger to Barbara carry over into Alice's utterances
to Cynthia? Is some carryover, on some channel, necessary in
order for Alice to be considered 'really' angry at Barbara at
all? Or, if Alice is angry at Barbara about topic T but not
about topic X, under what circumstances can there be a topic
switch? If the switch occurs, is there also some carryover of
Alice's display of anger? Again, is this necessary in order for
an observer to believe Alice is 'really' angry? Put another
way, what all this concerns is the relation of affect display to
problems of contextualization and the activation of multiple
roles and relationships.

(c) Finally, one more type of disjunction involves the use of
speech intermediaries (spokespersons)--that is, disjunction
across participants. A good example of this would be a Wolof
genre of insult and verbal abuse where the person who is the
source of the abusive message does not perform it, but hires
someone else to do so (usually a griot). The source maintains
silence and a decorous deadpan expression, while the griot
shouts angrily or mockingly. This type of disjunction does not
falsify the verbal message, but it may perhaps weaken the
affective load by its indirectness.[4]

What happens when affect signals over all channels are consistent? Most of the time we would expect that the various
devices and channels would reinforce each other and also indicate the seriousness, the 'for-real-ness', of the affect concerned. They might also suggest that the affect is more intense. But some caveats are necessary. Some of these devices
can be piled up to increase emphasis, such as reduplication, and
the use of emphatic particles, of which there can be several in
the same sentence; but, paradoxically, this accumulation of
emphatic devices does not always achieve more intensity. Many
of the devices listed here do not concern any specific type of
affect--they are just intensifiers that could be applied to any
affect--and if you have many intensifiers but not much
specificity, you end up with what Wolof sometimes calls empty
speech: all air and no content.

3. Conclusion: Social identities and cultural stereotypes. In
concluding this discussion, I want to return to the social aspect
of these semiotic devices. Earlier, I considered the social in
terms of a context of expectations about affect display--a baseline against which affect displays are marked or unmarked.
But although this is still the aspect of the social that I would
most want to emphasize, social identities and situations are not
just a backdrop that is not spoken about in its own right.
Rather, they may be invoked or alluded to much more directly;

and this has implications about affect. For instance, as indicated in Section D(6) of the Appendix, the speaker may label
an addressee by some term--say, a kinship term--that implies
a relationship having a particular emotional tone. Or, a
speaker may use some linguistic variant, or switch codes, to
take on some social identity or role which, in turn, is stereo-
typically associated with a type of affect.

However, since these communicative forms primarily signal
social identity, and only secondarily (by implication) signal
some type of affect, they do not really belong to quite the
same set of phenomena as most of the other material in the
outline (and perhaps D(6) should not be included there at all).
Instead, they represent a certain merging of the affective with
the social--analogous, perhaps, to the merging of affective with
referential which I mentioned earlier. So I am distinguishing
referential, affective, and social as three functional dimensions
of language that intersect in various ways. And I point this
out because it differs from what I see in much of the linguistic
literature which tends to draw a two-way contrast only. Various authors contrast 'cognitive' with 'expressive', where expressive (even if also termed 'emotive', as in Stankiewicz 1964)
seems to include anything that works through connotation instead of through denotation (and so includes code-switching
and onomatopoeia, but not lexical labels for emotion). [5] This
usage, I think, risks confusing form with function and an
individual level of analysis with a social level.

Although affect is a subjective feeling-state which thus applies
in the first instance to the individual, affective states (and
their display) are also socially defined. As I stated before,
social roles, identities, and situations all may have their associated expectations about display of affect. Take the Wolof cultural stereotypes of the noble and the griot--that is, expectations about how persons belonging to those social categories
typically behave. These are two cultural models for affective
display--the laconic and the aroused/arousing--which cross-cut
all levels of semiotic organization. The various communicative
devices of affective display cluster around these two poles.
(For some indication of how these devices cluster, see Section
F(2) of the Appendix, where I have indicated the prosodic phenomena corresponding to noble and griot behavioral styles.)
Now, these two are not the only behavioral models rural Wolof
find relevant, by any means. Nor are these two clusters of
communicative devices the only clusters where forms 'go
together' and jointly give rise to some conventional interpretation. Nor do these two models rigidly determine how actual
nobles and griots actually talk. Nevertheless, they are important parts of a frame of reference within which individual
uses of communicative devices are assessed (and affective states
imputed). These cultural images of person types are not
necessarily either entirely accurate or heavily constraining; but
they do provide us with a useful entrée to our original

question: the relationships among culture, affect, and communicative forms.

APPENDIX

Linguistic Expression of Affect in Wolof [6]

(A) Exclamations (which can occur alone):

ndei/ndei saan 'Alas!' (lit.: 'mother')
yaay Pity or sympathetic surprise ('mama')
e/ey/ay Surprise
ey waay/ay waay Shock (includes: anger, impatience, pity)
a? Nonsolidary surprise (common prelude to refusals and other-repair)
moo Indignation
ndégé-ndégé-ndégé Sympathetic surprise?
waaw kaay/wôw kay 'Right on!', 'Okay!'
ahàkay 'Yes it is too (like French si)'
hhh Supportive back-channel
mhm Supportive back-channel
tch (dental click) Supportive back-channel
kës 'Shoo!'
wuy/wo-wo-woye 'Boo-hoo (crying, report form)'

(B) Emphatic particles:

de, daal, waay, kat, kay Emphasizers (no clear difference among them, but can be piled up)
kwa (French quoi) Complaining?

(C) Morphological and syntactic devices for emphasis:

(1) Vowel lengthening in deictic determinants, e.g.:

mbote mii 'this lamb (vs. mbote mi)'
lamb det
      NCM
      prox
      emph

(2) Reduplication, e.g.:

lu bari 'a lot' vs. lu bari-bari 'a lot'

(3) Repetition

of own utterance: emphasis
of other's utterance: praise, understanding, approval

(4) Left-dislocation:

    (a) of modifiers, e.g.: Mii mbote 'this lamb'

    (b) of major sentence constituents, e.g.:

        Fatu Ture mii, Fatu Ture loxo-ëm moomu ko.
        (name) det-emph (name) hand her poss-neg pron-obj
        S   S   O   V Obj. pron.
        'This Fatu Ture does not possess her own hands
           (i.e. she has no control over them)'

        Compare neutral statement:

        Fatu Ture moomu loxo-ëm
        S   V neg   O

(5) Focus markers (some accompany left-dislocation), e.g.:

    Fatu-a   wax loolu, wante waxu   ma ko
    (name)-   say that but say-   I   it-(obj)
     (subj-focus)   (neg)
    'Fatu said that, but I didn't say it.'

(D) Lexical devices

    (1) Graded sets, e.g.:

        dara/darrra/tuus/gatt 'nothing/.../absolutely nothing'.
        lu-bari/lool/torop 'a lot/.../too much (a whole lot)'

    (2) 'Loaded' terms, e.g.:

        miikar-miikar 'be hoity-toity'
        maacipi 'a crummy little peewee'

        sa jôd-a-jôd, ak sa jëd
        your (?)   and your (?)
        'your awful way of walking very straight ahead
           (strutting?)'

    (3) Ideophones and hyperbolic expressions, e.g.:

        ba dee 'till dying'
          (as in ma ree baa dee, 'I laughed to death')
        ba reey 'till killing'

        sedd guii 'extremely cold'
        nyuul kuuk 'extremely black'
        wex tall 'extremely bitter'

(4) Lexical encoding of affect and affect-connoting speech acts, e.g.:

mere naa 'I'm angry'
ruus naa 'I'm ashamed'
bëgg naa la 'I like/want you'
bañ naa la 'I hate/refuse you'
sant naa la 'I thank/praise you'
gërëm naa la 'I thank you'
toñ naa la 'I'm teasing/annoying you'
bu la-i neexee 'If it's pleasing to you'

(5) Lexical descriptions (many insults and compliments are done this way), e.g.:

baax ngga 'You're good'
yaa di mbaam 'You're a pig'

(6) Address forms:

Kinship terms, praise-names, nicknames, etc.

(E) Oaths and imprecations:

bilaay 'by God'
ngir-Yalla '(I) swear to God'
ngir sama meen-u ndei ak sama geenyo-a baay 'By my
  mother's milk and my father's belt (i.e. matriline and
  patriline)'
sa gattay bu rëy, bu ma ko waxee, Yalla bu ma jôgé
  fii ma toog. '"Your great big shortness"--if I said it,
  may God make me go away from right here where I'm
  sitting.'
Praise-epithet of own patriclan (when very upset?)
Optatives and prayer-forms
Yall'na ngga dellusi fi ci Sengal 'May God grant you return
  here to Senegal.'
na ngga dellusi fi ci Senegal 'May you return here to
  Senegal'

(F) Phonological and prosodic devices:

(1) Lengthening of long vowels and continuants; also,
perhaps, geminates:

deeeedet 'No!!' (vs. deedet)
darrra 'Nothing!' (vs. dara)

(2) Intonational phenomena: pitch, volume, speed of talk, intonational contour.

low pitch low volume slow speed flat contour; dynamic and pitch nucleus last	'Noble speech' (wax-u géér; said to express sense of shame, self- control)
high pitch high volume fast speed varied contour; dynamic and pitch nucleus first	'Griot speech' (wax-u gewel; said to express excitement)

(3) Voice (e.g. breathy vs. clear)

(G) Nonverbal devices:

Facial expression, gesture, stance; especially: degree of animation (amount and energy of movement); open vs. closed arm positions

(H) Discourse and interactional devices:

(1) Sequencing, pauses, repetitions
(2) Use of intermediary spokespersons (e.g. hiring a griot to praise or insult someone)

NOTES

This paper grew out of discussions held at the Australian National University among members of the Working Group in Language and Cultural Context (sponsored by the Anthropology Department of the Research School of Pacific Studies). Many of the ideas in the paper actually come as much from other members of the group as from myself. Participating in those discussions were: Elinor Ochs and Bambi Schieffelin, who started us talking on this topic; also Penelope Brown, John Haviland, Leslie Haviland, Steven Levinson, Edward Schieffelin, and Michael Silverstein. Thanks are due to all, although they do not have to bear responsibility for what I say here.

1. For a sample of readings and a recent review of literature on the nature of emotion, see Arnold (1968) and Plutchik (1980).

2. I owe this point to Edward Schieffelin.

3. As Bambi Schieffelin has put it, 'hot and cold running emotions'.

4. What is weakened much more definitely, however, is the moral responsibility each party (source and spokesperson) must

bear for the abusive message. I have written on this point elsewhere (Irvine 1973, 1981).

5. So, many of the phenomena linguists have considered 'expressive language', such as the onomatopoeic 'plops, squeaks, croaks', etc., are not really particularly expressive of affect, except insofar as any attempt at vividness (of portrayal of a referent) expresses personal engagement with its object. In some uses, 'expressive language' seems to be a somewhat nebulous realm in which quite varied phenomena float about-- iconicity, metaphor, affective display, and social markers.

6. Wolof linguistic forms are rendered in the transcription system developed by the Centre de Linguistique Appliquée de Dakar and adopted by the Senegalese government in 1971 as the official orthography (cf. *Journal Officiel de la République du Sénégal*, No. 4141, 28 June 1971).

REFERENCES

Arnold, Magda, ed. 1968. The nature of emotion: Selected readings. Baltimore: Penguin.

Austin, J. 1962. How to do things with words. Cambridge, Mass.: Harvard University Press.

Bateson, Gregory. 1972. Steps to an ecology of mind. New York: Ballantine.

Bateson, Gregory, Don Jackson, Jay Haley, and John Weakland. 1956. Toward a theory of schizophrenia. Behavioral Science 1.4:251-264.

Birdwhistell, Ray L. 1970. Kinesics and context. Phila- delphia: University of Pennsylvania Press.

Darwin, Charles. 1872. The expression of the emotions in man and animals. London: John Murray.

Diffloth, Gerald. 1972. Notes on expressive meaning. In: Pro- ceedings of the Eighth Annual Meeting, Chicago Linguistic Society. Chicago: CLS. 440-447.

Diffloth, Gerald. 1976. Expressives in Semai. In: Austroasiatic Studies, Part 1. Edited by P. Jenner, L. Thompson, and S. Starosta. (Oceanic Linguistics, Special Publications 13, Part 1.) 249-264.

Eibl-Eibesfelt, I. 1972. Similarities and differences between cultures in expressive movements. In: Nonverbal com- munication. Edited by R. A. Hinde. London: Cambridge University Press. 297-312.

Ekman, Paul, and W. Friesen. 1969. Nonverbal leakage and clues to deception. Psychiatry 32.88-106.

Ekman, Paul, and W. Friesen. 1971. Constants across culture in the face and emotion. Journal of Personality and Social Psychology 17.124-129.

Ekman, Paul, E. R. Sorenson, and W. Friesen. 1969. Pan- cultural elements in the facial displays of emotion. Science 164.86-88.

Fudge, E. 1970. Phonological structure and 'expressiveness'.
Journal of Linguistics 6.161-188.

Goffman, Erving. 1961. Encounters. Indianapolis: Bobbs-
Merrill.

Goffman, Erving. 1974. Frame analysis. New York: Harper
and Row.

Irvine, J. T. 1973. Caste and communication in a Wolof
village. Ph.D. dissertation, University of Pennsylvania.

Irvine, J. T. 1981. Semantics and context in Wolof insults.
Paper delivered at meetings of the Australian Linguistics
Society and the Australian Anthropological Association,
Canberra, August.

Kagan, Jerome. 1978. On emotion and its development: A
working paper. In: The development of affect. Edited by
Michael Lewis and Leonard Rosenblum. New York: Plenum.
11-42.

LaBarre, Neston. 1947. The cultural basis of emotions and
gestures. Journal of Personality 16.49-68.

Leach, Edmund. 1972. The influence of cultural context on
non-verbal communication in man. In: Nonverbal communication. Edited by R. A. Hinde. London: Cambridge University Press.

Lewis, Michael, and Leonard Rosenblum. 1978. Introduction:
Issues in affect development. In: The development of
affect. Edited by Michael Lewis and Leonard Rosenblum.
New York: Plenum. 1-10.

Lutz, Catherine. 1982. The domain of emotion words on
Ifaluk. American Ethnologist 9.113-128.

Mithun, Marianne. 1982. The synchronic and diachronic behavior of plops, squeaks, croaks, signs, and moans. International Journal of American Linguistics 48.49-58.

Plutchik, Robert. 1980. Emotion: A psychoevolutionary
synthesis. New York: Harper and Row.

Samarin, William. 1970. Inventory and choice in expressive
language. Word 26.153-169.

Sapir, Edward. 1927. Speech as a personality trait. American Journal of Sociology 32.892-905.

Stankiewicz, E. 1964. Problems of emotive language. In:
Approaches to semiotics. Edited by T. Sebeok, A. S. Hayes,
and M. C. Bateson. Transactions of the Indiana University
Conference on Paralinguistics and Kinesics. The Hague:
Mouton. 239-264.

LANGUAGE AND BELIEF IN A MEDICAL SETTING

Aaron V. Cicourel
University of California, San Diego

Introduction. Discourse always occurs within complex contextual conditions wherein language use and paralinguistic and nonverbal information interact simultaneously at several levels of abstraction and attention. These complex processes mirror the fact that during discourse or social interaction participants must be capable of multilevel, parallel processing in order to perceive themselves and others as generating competent or unusual communication.

Discourse participants must be capable of assigning and assessing the significance of the immediate interactional setting. Several senses of normality are implied, including a person's technical, professional, and social status and actions. Many of these conditions are seldom made explicit, but subtle differences are often marked by the use of different linguistic registers. The setting itself can provide information about the appropriate forms of dress called for, the kind of turn-taking expected, physical distance and posturing, and specific or general motor actions.

The use of different linguistic registers presupposes that members of a group or society possess a theory of social stratification or schemata about the way material objects, beliefs, values, occupational pursuits, educational achievement, social activities, interpersonal attributes and behavior styles, and appearances are valued. Murray (1980) has noted the importance of identifying the rules and mechanisms that members of a group or culture must know and/or utilize in order to understand the rights and obligations or entitlements they can expect and exercise in different situations in order to produce appropriate speech acts. A stratification system requires that its members achieve a complex synchronization of speech and paralinguistic activities, nonverbal behavior, and appearances that in general will be appropriate to different settings. Participants of discourse in everyday life must know something about the social conventions and procedures necessary for sustaining the larger system as well as producing speech, paralinguistic, and nonverbal activities that may have only local appropriateness. But participants of discourse must also be sensitive to irregularities or deviations that can occur.

In its idealized form, discourse can be expected to follow the Gricean cooperative principle (Grice 1975) and the notion of conversational postulates wherein participants are expected to follow what are assumed to be tacitly agreed upon aims of the conversation. The speaker is expected to be as informative as possible without going too far vis-à-vis what seems to be called for, while not saying anything believed to be false or lacking adequate evidence. Furthermore, the speaker is expected to say things that are relevant, while also being brief, orderly, and clear.

The idealized forms of discourse outlined by Grice can be recognized as part of every competent speaker-listener's native knowledge, but this knowledge base must also include the ability to lie or to recognize a lie, the ability to perceive more than one message in an utterance, and to link a target utterance or a series of utterances to antecedent and subsequent utterances to create some kind of coherence or theme or to infer a goal. The speaker-listener's ability to produce and perceive or infer speech, paralinguistic, and nonverbal activities associated with terms like 'insults', 'deception', 'ridicule', 'teasing', 'intimidation', 'evasiveness', and the like, must be part of a native competence that can be observed in discourse.

A process model of discourse must be capable of addressing how participants track each other's speech, paralinguistic, and nonverbal activities while periodically assessing the degree of convergence or divergence in the way they communicate, make inferences about their actions, or seek to resolve apparent conflicts as they make attributions to each other.

The various mechanisms and processes associated with a model of discourse, therefore, amount to aspects of a theory of comprehension or understanding. Participants must be capable of interpreting and summarizing their own and others' activities throughout discourse. They must, therefore, develop theories of knowledge or schemata that will guide their perceptions of a setting and the talk and actions, while also reacting to environmental sources of information and perhaps modifying their views of the world.

The study of language and social context presumes an ethnographic setting that has been observed for an extended period of time. By making careful use of one case of doctor-patient communication, we can clarify the significance of an ethnographic approach for an understanding of language and social context as it seeks to reveal the important role of feelings and emotions in the necessary interaction between cognitive and organizational ways of framing decisions in discourse.

In this paper I examine materials from a series of doctor-patient interviews and some additional material from an interview I conducted with the patient some 16 months after her initial contact with the physician. The materials form part of a larger corpus; some of these materials have been used in other papers (Cicourel 1981; in press). This paper contains previously unpublished details from the interviews between the doctor and patient.

The reader will want to raise the question of the distortion that is likely to be inherent in the patient's memory of her encounters with the physician 16 months earlier. I sought to make this distortion both a topic and a resource for comparing what the patient could remember of what she and the doctor actually said 16 months earlier.

The interview materials make continual reference to organizational practices and contain occasionally dramatic confrontations between doctor and patient within the confines of a bureaucratic setting. In principle the participants observe the decorum of the setting, yet, throughout, the patient challenges the very trust upon which the doctor-patient relationship is said to be built.

On the basis of these interviews, several issues are discussed here, with primary focus on the following ones.

(1) The patient's beliefs about health care and illness are in contrast with the doctor's views about the same issues. Hospital social routines are known by the patient from her youth when she worked in a large midwestern hospital. She keeps bringing this knowledge into the medical interviews and the interview with me. She updates her beliefs about what she knows by referring to recent negative experiences at a university hospital and at the military hospital where she worked as a volunteer and where her husband died.

(2) The notion of psychological framing (Tversky and Kahneman 1978, 1981), or how decisions are made under conditions of uncertainty, as tested in experimental settings, is employed and combined with the idea of interactional and organizational framing in order to underscore the complex circumstances under which decisions are framed in natural settings. If we think of the patient as a subject and the doctor as the experimenter, we have a situation in which the experimenter tells the subject what is wrong and what is to be done about it. For the most part, however, the subject does not believe the frame provided for her and thinks the action (treatment) recommended and subsequently followed was unnecessary. The bureaucratic setting and the physician's professional authority carry the patient through the radiation treatment and surgery despite the patient's strong doubts about what is happening.

(3) The notion of schemata as problem-solving, hypothesis-testing theories that guide one's perception and interpretation of incoming information while also being shaped by the information, is contrasted with the notion of beliefs as schematized

knowledge driven by feelings and emotions. The idea of a
schema employed in everyday settings as an interaction of cognitive and emotional elements helps us understand the patient's
refusal to accept certain evidence while following bureaucratic
practices about which she has raised serious doubts.

(4) The patient's doubts about the physician's speech acts
suggest a slight change in the role of the Gricean (Grice 1975)
cooperative principle and the conversational postulates it gener-
ates.

Finding social context in discourse and textual material. The
importance of studying language in a social context has been
presented forcefully by many researchers in recent years (Bauman and Sherzer 1975; Bernstein 1971, 1973; Bright 1966;
Cicourel 1968, 1974a; Corsaro 1981; Gumperz 1971; Gumperz
and Hymes 1972; Hymes 1962; Labov 1972; Labov and Fanshel
1977). Labov and Fanshel's analysis of therapeutic talk between
a therapist and a 19-year-old female patient called Rhoda is a
clear example of linking organizational and institutional status
and role relationships to the study of discourse. I briefly
paraphrase the background and circumstances that emerge in
the therapy talk and then address Labov and Fanshel's notion
of a web of rights and obligations between the patient and her
mother to explain the intent and content of the discourse they
examine.

From the discourse it can be inferred that Rhoda, age 19, a
college student, lives with her mother and an aunt, Editha.
Rhoda's sister, Phyllis, is married and has a child. Since
Phyllis works part-time, the mother often visits her daughter
to help with the baby, thus taking her away from her normal
duties at home with Rhoda and the aunt. Labov and Fanshel
call attention to the patient's adult status and the rights and
obligations normally attributed to this status, which in this
context include the obligation to perform particular household
duties such as cleaning the house, buying food, and preparing
meals. The therapy talk reveals a patient who is complaining
that her mother has been away from home longer than usual,
helping her sister. The extended absence is said to be creating small problems that the patient is trying to resolve using
principles learned from the therapist, especially the idea that
one should express one's needs and emotions to key persons.
We are led to the conclusion that family problems have altered
the patient's perceived role obligations, thus creating role
strain for Rhoda.

The analysis of therapeutic discourse by Labov and Fanshel
helps one to understand the need for a therapist to assess the
social norms involved in family problems as a means of helping
the patient resolve her difficulties. The authors address the
kinds of role strain evident from the therapy talk and their
consequences for Rhoda at home and in the therapy sessions.
The role obligations and role strain become explanatory themes

for understanding the patient's problems of housecleaning and shopping with an aunt who is perceived as not helpful, as well as Rhoda's concerns with her school studies. The analysis by Labov and Fanshel is a good example of how a sociolinguistic study must address external organizational conditions as they are revealed by the therapy talk. The authors were not able to extend their study into the home environment, thus adding an ethnographic dimension to their reliance on organizational conditions for explaining the therapy talk. But the work of Labov and Fanshel underscores the necessity of pursuing the organizational or institutional constraints and resources that help to shape the participants' discourse.

This study is similar to that of Labov and Fanshel. The organizational setting is a medical clinic and a series of doctor-patient interviews and physical examinations. A similar physical setting exists in the two studies that immediately constrains what the participants can expect to happen and also indicates the kinds of status and power differences that exist. The organizational element which differs is the existence of medical interviews and written progress notes or elements of a medical history, as well as laboratory reports that can be contrasted with transcripts of the interviews.

The single case presented here is part of continuous research by the investigator on medical interviews and diagnostic reasoning in a variety of clinical settings. Familiarity with the medical speech community has been enhanced by teaching aspects of medical interviewing to medical students for over 10 years while also observing these students interviewing patients, listening to their tape-recorded interviews, and assessing their adequacy for two required courses on doctor-patient relations and an introduction to clinical medicine.

The necessity of ethnographic or organizational information for understanding discourse can be underscored by choosing settings in which fairly clear constraints exist on institutional procedures and routines to be followed. The bureaucratic context of a hospital or private clinic is an ideal setting because aspects of a professional role and the expectations and constraints that are likely to occur can be identified. There are routine occasions when specific transfers of information occur-- such as the kind of information that is to go into a medical history and the results of laboratory tests. Common elicitation procedures are followed and a specific written protocol designed to clarify and summarize the information is obtained. Fairly precise procedures exist for various medical subspecialties, as Petinari (n.d.) notes in her description of a particular surgical procedure. Hence there are many top-down or hypothesis-driven aspects of discourse that can be specified in these bureaucratic settings.

An essential common element of the study of discourse materials as relatively self-contained, that is, without explicit data on the ethnographic or bureaucratic context, versus the study of discourse in natural organizational settings, is that an interactive theory of comprehension is always presupposed (Rumelhart 1977). Comprehension necessarily assumes several levels of information processing, for example, an understanding of features, letters, and words; the way a referent is expressed in one part of a long dialog and then suspended, only to be resumed much later (Reichman 1978); the recognition of linguistic registers; and the perception of activities labeled 'polite' or 'rude'. The inclusiveness or exclusiveness of levels of processing identified in studies of discourse varies with the particular academic discipline and theoretical problem addressed by the researcher, while the participants' comprehension of discourse is always constrained by their understanding of the natural or laboratory organizational setting, the kinds of social interaction perceived to be permitted or encouraged, and the knowledge base they bring to the setting.

Participants of discourse or readers of a text are always engaged in selective use of the information they can attend to. Limited capacity processing constraints imposed by a complex setting and the participants' knowledge base can sharply reduce the participants' comprehension of what is taking place. The researcher faces similar problems. We normally examine single utterances or connected discourse that run for a few lines, giving careful attention to lexical items, pronominal usage and repetition, the repetition of clauses that give referential prominence to a person, object, or event, WH-cleft constructions, IT-cleft constructions, relative clauses, rhetorical questions, and the like; yet we may avoid or be unaware of information that presupposes organizational constraints and complex social relationships that can be obtained only by ethnographic field research.

We are not always sensitive to complex organizational issues because they seem remote or make substantial demands on our time, yet we must also devote considerable time to variations in intonation and stress that seem to signal what we already think we know of as status conflict or role strain between participants. These subtleties cannot be ignored, but their relative importance depends on our general sociocultural knowledge, our familiarity with specific bureaucratic settings, and our understanding of power and role relationships within the organization. We may not always be able to show that one person is exerting power over another by virtue of dominating a conversation or using relative clauses or remarks that are intended to mitigate the other's status or the importance of what is said. There is, therefore, a top-down, bottom-up trade-off between what we can predict about the way people will and do talk to each other because of what we know (and assume they know) about organizational constraints and existing status relationships. There is also the further question of what aspects of these predictions we can document, or what we can learn about

organizational constraints and existing status relationships from
a careful examination of an audio or video tape.

   Bureaucracy, beliefs, and discourse. Recently, I have
studied the case of a patient referred to a gynecological clinic
of a teaching hospital to illustrate the recoding process used
by a physician to represent his understanding of the patient's
illness (Cicourel 1981; in press). Unlike previous work of a
similar nature (Cicourel 1974b, 1975), this recent work covers
several interviews and seeks to obtain from the patient independent information on her perception of prior interaction with
the physician during formal interviews at the clinic.
   Some readers will want to know why the patient we have
studied in this paper became the focus of attention. The case
emerged by chance from a larger study of patients in an ob-
stetrical oncology clinic. The case was called to my attention
because of an interest in patients who spontaneously expressed
their own views to the physician about their own health as well
as their views on health care delivery. The present case did
not fit the criteria for the larger study but seemed to be ideal
for my interests in medical communication. I wanted to explore
aspects of memory and comprehension that would enable me to
compare the original setting of interaction, the doctor's written
account, and the patient's long-term memory of the original
interaction. I had expected to wait about one year for the
course of treatment to be completed. But the treatment per-
sisted and I finally decided to pursue my interview with the
patient in her home after some 16 months had elapsed.
   The case history is augmented by using new materials from
the medical interviews and my interview with the patient some
16 months after her initial contact with the gynecologist. High-
lights of the case are presented briefly in order to focus on
details that clarify how the patient's beliefs are linked to
organizational constraints and practices, and the structure of
discourse. The patient's beliefs about her illness provide us
with an independent source of information about the formal
medical history, the medical interviews, and bureaucratic procedures that seemed to have a direct bearing on the patient's
beliefs about her illness and the practice of medicine.
   The patient, Mrs. Muir, initially visited Dr. B on 21 March
1977. I was able to record her visit of 21 March, as well as
visits on 25 March, 30 March 1977, and 15 April 1977. The
physician's initial examination did not produce any serious
findings and he told the patient: 'Well...from uh...uh standpoint of uh, a gynecologist, I think everything is, is really
pretty good.' In the course of a routine physical, the doctor
took a pap smear test. The results were positive and the
physician proceeded to call the patient and asked her to return
to his office for biopsies. The patient returned on 25 March
1977. The visit was brief, the biopsies were performed, and
the doctor told the patient he would call her with the results.

The doctor called the patient to report that the biopsies indicated cancer in the inner lining of the uterus and that she should return to his office for further consultation and treatment plans. The patient returned to the physician's office with her daughter on 30 March 1977. The biopsy findings were described to the patient and the doctor also described the radiation treatments and surgery that would be necessary. The descriptions were quite detailed. He also noted that he would explain what he had told the patient on the telephone; that from the biopsies an unequivocal diagnosis was established and that a previously discussed D and C (dilation and curettage), or 'scraping' of the uterine cervix, would be unnecessary. The physician stopped on several occasions to ask the patient if she understood everything he had said; her responses were always in the affirmative. However, she then expressed doubts about the diagnosis and about medical bureaucratic practices and policies. The patient completed her radiation therapy and the surgery was performed.

When I interviewed the patient some 16 months after her initial visit to the gynecologist, she presented me with a series of remarks which both reiterated and contradicted many things contained in the tape-recorded medical interviews and the doctor's account of his experiences with Mrs. Muir over a period of four years. Briefly, the patient confused three interviews at the physician's office with two telephone conversations. She noted that, based on the first interview, there appeared to be nothing serious about her condition. The doctor called after receiving a laboratory report indicating an abnormal pap smear test, and, according to the patient, suggested that a D and C might still be the only treatment necessary if the biopsies he now wanted performed were negative. Based on the medical interview material and my interview with the patient, she continued to believe that her condition was not serious when she visited the doctor on 25 March 1977, at the time the biopsies were performed. A second telephone call by the physician was made on 28 March 1977, and the biopsies were reported as confirming cancer of the inner lining of the uterus. On 30 March 1977 the patient was given an extensive explanation of the diagnosis and treatment to be followed. The patient was accompanied by her daughter, but the doctor's remarks did not convince the patient that everything had proceeded routinely. The patient's doubts about her diagnosis and treatment seemed to be related to several independent events.

When I interviewed the patient, she confronted me with a routine hospital report that had arrived when she was in the hospital recovering from surgery. There was no name or date on the letter and only a stamped signature of the gynecologist. The envelope was dated 3 May 1977. The patient assumed a mistake had been made but her remarks were not clear. First she stated that someone's letter had gotten into her envelope, but we could also infer from her remarks that perhaps she was

thinking that her pap test was normal: 'And somebody in,
along the line somewhere said it wasn't normal...' The patient
seems to have questioned the original diagnosis and the operation performed because there had perhaps been a bureaucratic
mistake. The patient called this letter about a 'normal' pap
smear report a 'shock' that reminded her of the 'shock of my
husband's death...' The letter and the test results triggered
prior doubts about her illness and the surgery, and led to re-
newed thoughts about her husband's death.

Another source of possible confusion for the patient was the
mention of the D and C during the first telephone call from the
doctor, and the physician's remarks at the close of the initial
interview to the effect that she appeared to be in good condition. The patient seems to have interpreted the idea of a
D and C as a fairly routine procedure to be pursued if the
biopsy proved negative. The diagnostic importance of a
D and C, if it was performed, did not seem to be part of the
patient's knowledge base, and hence she did not realize that
this procedure could be used to confirm problems rather than
being a fairly benign terminal treatment for her gynecological
problems.

The bureaucratic procedure of sending out test results without a name or a date on the letter, and the patient's unfamiliar-
ity with the significance of a D and C procedure, are part of
a knowledge base embedded in complex ethnographic or organizational settings that force the participants of discourse and
the researcher continually to integrate organizational and technical knowledge. Under simulated experimental problem-solving
conditions, we would expect a person to assimilate the doctor's
explanations into the construction of schemata or to modify or
confirm existing schemata or theories about medical domains of
knowledge. But when we compare what the physician told the
patient in the presence of her daughter with what the patient
told me some 16 months later, we realize that a problem-solving
model of comprehension needs some modification if we are to
understand the patient's reasoning and feelings about her illness and the treatments given her.

The patient's conception of her illness and how she developed
cancer contains contradictory elements that are sometimes striking in their differences. Having consulted her own internist
first, and having been told that she had an uncomplicated infection that could easily be treated, the patient nevertheless
turned to the gynecologist for a second opinion. Finding the
letter from the hospital announcing a negative pap smear test
after returning home from surgery seems to have led the
patient to question the gynecologist's diagnosis and perhaps
even the biopsies. She suspected that someone else had the
cancer for which she was diagnosed and received treatment.
Her beliefs contrast sharply with the fact that she was aware
of many of the factual explanations and data given to her by
the gynecologist.

The basic elements of the patient's belief can be stated as follows.

(1) She questioned the diagnosis of cancer because of her internist's original diagnosis of an uncomplicated infection and the gynecologist's remark at the close of the initial interview and physical examination that she seemed to be in good condition.

(2) She noted the doctor had told her that only a D and C had initially been indicated as necessary.

(3) The after-surgery report from the hospital that her pap smear was normal and the bureaucratic format of the letter provided support for her belief that perhaps the wrong person had received the surgery.

(4) She ignored the negative pap test and biopsy performed by the gynecologist.

The patient's belief also contained the following elements which contradict the foregoing views:

(1) She consulted the gynecologist in order to obtain a second opinion, despite the seemingly routine and benign diagnosis by her internist.

(2) She suggested that cancer is contagious and that she and her children probably contracted the disease from her husband.

(3) This view of cancer was further supported by the remark that 'maybe the cancer is contagious and nobody warned us, and my, me dear son, he always kissed his dad on the forehead and, uh my uh daughter did too, and you know that last three weeks or so, they really perspire and I wonder if the germs don't come out with the perspiration...'

(4) The patient cited a television program where she claimed there was a reference to the possibility that leukemia could be contagious.

The interaction of the patient's beliefs and factual knowledge. Tracing the way in which the patient acquired her beliefs about health care delivery practices and the cause of cancer is at best a weak reconstruction based on fragments of data from several doctor-patient interviews and a follow-up interview conducted in the patient's home some 16 months after her initial visit to the gynecologist. The third interview with the physician, in which he explained the nature of her illness and the treatment to be followed, revealed elements of the patient's beliefs that were not to become clear until I conducted my interview with her more than a year after her surgery. By reference to the patient's remarks during the third medical interview and her remarks to me, I hope to show how her beliefs and her experience with bureaucratic organizations contributed to her maintaining two contradictory beliefs about her own illness and about the harm that health care practitioners can do to their patients.

During her first visit to the gynecologist, the patient was told that she appeared to be in good condition. The pap smear taken, however, revealed an abnormal reading and the doctor called the patient to ask that she come in for a biopsy of the uterus. During his telephone conversation, he stated that the patient might have to return to his office for a D and C if the biopsy proved negative. The biopsy revealed the presence of cancer in the endometrium or lining of the uterus. The doctor called the patient a second time and asked that she come in as soon as possible for a discussion of treatment plans.

The third interview opened with a few usual pleasantries, including the introduction of the patient's daughter to the physician and to my former doctoral student. The doctor asked whether the patient had had any bleeding and whether she was still taking estrogen. The patient referred to having had a pap smear done a few months earlier by one physician, and having seen another doctor for 'cracking in the you know vulva'. The doctor reviewed the estrogen taken previously, covering the same ground he had asked the patient about during their first meeting. The patient revealed a similar story that she told during her first visit about deciding to see the gynecologist after consulting with another one of his patients. The patient made this decision despite having been told by the internist she had consulted two months earlier (January, 1977) that her pap test was negative and that she had only experienced an infection. The patient stated: 'I felt there was something wrong, even though they said second pap [Dr: Right] tests was all right. I could tell it in my eyes and the way I, way I feel, there was something wrong.' The doctor then provided the patient with a long narrative explanation of his findings and the course of treatment to be followed (Figure 1).

In Figure 1, the doctor begins his remarks by mentioning what he had already told the patient during their recent telephone conversation: the biopsies taken during her second visit to the clinic showed a clear diagnosis. Therefore, a D and C would not be necessary. The physician states the diagnosis as cancer of the endometrium and assures the patient that there is a 'very excellent chance of curing this.' He suggests a combination of radiation treatments and a hysterectomy. He explains that 'the surgery consists of removing the uterus and the tubes and the ovaries.'

When the doctor completed the explanation contained in Figure 1, he asked (line 30) 'Uh, okay so far?' The patient's reply was 'yes.' He then told the patient and her daughter that he wanted them to ask questions when he completed his explanation. The physician continued to explain aspects of the procedures to be followed during treatment and once again asked if there were any questions the patient wanted to ask. The patient asked about the purpose of the radiation treatment to be given before the hysterectomy.

Figure 1. Physician's explanation of findings and suggested treatment.

1	Dr:	Right. Well, to explain again what I explained to you on the phone,
2		what we found from the biopsies that I took in the office, very
3		clearly establishes the diagnosis. So that we don't have to do a
4		D and C or anything like that. We know what's wrong with you, and we
5		know uh what needs to be done. This is a very common kind of cancer.
6.		Many women at your age get it, nowadays, in the United States. It's
7		called cancer of the inner lining of the uterus--we call it cancer
8		of the endometrium. Uh, it's also, if you're going to have to get
9		something like this, one of the uh, most favorable, from our stand-
10		point, to treat. The results of treatment are very, very good. Uh
11		very excellent chance of curing this. But treatment can't be delayed.
12		It's got to be done right, it's got to be started promptly. Now we
13		feel the best way to treat something like this, on the basis of the
14		information we have, and we're going to have to do some more tests,
15		by the way, to to uh uh check out other things, to make absolutely
16		sure there aren't other problems. Uh, and I'll explain those to
17		you. But, basically, we feel the best way to treat this, to give
18		you the best chance to cure it, is a combination of radiation
19		treatments and a hysterectomy. The radiation treat- ment, and I want
20		you to go over this morning, if possible, to see Dr. Birch who's
21		a colleague on the university faculty, who is head of the radiation
22		therapy department at the university. The radiation treatment
23		consists of external radiation which is painless, really doesn't
24		involve much more than just lying on the table while they direct the

Figure 1.   Continued.

25	machine. Uh, and that goes on for a period of about four weeks,
26	Monday through Friday, or weekdays, and then as soon as that finishes,
27	within uh, just a short period of time, one or two days, or two or
28	three at the most, we'd like to go right ahead with the surgery. And
29	the surgery consists of removing the uterus and the tubes and the
30	ovaries...Uh, okay so far?

Each dot = 1 second.

The doctor provided her with further details on the importance
of the radiation therapy: 'it reduces the chances of the cancer
spreading..uh...and it reduces the chance, it increases the
chances of cure by about 15 or 20 percent, which is significant.' The doctor gave the patient a somewhat formal but detailed explanation, using the following terms:

> Uh, the radiation treatments cause some symptoms while
> you're having the radiation. Usually a bit of loss of
> appetite, maybe some bowel irritability, and some bladder
> irritability, which the radiation therapy doctors will ex-
> plain it to you in much more detail. That subsides also,
> usually within a very short period of time begins function-
> ing normally.

The patient expressed concern about the possibility of the
radiation affecting her eyes, but did not question the physician's remarks. The doctor's use of terms resembled a medical
linguistic register that implies a fairly sophisticated audience.
There does not appear to be any indication thus far of the
patient harboring doubts or beliefs that might challenge or
contradict the physician. But immediately following the remarks about the possibility of the radiation affecting her eyes,
and the doctor's assurances that it would not, and a few additional remarks by the patient describing some discomfort she
experienced the night before, the physician shifted the topic
to the biopsy that was taken a few days earlier; perhaps he
was thinking that it could be causing the reported discomfort.
Figure 2 indicates the topic shift by the physician, but also
reveals a more abrupt topic shift by the patient that is noteworthy for the rather abstract deictic expression *there* ('Do
you feel that's been there?' line 4) to refer to the cancer of
the endometrium previously mentioned by the doctor. The
patient seems to be saying: 'Do you feel that the cancer has
been in the lining of the uterus all the time that I was given

earlier pap smear tests?' We can create this expansion because
of the remarks that follow, in which she refers to previous
pap tests that were performed.

The patient's remark clearly indicated that her own beliefs
about her illness were heavily influenced by a number of facts
which she proceeded to describe (lines 5-6), referring to a
'pap test' taken in 'September, and the last one they took, I
asked the nurse, I didn't see the doctor...' Two different
tests can be inferred here: one in September, and one noted
elsewhere in the interview, taken in January, 1977. The
significance of these remarks for the patient seems to be that
the tests were normal, but the gynecologist has just told her
that she has cancer of the endometrium, based on a positive
pap test and a biopsy that confirmed a diagnosis of cancer.

Figure 2.   Patient's doubts about diagnosis and doctor's
            explanation of pap test limitations.

1 Dr: Did you have much problem after we took the biopsy
        the other day?

2 Pt: Not over the weekend. Not until yesterday, really.
        (unintelligible)...
3   but over the weekend I didn't. It just seemed like
        last night I had
4   quite a bit. Do you feel that's been there? Now, as
        I say, I had this
5   paps test taken, taken one in September, and the last
        one they took,
6   I asked the nurse, I didn't see the doctor, and I
        said, 'Was that test
7   all right?' Because I called her, and she said, and
        she looked it up,
8   and she said, 'Yes.'

9 Dr: Yeah, I'm not surprised at that, because the pap test
        is not at all
10   good when it comes to diagnosing this kind of cancer.
        It's fortunate
11   that the pap test that I took was positive, because it
        could have been
12   missed for a longer period of time. Ordinarily, we
        wouldn't take a
13   biopsy unless you had some bleeding...And the thing
        that led me to take
14   a biopsy was the pap test, and it's just fortunate that
        it was positive...
15   Uh, I always try and take a smear from up inside the
        cervical canal in

Figure 2. Continued.

16	addition to the outside of the cervix, and that's prob- probably why it
17	was positive. The ordinary pap smear wouldn't have been positive.

18 Pt: Uh and then the biopsy

19 Dr: The biopsy, there was no question about that at all.

20 Pt: Is it up in the cervix ⌐or

21 Dr: ⌊No, it's up above the cervix,
        up inside the
22   uterus itself.

23 Pt: Uh hmm.

24 Dr: That's why we call it cancer of the inner lining of the
        uterus, or cancer
25   of the endometrium.

The spontaneous topic shift by the patient and her reference
to prior pap smear tests that were considered negative suggest
for the first time doubts about the diagnosis of cancer. Yet
the patient had already told the physician that she had come
to see him because of a concern that she might not be well,
having asked a former patient of the gynecologist for help in
seeing someone other than her internist. It is as if the patient
were trying to assess her own feelings about not being well,
and the accuracy of independent pap smear tests and a biopsy.

The external bureaucratic information called 'laboratory tests'
becomes a significant aspect of her beliefs about her illness,
yet there is marked indecision. On the one hand, she reported
concern for her health and the fact that she sought independent
medical help despite the negative pap tests with the internist
and a diagnosis of vulva irritation and an infection. The gynecologist confirmed this diagnosis after his initial examination,
but this was before the positive pap test and biopsy during her
second visit. On the other hand, she suddenly began to
'wonder out loud' in the presence of the gynecologist about the
fact of the previous pap smear tests taken by the internist;
yet this occurred immediately after the gynecologist had
explained that the laboratory tests clearly revealed that she
had cancer of the endometrium. The patient said nothing
immediately after the phyician confirmed the presence of cancer,
repeating what he had told her in a telephone conversation a
couple of days earlier. Yet after hearing the doctor explain

the treatment process, the patient suddenly asked if the cancer had been in her uterus all along and then referred to the fact that there had been previous pap smear tests.

Lines 9-17 of Figure 2 give the doctor's response. He immediately picked up the topic shift and its implication for the patient that there seemed to be conflicting evidence here, and provided an explanation that mitigated the importance of the pap test for diagnosing cancer of the endometrium, while also noting that if a smear had not been taken 'from up inside the cervical canal', and if the pap test had not been positive, the diagnosis could have been missed. The physician's remarks here and in earlier interviews imply that no biopsy would have been taken unless there had been bleeding or the pap smear test was positive. When the patient reported no bleeding at the initial interview, there was no discussion about doing a biopsy or even a D and C. The D and C emerged as a possibility during a telephone conversation only after the pap test came back positive, and only under the further contingency that the biopsy that was then felt to be necessary proved to be negative. The patient either was unable to comprehend these facts, or else was reluctant to revise her conception of what had happened in light of new facts. She was motivated to seek further medical help, but was unable to accept the facts as explained by the gynecologist.

I want to jump ahead of the story quickly to note that in her interview with Cicourel some 16 months later, the patient stated that she had returned to her internist to report the gynecologist's findings and diagnosis. The patient stated (lines 31-32, Figure 4) that the internist had told her that the gynecologist 'must have really hit a particular spot where it started.' So, for the patient, perhaps the internist was saying that the gynecologist's procedure was on target because of luck. The gynecologist implied something similar in his remarks ('It's fortunate that the pap test that I took was positive'), but we could also infer (lines 15-17, Figure 2) that it was his experience and specialty that led him 'to try and take a smear from up inside the cervical canal in addition to the outside of the cervix, and that's prob-probably why it was positive.'

The patient then questioned the doctor about the extensiveness of cancer and whether there was some reason for waiting for surgery. The physician then reiterated his point about the importance of doing the radiation therapy first and then asked if there were any questions. The patient's daughter entered the conversation at this point to say:

The only thing that really shocked me was when you said that, this doesn't have to do with Ma, it's that, more of my own curiosity, that's what, you know, I always felt like that was what a pap was for, and so I always walked away feeling secure, but now I don't know.

The daughter's questioning of the accuracy of the pap smear test seemed to leave her rather insecure about the doctor's previous remarks. The physician proceeded to note that cancer of the endometrium tends to occur after menopause and that in general a pap smear does not catch several important gynecological problems. He also repeated that this type of cancer is easy to treat and that had the pap test not been positive, things could have been considerably worse if they had to wait until bleeding occurred before taking the biopsy. So what was seen as good fortune from the doctor's perspective was seen as doubtful from the patient's perspective, and left the daughter feeling insecure about pap smear tests.

The physician then changed the topic to the previously mentioned importance of a projected visit by the patient to the radiologist, the desirability of radiation therapy, and the possibility of surgery about four and one-half weeks later. The patient then shifted the topic (lines 1-2, Figure 3), asking if the gynecologist were connected with the university. The doctor replied, 'That's right'. The patient shifted the topic again and asked if he would do the surgery, and then followed this question with the remark that 'After that '60 Minute' program where I wonder whether the doctor does', only to be cut off by the physician, who reported that this is a frequently asked quesion. The patient seemed to be questioning the adequacy of treatment at a university hospital and also challenging the doctor's professional integrity.

Notice how medical bureaucratic practices are again foremost in the patient's thinking about her illness and what could happen to her. The doctor patiently tried to address these doubts and acknowledged that other patients have similar concerns. The physician also indicated that residents help him and that he also works with an associate, taking some pains to assure the patient about the quality of care to be received. The patient then (lines 15-19, Figure 3) referred to her experience at a large private hospital in the Midwest where she had worked many years ago, noting how irregularities had occurred during the delivery of babies by someone other than the designated doctor. The physician once again agreed that such activities are very unfortunate. The patient then recalled an operation on her eye at a university hospital in the Los Angeles area, where she had asked the surgeon the same question, even though it was before she had seen the program on '60 Minutes'. The doctor's brief remarks acknowledged the activities.

The patient recalled her personal experiences while working in a large, private midwestern hospital as a young woman, and then in recent years as a volunteer at the military hospital where her husband had died. These experiences seemed to be the basis for challenging the physician's professional conduct, and placed the doctor in an awkward situation toward a patient whose trust he needed and hoped to have before pursuing a course of treatment.

Figure 3. Further indication of patient doubts about medical bureaucratic practices.

1 Pt:	I have one question there. You're you're connected with the university,
2	right?
3 Dr:	That's right.
4 Pt:	Now, you do the surgery? After that 60 Minute program where I wonder
5	whether the doctor does
6 Dr:	Yeah, I get that asked by about every other patient,
7	Yesterday, I operated on a lawyer's wife and, needless to say, he asked
8	me that question about six times. And, yes, I do the surgery, yes that's
9	correct. Uh, residents help me and, as a matter of fact, I have a full-
10	time associate who's fully trained, a gynecological cancer doctor,
11	Dr. Rob and he often helps me too, and we help each other. Uh, that
12	was a very unfortunate program because, in many respects, the best care
13	that anybody can possibly get in a university hospital. And uh I wish
14	that...
15 Pt:	Well, even in private hospitals, see, I worked in Queen's in
16	Chicago, and I, I remember that, I worked the desk. When they called
17	down and gave me a delivery and said Dr. Frank, for example, delivered
18	the baby, and I'd see him walk in ten minutes later. So, he wasn't
19	anywhere near that delivery.
20 Dr:	Yeah, I think that...
21 Pt:	And I didn't think that was right either.
22 Dr:	I agree.

Figure 3. Continued.

---

23 Pt: For the hospital records to say he delivered that baby.

24 Dr: I, I agree with you.

25 Pt: Because I worked there, and did as I was told.
    [Dr: I, I] I was very
26   young.

27 Dr: I couldn't agree with you more about something like
    that.

At this point, it may be helpful to summarize the material
presented thus far.

(1) The patient visited her internist to check on vulva irritation approximately seven months and again two months prior
to seeing the gynecologist, and presumably had pap smear
tests done on each occasion. The second test was reported
as negative and her problem was diagnosed as having been an
infection. The visit in September, 1976 occurred a few weeks
after her husband had died of pancreatic cancer in a military
hospital.

(2) Despite a benign diagnosis, the patient noted 'I felt
there was something wrong, even though they said second
pap [Dr: Right] tests was all right. I could tell it in my
eyes and the way I, way I feel, there was something wrong.'
We do not know if the patient rejected the medical frame provided by the internist because of her husband's death from
cancer, but she was sufficiently concerned to consult a gynecologist.

(3) During the first interview, the gynecologist told the
patient that on the basis of his preliminary examination she
appeared to be in good gynecological health. He took a routine pap smear. The patient did not reveal her beliefs about
cancer or medical bureaucratic practices and policies during
this initial interview, but she did mention her husband's death
from cancer and the physician indicated in his progress notes
that she seemed depressed.

(4) The doctor called the patient a few days later to report
that the pap test was abnormal and that she should come in for
a biopsy of the uterus. According to the patient, he mentioned
that if the biopsy was negative, all that might be required
medically was a D and C. The medical perspective changes
here.

(5) The patient returned for the biopsy four days later. The
results were telephoned to the patient three days later and she
was in to see the physician about a course of treatment two
days later. During the telephone conversation and the third
visit, the patient's medical perspective was changed again by

the physician. He stated that she had cancer of the inner lining of the uterus or endometrium.

(6) During the third visit, the patient's views about her illness began to emerge, suggesting that she had doubts about the results of the pap test and biopsy performed by the gynecologist. She also expressed her negative views on irregularities in medical bureaucratic practices and policies. Her knowledge of bureaucratic practices and policies, and her reference to a television program on 60 Minutes about doctors who, by allowing other doctors to replace them, fail to fulfill their obligations to patients, became the basis for challenging the gynecologist's practices and policies regarding health care delivery.

(7) The patient's remarks suggest two perspectives, both of which challenged the physician's integrity: she began to doubt the validity of the doctor's diagnosis by comparing earlier pap tests taken by her internist with the one taken by the gynecologist, despite her own feeling that she was not well; and she invoked her experiences with medical bureaucracies and a television program to elicit guarantees from the doctor that he would be the one to perform the surgery on her.

(8) Despite direct confrontations between doctor and patient over the significance of the pap test and biopsy performed by the gynecologist, and the doctor's attempt to mitigate the idea that irregularities known to have happened elsewhere could result in the doctor not performing the surgery on the patient, the patient seems to have sustained her beliefs about her illness and the practices and policies of medical bureaucracies. The patient seems to have used her belief system to challenge the factual information offered by the doctor and his assurances that he would perform the surgery. The patient's knowledge of social structure and organizational practices and policies takes on a significant role in her use of language to challenge the physician's views.

Returning to the discourse after Figure 3, we find the doctor responding to the patient's reference to the 60 Minutes program. The patient seemed to feel that such practices are fairly common. She made the following pointed observation: 'And you put your faith in this doctor, and I put my faith in you, because you're here, and then if someone else turns around and does the surgery, I don't appreciate that' (laughs). The physician responded as follows:

No, I understand exactly how you feel, and you, you're going to have to take my word for it, obviously. I should also say that, that uh, you know, you, it's up to you to choose your physician, and you should choose whoever you want. You know, you don't have to come to me for care. You can go to anybody you want.

The doctor was placed in a situation where he had to defend himself and simultaneously remind the patient that she was perfectly free to go elsewhere for her medical care. The matter of trust is the issue here and the exchange signifies a possible breach in the doctor-patient relationship, although the voice intonation and stress employed by the participants of the discourse did not imply any animosity or even impatience. The patient and the physician then moved to repair any sense of a serious confrontation, with the patient stating clearly to the doctor that she 'would like to have you do it, and I have a lot of confidence in you'. The doctor stated that he wanted to take care of the patient and noted that 'I want to reassure you that I will be taking care of you through every step of all this, and following along afterwards, which is just as important to me.' But this exchange did not end the patient's doubts nor the continued efforts made by the physician to convince the patient of the accuracy of his diagnosis and treatment.

During the final interview we were able to tape record (15 April 1977), the patient suddenly asked the doctor if he performed surgery at any other hospital than at the one managed by the university, noting that she was not comfortable with 'all of the students around.' This remark by the patient opened another lengthy discussion on the merits and problems of a university hospital. The physician was again put in the position of having to defend his professional judgments and the quality of care at the hospital. The patient again brought up her unpleasant experiences with military hospitals and that her observations at the university hospital seemed to indicate that they were run in similar ways. The patient specifically mentioned waiting for what seemed to be treatment or for a prescription (the context is not clear), and overhearing another patient talking to a nurse about an injection for the 'wrong' person. The patient complained that it reminded her of the military and that what she observed was quite upsetting. These remarks semed to be her way of showing how the medical bureaucratic practices she observed were faulty, leading to her topic shift again and to spontaneous discourse about the quality of care she might receive at the university hospital. Her experiences with hospital practices seemed to trigger what appears to have been a long-standing set of beliefs concerning medical bureaucratic practices and policies to which she objects.

The patient, during this fourth interview, was in to see the doctor about scheduling the surgery and was in the process of completing her radiological treatments. While one can acknowledge that the radiological treatments and pending surgery could be serious sources of stress for any patient, resulting in an emotional overload, the remarks are consistent with previous ones reflecting her general and specific negative beliefs about medical bureaucracies and their practices, especially those with a public, institutional sponsorship. The stress could be seen as exacerbated by the experience of her husband's death from pancreatic cancer some months earlier. In each case, the bureaucratic organization of the health care system involved was cited as contributing to or as a possible cause of inadequate care. Her experiences at the university hospital supported her beliefs.

When the patient mentioned that 'I hate to go to somebody new', the physician quickly pointed out that this is her choice, and then noted that the hysterectomy should be performed as soon as the radiation treatments are completed. The patient then asked again about the possibility of the gynecologist recommending another hospital, mentioning two places in particular and again citing irregularities observed at the military hospital where her husband had been, and at a university hospital. Again the doctor was put in the position of having to defend his own training and experience. He noted, however, that he was not in a position to recommend someone else, pointing out that there were 110 gynecologists in the country who could perform the hysterectomy. The discussion was extensive and the physician continually reassured the patient about the care she would receive. The patient then shifted the topic by asking for the date the doctor wished to set for the surgery, and this remark terminated her complaints and misgivings for this interview.

It is important to note that at no time did the physician or the sociologist feel that perhaps they were dealing with an unbalanced person, despite the occasional confusions in the patient's remarks and her own reference to her confusions. It is also important to note that no one was suggesting that the patient's observations about medical bureaucratic practices and policies did not have any truth to them. No one attempted to tell the patient that she was simply wrong, but that her observations and fears did not warrant the level of generalization to which she had elevated the issue. There was, however, a clear confrontation with the physician in the sense of putting him in the awkward position of having to defend his own integrity and that of the hospital in which he worked. Organizational facts were brought into the discourse in a direct manner and they seem not only to have influenced the structure of the patient's beliefs, but could be perceived as shaping her perception of the information to which she was exposed and her rejection of aspects of this information that might be seen by others as damaging or contradicting her beliefs.

The persistence and strength of the patient's belief system about her illness can be grasped by a quick perusal of Figure 4, based on my interview with the patient some 16 months after her initial visit to the gynecologist. The remarks in Figure 4 suggest a series of confusions going back to the initial interview and physical examination. The upshot of the confusion revolves around an apparent discrepancy between the seemingly routine nature of the doctor's remarks about her condition and the progressively serious depiction of her subsequent tests

leading up to radiation therapy and surgery. The confusion
is evident from the way the patient talked about going to see
her internist (lines 20-33) about the results of the biopsy done
by the gynecologist. There is a fairly close relationship be
tween her remarks during the third interview and the comments
expressed 16 months later. The same doubts were expressed
and the same point was made about the apparent luckiness of
the gynecologist's pap smear test.

Figure 4.   Patient's reconstruction of confusion about post-
operative pap test results and physician contacts
prior to the operation (16 months after initial
interview).

14 Pt: ...But, uh, Dr. B. gave me the examination, and took
this pap test and

15   then I don't remember, it wasn't very long after he
called me and he, on the

16   phone, and he said that...uhm...uhm we found cancer
cells. Or cancer,

17   cancer cells, I don't remember just how he said it, and
of course I was, as I

18   say, still in shock from my husband's death. It didn't
faze me that I had

19   cancer at the time. It didn't, I, it didn't register. I
just asked him what

20   comes next. But, he mentioned prior to this, that if
there was anything, and

21   I don't know why, we were talking about if there was
anything. This, what,

22   as Dr. B. brought up. I stopped to think why was
that brought up; I can't

23   remember, but, uh, that he would then take a D and C.
But when, when he

24   called me, he said there would be no need for a
D and C, that there was

25   definitely cancer....and so he would take a biopsy...
and he took a

26   biopsy...and told me that there was. I guess, and
uh, as I say, I got the

27   two kind of mixed up because, uh, he called me and
asked me to come in

28   for a biopsy and (not?) do a D and C, and then he
said there was no need to

29   do a D and C. That there was, that it was definite.
So I went to see my

30   intern, internist, and he said well....uh...what did
he say? He said

31   something about, he said he must have really hit a
particular spot where it

Figure 4. Continued.

32	started because, I guess, according to him, and he had taken a pap test
33	prior to that about four or five months before that. An then, un, I think it
34	was uh, probably a Class 2 or something and I had a little infection that he
35	was treating but, uh...I was uh...sort of going fairly early just to double
36	check and talking to this widow, she thought so much of Dr. B. that she,
37	she said go see him you'll feel better if you do. But, uhm, then reading that
38	letter I thought well, something got mixed up there. Maybe somebody is
39	walking around with cancer and I didn't have it. I, all this was going
40	through my mind, you know...
41 I:	All right, but that was going through your mind after you came out of the
42	hospital in terms of the letter..is that right?
43 Pt:	Well, uh...my friend said, why don't you double check with another
44	doctor.
45 I:	Oh, I see.
46 Pt:	And I said, I'm just so mixed up now, I'm, I, I said.... if I need surgery, I
47	would want Dr. B. to do that (?), I've heard he's such a good surgeon. So,
48	even my internist said that he's probably done 2,000 of them so don't
49	worry about your surgery. You'll be all right (laughs). So, I got that....
50	part, but, I, I, no, I kind'a went into it not sure that I had cancer.

The patient (lines 35-40, Figure 4) confirmed her previous point about looking for a second opinion for the internist's treatment of her infection, yet she referred to the letter she received about the normal pap smear test after returning from the hospital. Her remarks (and also lines 40-50 of Figure 4) implied that perhaps there had been a mistake and that she did not have cancer but that someone else did, someone who was unaware of it. There is an implication here that the biopsy was also incorrect. The bureaucratic procedure of sending a laboratory test report without the patient's name or date is tied directly to the possibility that there had been a mistake all along, despite the patient's independent remarks that she wanted a second opinion because she did not feel right

after the internist had indicated that there was nothing
seriously wrong with her.

Concluding remarks. An important consequence of studying
language use in ethnographic or organizational settings is that
we can often obtain a glimpse of the way participants of discourse employ multiple frames in order to understand several,
possibly conflicting, sources of information and courses of
action. When we can also elicit additional information from the
participants about the setting and their views of what is
happening, we can strengthen our control over the analysis of
the data obtained.

The doctor-patient exchanges discussed here can be seen as
an emotionally difficult situation for all parties, including the
daughter, who at one point was on the verge of tears after
hearing her mother link her present illness to the husband's
suffering and death. There appears to be a case of misunderstanding here between doctor and patient, as if they are 'talking past each other'. But my transcripts of the interviews
suggest that the term 'misunderstanding' oversimplifies the
clash of different belief systems.

Despite the patient's frequent objections to what she was
told about laboratory tests, medical practices, and the nature
of her illness, there was compliance with the physician's
speech acts throughout the interviews. It is difficult for a
patient to seek information that would challenge a doctor's
professional authority and evidence. The patient was faced
with the expensive and time-consuming necessity of seeking
additional medical opinions or else had to contemplate serious
consequences if nothing were done about the way she felt and
the diagnosis rendered by the physician. It is easier to move
along with the organizational machinery that results in treatment and surgery than to seek another opinion and another
hospital.

The patient's disbelief of the doctor's speech acts suggests a
small addition to the Gricean notions of the cooperative principle and conversational postulates. Normally, the patient would
follow the tacitly agreed upon aims of the conversation (sub-
mitting to a medical interview and examination), and would believe the speech acts expressed (the diagnosis and the action
being offered). But everyday settings can also reveal the
following: (1) the patient follows the action (radiation treatment and surgery) offered by the physician, but (2) the patient
does not agree to the truth of what is being offered.

In the everyday social world, we routinely express and imply
intentions and propositional meanings, while seeming to accept
the expressed or implied intentions or propositional meanings
of others. Yet there are interactional and organizational pres-
sures and constraints that propel a person into action or
gradually seduce or coerce action even when the person disagreed with or does not believe what is proposed. We are

often pulled into action because it is difficult to find enough
convincing information to permit alternative courses of action
that can compete with the authority, size, and appearance of
objectivity afforded a bureaucracy, even when there are conversational exchanges with helpful personnel in which Gricean
conversational maxims are followed.

The patient's beliefs about medical bureaucratic practices and
policies, and her beliefs about the cause of cancer, do not appear as the kind of schemata we associate with a fairly narrow
experimentally studied problem-solving task in which the person is continuously updating hypotheses about the meaning of
a story being read or a task being followed under controlled
conditions. There are many elements of a psychological frame
created by the physician that are being challenged by the
frame that emerges from the patient's beliefs about medical
bureaucratic practice and policies and the cause of cancer.

The doctor does not directly challenge the existence or
occurrence of the practices by physicians noted by the patient,
such as sometimes not performing an operation or the delivery
of a baby. Nor is there a denial of inefficiency in military and
public hospitals. But the doctor questions their generality or
widespread existence and, in particular, is quick to insist that
he would never be a party to such practices.

The patient's beliefs about the cause of cancer were never
directly raised in the doctor-patient tape-recorded sessions,
but emerged indirectly by way of challenging the diagnosis
and laboratory tests, and then were raised explicitly in my
interview with the patient many months later. The patient's
beliefs led her continually to find confirmatory evidence for
them in the doctor's remarks after his examination of her, in
her perception of conflicting laboratory test results, in
bureaucratic practices she observed at the hospitals, and in
the kind of laboratory report sent to her home after surgery.

There is a family resemblance between the notion of schema
when used to discuss a subject's on-line comprehension of a
story (deciding from among two or more options as defined
by the notion of a psychological frame, pursuing different
conceptually driven and data-driven ideas that extend over
time, as in the case of the physician or scientist) and the case
of the patient who selects from among contradictory data only
those elements that support her belief system. We are reminded, therefore, of the close relationship between cognition
and affect as related aspects of meaning systems (D'Andrade
1981).

But when we use the notion of a schema as a belief employed
in understanding everyday life events that create their own
historical conditions, in contrast to a problem-solving situation
with a closed psychological frame imposed by the experimenter,
there is an additional element we cannot ignore: the ethnographic or organizational framing of events that have repeated,
serious consequences for the person.

From the opening remarks by the patient during her initial interview with the doctor and her comments about the death of her husband from pancreatic cancer, there were continual references to her own illness and her negative views about medical bureaucratic practices and policies. Throughout her discussion with the physician, and during my interview with her many months after her initial visit, persistent concerns were always expressed about the drawbacks of medical bureaucratic practices and policies and the actions of physicians toward their patients. This concern about health care delivery was always intimately linked to emotionally charged preoccupations about the care given to her husband, the patient's remarks about her own illness, and the health of her children.

The patient's views about medical bureaucratic practices and policies, her belief about the cause of cancer, and her preoccupation with her own illness are part of a belief system that remains viable and consistent across the actual settings for which we have data. The patient's views or beliefs, therefore, incorporate specific schemata about events, acts, outcomes, and contingencies. We are talking about schemata whose emotional elements permit the inclusion of specific domains of knowledge that contain contradictory facts, but where these facts are not permitted to challenge metapropositions that make up the belief system. Thus, the patient is aware of different medical options and the doctor's remarks about the results of the pap test and biopsy he performed.

The patient's schematized beliefs about the illness attributed to her and for which she received surgery, and her views about medical bureaucratic practices and policies, were always expressed within organizational settings whose routine procedures both governed the discourse and activities that occurred, and also permitted her to challenge what for her were excessive irregularities in practices and policies. The same setting permitted her to observe practices she viewed as damaging or unnecessary and to express beliefs that challenged the hospital's and physician's authority and credibility. The extensive interview material enabled us to obtain a partial understanding of the way belief schemata combine cognitive and emotional elements that tend to be absent in task-oriented problem-solving studies. The patient incorporated and challenged (yet observed or followed) medically organized scientific facts, and routine health care bureaucratic practices and policies, while under emotionally delicate conditions associated with her husband's death. The patient's language consistently revealed strong negative feelings about health care delivery practices, and these feelings continually influenced her thinking about the interpretation of the physician's framing of a medical diagnosis and clinical decisions about treatment.

In order to place the patient's beliefs within an explanatory conceptual framework, we can draw upon the useful work of Tversky and Kahneman (1978, 1981) and their notion of a psychological frame. For Tversky and Kahneman, the decision-maker's particular choice revolves around a 'decision frame' that refers to the decision-maker's conception of the acts, outcomes, and contingencies associated with a particular choice. So if we create variations in the framing of acts, contingencies, or outcomes, we can expect subjects to alter their choices when a decision problem is framed in more than one way. We want to extend this framework to the case of our medical patient where there are additional elements that must be addressed, while taking into account the actions of the physician in reaching a decision about the patient's diagnosis and course of treatment.

The doctor-patient interviews and the interview by Cicourel include elements of the patient's and doctor's respective perception of acts, outcomes, and contingencies associated with the events of a particular interview or some part of an interview, but there is also the continuous interaction or discourse wherein information is challenged directly or indirectly, and there are continual references to organizational practices and policies that are invoked during the interviews. The interactional setting provides patient and doctor with an occasion for presenting and reviewing the psychological and organizational frames that structure decisions.

The organizational frame includes bureaucratic practices and policies that are recalled by the patient and refer to the activities of the hospital before, during, and after the medical interview. The patient seeks to negotiate with the physician the relative significance and meaning of laboratory tests, the diagnosis, the course of treatment, who will perform the surgery, and where the surgery will be performed.

The psychological and organizational frames that emerged over the course of different interviews refer to the way in which the patient follows but does not believe the physician's way of framing the problem. The patient's beliefs weakened or mitigated or defied the way in which options were framed by the doctor, and the decision frames were not perceived by her as leading to acts or outcomes that should be accepted as warranted.

The Tversky and Kahneman study provided subjects with clearly bounded options and assumed a common knowledge base obtained. Differences in the belief systems of the subjects are implied, but the structure of these implied beliefs is not part of the study. The subjects seem to employ a form of rationality in which acts, outcomes, and contingencies are initially assessed or framed, and then a specific choice is made. The internal structure of the beliefs and feelings activated by the decision frames posed for the subjects remain real but implicit aspects of the reasoning leading to the way decisions are made. The kinds of interactional conditions of the medical interview and my subsequent interview were not intended to be part of the Tversky and Kahneman framework, but they are consistent with the idea of psychological framing.

An important aspect of the medical case is the fact that the patient continually challenged the doctor's professional responsibility and the adequacy of the hospital's practices and policies. She nevertheless followed the radiation treatment and submitted to surgery and a lengthy follow-up period of checkups for several years, despite very strong beliefs to the contrary. The organizational frame, therefore, imposes a powerful set of conditions; the patient must either comply with these conditions or else reject them despite the way her beliefs lead to specific and general constructions about her illness, its cause, and the potential dangers of medical bureaucratic practices and policies.

The laboratory conditions devised by Tversky and Kahneman are free of the changes in the kind of data (subsequent laboratory reports, the patient's reactions) available to the physician, and the patient's observations of organizational practices over several occasions. But in laboratory and natural settings there are similar if not invariant conceptual and data-driven processes at work, as well as computational devices that are employed to evaluate the fit between the elements of the schemata and whatever data are admitted as valid. For the patient, the validity of different sources of data she could obtain from her own observations, from listening to the doctor, and from watching television, clearly creates a complicated notion of goodness of fit between theory and data. The fit between theory and data is influenced by important feelings and emotions.

The Gricean and the Tversky and Kahneman models both presuppose a cooperative principle and idealized conversational postulates that are said to govern discourse and the way instructions are followed. There are, however, differences between the idealized conditions of discourse as postulated in Gricean terms and the experimental conditions of the Tversky and Kahneman model. The Tversky and Kahneman experiments provide the subjects with conditions of uncertainty that seem to presuppose affective and cognitive elements that interact within causal schemata and that simulate what happens in the everyday world. We would expect their findings to hold in everyday life settings where people must also address hypothetical and real monetary outcomes and decisions that can seriously influence the loss of human lives. Their use of experimental conditions enables them to obtain clear measures of the way decision processes can vary with changes in the framing of a problem or event.

In this study of a medical patient, I have examined the manner in which hypothesis testing and emotional elements of schemata or beliefs interact in a natural setting. The setting introduces additional elements of framing; the patient must integrate the psychological framing of the doctor with the framing provided by local conditions of social interaction and ethnographic or organizational practices and constraints over different occasions.

Within the Tversky and Kahneman model, framing a problem in two different ways does not alter the facts of the case, but does influence the subject's perception and interpretation of the facts. Different framing conditions could be evoking different affective elements and thus influence the decision process, in contrast to experimental problem-solving tasks that do not simulate everyday life conditions.

I have suggested that beliefs which are instantiated in a natural interactional context and which incorporate psychological and organizational frames, have as part of their schematized knowledge base a set of metapropositions. The metapropositions are driven by emotional elements that can lead the patient or subject to deny or resist accepting contradictory facts, yet reveal an awareness of them; there is a general reluctance to revise beliefs in light of new evidence, while an active cognitive search continues for new information from the environment or organizational practices of everyday life that would support the metapropositions.

NOTE

The medical information used in this paper was obtained as part of a larger study of a gynecological oncology clinic. I am grateful to Dr. Sue Fisher, a former student, for her help in obtaining the doctor-patient interview materials. The analysis of these materials and my own interview with the patient are entirely my responsibility. I am indebted to Dr. B. for his generous help. I am grateful to Roy D'Andrade and Pat Murray for their helpful comments and suggestions on the first draft of the manuscript.

REFERENCES

Bauman, R., and J. F. Sherzer, eds. 1975. The ethnography of speaking. In: Annual Review of Anthropology. Stanford, Calif.: Stanford University Press.
Bernstein, B. 1971. Class, codes and control. Vol. I: Theoretical studies towards a sociology of language. London: Routledge and Kegan Paul.
Bernstein, B. 1973. Class, codes and control. Vol. II: Applied studies towards a sociology of language. London: Routledge and Kegan Paul.
Bright, W., ed. 1966. Sociolinguistics. The Hague: Mouton.
Cicourel, A. V. 1968. The social organization of juvenile justice. New York: Wiley. London: Heinemann.
Cicourel, A. V. 1974a. Cognitive sociology. New York: Free Press.

Cicourel, A. V. 1974b. Interviewing and memory. In:
Pragmatic aspects of human communication. Edited by C.
Cherry. Dordrecht: D. Reidel. 51-82.
Cicourel, A. V. 1975. Discourse and text: Cognitive and
linguistic processes in studies of social structure. Versus:
Quaderni de Studi Semiotici 12.33-84.
Cicourel, A. V. 1981. Language and the structure of belief
in medical communication. Studia Linguistica 35.
Cicourel, A. V. (in press) Hearing is not believing: Lan-
guage and the structure of belief in medical communication.
In: The social organization of doctor-patient communication.
Edited by S. Fisher and A. D. Todd. Washington, D.C.:
Center for Applied Linguistics.
Corsaro, W. A. 1981. Communicative processes in studies of
social organization. Text 1.5-63.
D'Andrade, R. G. 1981. The cultural part of cognition.
Cognitive Science 5.179-195.
Grice, H. P. 1975. Logic and conversation. In: Syntax and
semantics. Edited by P. Cole and J. Morgan. New York:
Academic Press. 41-58.
Gumperz, J. 1971. Language in social groups. Stanford:
Stanford University Press.
Gumperz, J., and D. Hymes, eds. 1972. Directions in socio-
linguistics. New York: Holt, Rinehart and Winston.
Hymes, D. 1962. The ethnography of speaking. In:
Anthropology and human behavior. Edited by T. Gladwin
and W. C. Sturtevant. Washington, D.C.: Anthropological
Society of Washington. 13-53.
Labov, W. 1972. Sociolinguistic patterns. Philadelphia:
University of Pennsylvania Press.
Labov, W., and D. Fanshel. 1977. Therapeutic discourse:
Psychotherapy as conversation. New York: Academic Press.
Murray, P. H. 1980. Directive speech acts: A theoretical
investigation. Dissertation. Department of Linguistics, Uni-
versity of California, San Diego.
Petinari, C. (n.d.) The function of a grammatical alternation
in 14 surgical reports. Typescript.
Reichman, R. 1978. Conversational coherency. Cognitive
Science 2.4:283-327.
Rumelhart, D. 1977. Toward an interactive model of reading.
In: Attention and performance VI. Edited by S. Dornic.
Hillsdale, N.J.: Lawrence Erlbaum Associates.
Tversky, A., and D. Kahneman. 1978. Causal schemas in
judgments under uncertainty. In: Progress in social
psychology. Edited by M. Fishbein. Hillsdale, N.J.:
Lawrence Erlbaum Associates.
Tversky, A., and D. Kahneman. 1981. The framing of deci-
sions and the psychology of choice. Science 211.453-458.

PSYCHOLOGICAL MEANINGS:
HOW MUCH WE SHARE, HOW MUCH WE DIFFER CULTURALLY

Lorand B. Szalay
Institute of Comparative Social and Cultural Studies

You are probably all thoroughly familiar with the Perkins Commission's report on the status of American language training and international studies. In its classical language, the report concludes (President's Commission...1979:1):

>...increasingly hazardous international military, political and economic environment is making unprecedented demands on America's resources, intellectual capacity and public sensitivity...At a time when the resurgent forces of nationalism and of ethnic and linguistic consciousness so directly affect global realities, the United States requires far more reliable capacities to communicate with its allies, analyze the behavior of potential adversaries, and earn the trust and the sympathies of the uncommitted. Yet, there is a widening gap between these needs and the American competence to understand and deal successfully with other peoples in a world in flux.

There are several reasons for this widening gap. My presentation focuses on a single main factor which, during my intensive involvement with this problem area over the last 20 years, I have found to be a major source of confusion.

At a more abstract professional level this involves the complex concept of culture, its role in our way of thinking. At a more concrete level it involves the practical question which I have chosen as the title of my presentation, 'how much we share, how much we differ culturally'. Probably most of us have wondered at one time or another how our view of the world compares to that of others: how similar, for instance, are Blacks and Whites; or to what extent do Americans and Chinese view the world differently? While these kinds of questions are intriguing, they also appear to be unanswerable.

Nonetheless, the work and findings presented here are the outcome of several studies which do bear on such questions, and the purpose of my paper is to share with you my results. Before doing so, I will define a few basic concepts and briefly describe my approach, at least to the extent necessary for understanding the following observations.

Subjective meaning, culture, psychocultural distance. My work has been centered on the in-depth comparative study of cultures, with emphasis on their characteristic views, beliefs, and frames of reference. This general problem area falls into an interdisciplinary no-man's-land, somewhere between psychology, anthropology, linguistics, international relations, and communication research, to mention only its main neighbors.

Cultural anthropologists have done a monumental work in studying and describing vast numbers of cultures, focusing primarily on remote tribes, exotic populations, their folkways, artifacts, life styles, etc. While much of this has become popular reading, Hall (1959) observes that the recognition of culture as a hidden but powerful psychological reality progresses slowly. It is still little understood that culture as a psychological disposition influences our own views, our own behavior as much as it does that of other peoples. As Hall (1959) puts it:

> Culture is not an exotic notion studied by a select group of anthropologists in the South Seas. It is a mold in which we are all cast, and it controls our daily lives in many unsuspected ways...many of which are outside our awareness and therefore beyond conscious control of the individual.

Along with many others in his field, Hall (1966) underlines the importance of cultures in creating these strong dispositions to see and understand the world in particular ways:

> People from different cultures not only speak different languages, they inhabit different sensory worlds. Selective screening of sensory data admits some things while filtering out others. This means that experience as it is perceived through one set of culturally patterned sensory screens is quite different from experience perceived through another.

Under such conditions, it is clear that cultural understanding turns into a complex and demanding task. As Hanvey (n.d.) observes, the task goes beyond learning geography or demographic information of recent origin:

> It is one thing to have some knowledge of world conditions. The air is saturated with that kind of information. It is another thing to comprehend and accept the consequences

of the basic human capacity for creating unique cultures--
with the resultant profound differences in outlook and
practice manifested among societies. These differences
are widely known at the level of myth, prejudice, and
tourist impression. But they are not deeply and truly
known--in spite of the well-worn exhortation to 'understand others'. Such a fundamental acceptance seems to
be resisted by powerful forces in the human psychosocial
system. Attainment of cross-cultural awareness and
empathy at a significant level will require methods that
circumvent or otherwise counter those resisting forces.

The methodological problem is serious and delicate indeed.
Researchers are frequently unaware that by selecting questions,
no matter how simple and common sense they may be, and by
offering multiple choice alternatives, the respondents are led
involuntarily to respond according to the framework offered by
the researcher. Pike (1966), a leading anthropologist, has
addressed this source of research bias by stressing the importance of using an emic approach, that is, using the
respondents' own terms and categories, when studying foreign
cultures:

Emic descriptions provide an internal view, with criteria
chosen from within the system. They represent to us
the view of one familiar with the system who knows how to
function within it himself.

Pike contrasts the emic approach with the etic approach
which uses the researcher's own frame of reference, running
the risk of producing empirical findings which distort the
actual meanings and priorities of a particular foreign culture.
The main empirical approach developed by psychologists
(Osgood 1957, Triandis 1964, Miller 1967) to gain access to
this hidden realm of reality relies on subjective meanings. In
contrast to linguistic or lexical meanings specified by dictionaries and lexica, subjective meanings are psychological reactions: perceptions, images, affects stored by the individual.
To illustrate this distinction one may think, for instance, of
the different subjective meanings the word *drug* has for a
pharmacist, a Christian Scientist, or a drug addict, etc.; or
how the subjective meaning of *ancestors* is likely to differ for
members of the aristocracy, e.g. the House of Lords, or for
the abandoned growing up in an orphanage.
The main reasons why subjective meanings are considered of
special information value relate to their key role in human
understanding and in the influence they exert on human behavior. As Osgood (1957) puts it:

Of all the imps that inhabit the nervous system--that little
black box in psychological theorizing--the one we call

meaning is held by common consent to be the most elusive. Yet again by common consent of social scientists,
this variable is one of the most important determinants of
human behavior.

Triandis and Vassilou (1967) observed that psychologists tend
to share the assumption that 'the system of cognitions of subjects constitutes a map of the ways they conceive the environment' and that different cultural maps offer the key to different
cultural behavior. In fundamental agreement with this position
there has developed the concept of subjective culture, which
involves essentially a system of subjective meanings encompassing in their globality a subjective representation of the universe.

Authors addressing this field use different labels like 'subjective lexicon' (Miller 1967), 'meaning systems' (Osgood, Suci,
and Tannenbaum 1957), 'cognitive map' (Tolman 1948), 'maze-
ways' (Wallace 1956), 'world view' (Black 1973), 'belief systems'
(D'Andrade et al. 1972), 'thought world' (Whorf 1956), and
'ethnographic dictionary' (Werner 1969). While these and
other labels sound different, they essentially refer to the same
psychological reality of behavioral dispositions (Campbell 1963).

Behind these diverse systemic concepts there is a consensus
among the authors that they can be effectively analyzed through
the empirical study of meanings.

Approach. In fundamental agreement with the main thrust of
the theoretical orientation just outlined, I approach subjective
culture as a system of perceptual/semantic representation as
developed by a group of people of the same background and
similar experiences. The elementary units of this system are
subjective meanings and images extracted and retained from
past experiences. A schematic model of the system of perceptual-
semantic representation is shown in Figure 1. In this model
the mosaic pieces of subjective meanings form a global subjective
representation of the environment and serve as a base for
organizing and understanding new experiences. These meanings
develop around key words or concepts; I call these 'themes'.
Individual themes form clusters based on their shared meanings
and also larger units that I call 'domains'. Thus, for example,
themes like 'father', 'mother', and 'children' form the domain
of 'Family'.

The overall perceptual/semantic representation of the world is
thus conceived as a system determined by an organized structure
of themes and domains. Within this system three main organizational dimensions are identified: 'dominance', the relative
importance of themes and domains; 'affinity', the relatedness
of representational units, based on the overlap of their content; and 'affect loading', the intensity of positive/negative
evaluations of representational units.

Figure 1.   Schematic model of perceptual/semantic representation of the world.

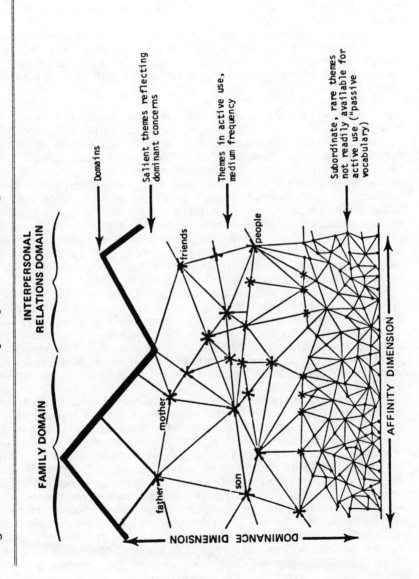

In terms of this model, an analysis of subjective culture involves a reconstruction of the system of perceptual/semantic representation by its basic units and main dimensions of organization (Szalay and Maday 1973). By measuring the similarities or differences between the culturally shared subjective meanings of two or more groups, one can then arrive at a measurement of their cultural distance (Szalay and Bryson 1973). However, to obtain results which are generalizable over very diverse cultures and to do so without exorbitant cost, requires a systematic strategy for selecting themes and a sensitive measure for gauging their similarities.

While in its theoretical orientation the method advocated here converges with those relying on meaning, it offers a new solution in the analysis of subjective culture, in its reliance on free word associations and its unstructured and open-ended approach.

Assessment of cultural meanings through Associated Group Analysis (AGA). AGA takes systematic advantage of previous observations that free associations offer a rich source of information on selected dimensions of subjective meaning (Noble 1952, Deese 1963). To reconstruct cultural meanings, AGA elicits free associations in continued free association tasks from medium-size cultural samples (50 to 100 respondents) to selected stimulus themes such as 'ancestors' or 'mental health'. The several hundred responses elicited to each theme were found to provide rich information on the group's shared subjective meaning of the stimulus. Several analytic methods have been developed to assess various parameters of the group's meaning: perceptual/affective composition, dominance, etc.

In its most common form the association task is administered in written form to members of selected sample groups. They receive the stimulus themes (e.g. 'ancestors') printed several times on slips, and are asked to write down as many ideas or associations as they can think of in one minute. The responses produced by all the group members to the same theme (e.g. 'ancestors') are tallied, scored, and accumulated into response lists, as shown in Table 1.

The response distributions shown deserve special interest at this point. They serve as the rough data for all the subsequent analyses, but, most importantly, they illustrate the central assumption, the critical principle, which serves as the foundation of the measurement of psychocultural distance. The response distribution formed of several hundred responses and characterized by high, middle, and low frequency responses provides a detailed and inclusive description of the shared subjective meaning of the stimulus theme which characterizes the group under study. Furthermore, a quick visual inspection of the distribution of the responses from the groups with which we are familiar will demonstrate that none of the responses or their specific scores are accidental; rather they reflect integral mosaic pieces of the group's shared experiences.

Figure 2. Members of medium-size sample groups produce multiple free responses to selected themes, like 'ancestors'. To account for the differential importance of reactions the following empirically derived weighting scores are used: 6,5,4,3,3,3, 3,2,2,1,1...

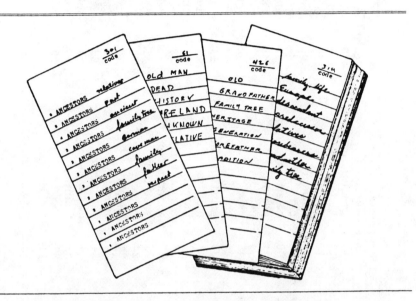

Associative Group Analysis utilizes several analytic methods which have been developed to reconstruct various parameters of the group's shared subjective meanings. Probably the most common one identifies the most salient meaning components of two or more groups compared. A content analysis of the group response leads to clusters of related responses (e.g. past, old, ancient) which convey the main elements of a theme's subjective meaning (e.g. emphasis on the past), as shown in Table 2.

The size of these clusters informs on the salience of a particular meaning component. While certain aspects could perhaps be elicited directly or are even common knowledge (for example, the Koreans' emphasis on rites), others, such as the relative timelessness of the ancestral role for Koreans, could hardly emerge by the asking of direct questions.

In a further step, the scores of each of these content categories--in our example the most salient components of the groups' contemporary meanings of Ancestors--are converted to percentages of the respective total scores in order to make them directly comparable (Table 3).

Table 1. Top 25 responses to 'ancestors'.

Anglo Americans		Black Americans		Hispanic Americans		Koreans	
Score	Response	Score	Response	Score	Response	Score	Response
173	family	113	relatives	193	grandparents	420	grandfather
145	old	107	family	97	history	198	rite
126	relatives	105	old	79	family	125	forefather
108	people	117	slaves, slavery	70	ancient	106	grave, visit -
87	past	114	Africa, Africans	61	old	84	respect
63	heritage	90	people	60	relatives	82	elders
62	dead	70	past	51	parents	81	Tau gun
61	ancient	66	grandparents	49	dead	77	burial ground
46	history	63	parents	48	past	58	father
45	forefathers	58	grandfather	44	good	58	genealogy
42	England, English	52	father	39	great grandparents	55	generation
37	grandmother	49	ancient	34	culture	49	days gone by
34	background	48	Black	30	former ones	35	primitive man
32	family tree	46	history	28	remembrance	33	human being
32	grandfather	45	dead	27	grandfather	31	relatives
25	monkeys	43	forefathers	25	yesterday	31	founder
23	parents	38	mother	24	respect	30	history
22	Mayflower	37	Indians	24	people	28	tradition
21	love	36	grandmother	24	ancestry	28	family, - life
21	Ireland, Irish	36	before	24	background	25	ties
19	mother	32	relatives	24	bad	24	serve
18	American	31	away	23	tradition	19	deceased
18	long term	30	love	20	race	19	home
17	tree	30	tree	18	inheritance	18	lineage
17	linkage	28	generation	28	Italy	17	hill

Table 2.   Categorization of U.S. and Korean responses to 'ancestors'.

Rites, veneration, worship	Score U.S.	K.	Time: Past, old	Score U.S.	K.	People, foreigners	Score U.S.	K.
Worship	10	--	Past	97	--	American	8	--
Respect	6	34	Old	91	--	Europe	10	--
Veneration	--	84	Before,-me,-us	56	--	German,-y	15	--
Serve	--	24	Ancient	54	--	Ireland,-ish	24	--
Great	17	--	Long ago	32	--	Indians	26	--
Rite	--	198	Early,-ier	11	--	Foreign,-er	14	--
Other	6	44	Unknown	6	--	Human being	--	33
			Days gone by	--	49	Man	5	--
			Year	7	--	People,person	85	--
			Posterity	--	10			
	39	384		354	59		187	33

Table 3.   Perception and evaluation of ancestors by Americans and Koreans.

Meaning components	U.S. group Score	%	Korean group Score	%
Time: past, old	354	20	59	3
Relationship, family tree	335	19	196	9
People, foreigners	187	10	33	2
History, tradition	152	8	84	4
Prehistoric man, ape	73	4	35	2
Forefathers, grandparents, relatives	546	30	824	39
Rites, veneration, worship	39	2	384	18
Grave, dead	91	5	233	11
Legendary figures	--	0	52	7
Miscellaneous	25	1	108	5
Total Scores (dominance)	1,802		2,100	

A 'semantograph' presentation (Figure 3) of the results of content analysis helps the reader to identify quickly those meaning components on which his own group and the other culture group are in agreement or disagreement.

This analysis can be used to show how important issues, dominant themes (from welfare to work) are perceived and understood by various culture groups. As our communication lexicons illustrate (Szalay et al. 1971, 1975, 1978), this approach goes beyond single themes; it can be used to reconstruct the main domains as well as the broader cultural frame of reference of the groups compared.

The measurement of distance.   Using Pearson's product-moment, we arrive at a measurement of psychocultural distance[1] which is based on the reasoning that, since response distributions describe a group's meaning range, groups producing

Figure 3. Semantograph presentation of the results of content analysis of U.S. and Korean responses to 'ancestors'.

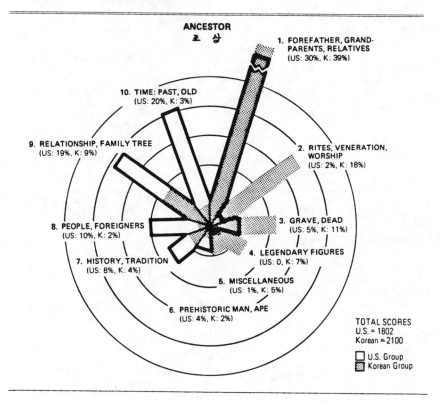

ANCESTOR
조 상

1. FOREFATHER, GRAND-
PARENTS, RELATIVES
(US: 30%, K: 39%)

10. TIME: PAST, OLD
(US: 20%, K: 3%)

9. RELATIONSHIP, FAMILY TREE
(US: 19%, K: 9%)

2. RITES, VENERATION,
WORSHIP
(US: 2%, K: 18%)

8. PEOPLE, FOREIGNERS
(US: 10%, K: 2%)

3. GRAVE, DEAD
(US: 5%, K: 11%)

7. HISTORY, TRADITION
(US: 8%, K: 4%)

4. LEGENDARY FIGURES
(US: 0, K: 7%)

5. MISCELLANEOUS
(US: 1%, K: 5%)

6. PREHISTORIC MAN, APE
(US: 4%, K: 2%)

TOTAL SCORES
U.S. = 1802
Korean = 2100

☐ U.S. Group
▨ Korean Group

similar response distributions reflect great psychocultural similarity, while those with significantly different distributions exemplify psychocultural distance.

Using this measure, one finds, for instance, a higher correlation, a greater similarity between the responses of White and Black Americans to 'ancestors' (.39); between White Americans and Koreans it is only .07. Associations to 'ancestors' (see Table 1) are used here merely to illustrate the nature of response distributions and the principal assumption that the distribution of spontaneous associations offers an empirical basis for gauging psychocultural similarity or distance between groups on selected issues or themes. The relationship between response distributions and cultural meanings which reflect cultural experiences and provide information on the perceptual/semantic world shared by group members becomes increasingly apparent when the response distributions are subjected to content analysis.

The measurement of psychocultural distance requires that two groups be systematically compared. The similarity of two perceptual/semantic representations cannot be decided on the basis of a few arbitrarily selected characteristics. To obtain measurements which are broadly based and generalizable following our model of perceptual/semantic organization, it is desirable to select the same number of dominant themes in the representation of each cultural system. The procedure developed to achieve this objective has three steps (Szalay and Maday 1973). First, members of each cultural sample are asked to list 25 important areas or domains of life (family, work, religion, etc.). (When tallied, this gives a ranked list of high-priority domains for each sample.) Second, they are asked to give free associations to each of the important domains they have listed. (When tallied, this provides a priority list of themes representative of high-priority domains.) Third, taking equal numbers of the top-priority domains and their top themes from each culture, a master list is developed which provides the themes (about 160 to 200) to be administered to samples of respondents selected from both cultures. The many hundred thousand free associations elicited from each cultural sample (N = 50 to 150) provide a broad base for measuring distances between dominant themes.

In the following I illustrate actual measurements of psychocultural distances among subcultures, such as Black, White, and Hispanic Americans; among groups of different socioeconomic status; among cultures; in a process of adaptation (acculturation); and on particular themes of practical importance.

Example 1. Distance between domestic groups. A study of the psychocultural similarities among Black, White, and Hispanic American groups in the Washington, D.C. area (Szalay et al. 1976) produced the results shown in Figure 4. The psychocultural distance between Blacks and Whites is relatively narrow, while Hispanic Americans (in this study, mostly Latin American immigrants) are very distant from both Black and White Americans. These findings may come as a surprise to those who had assumed that minorities share more perceptions and values with other minorities than with representatives of the majority. They are consistent in showing that Hispanic Americans share no more cultural content with Black Americans than with White Americans. [2,3]

Figure 4. Distances between the perceptual/semantic representations of the world of White, Black, and Hispanic Americans.

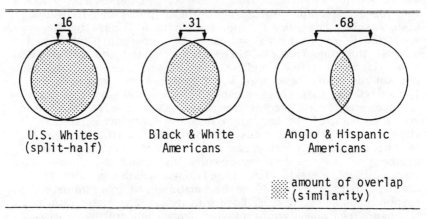

| .16 | .31 | .68 |

U.S. Whites
(split-half)

Black & White
Americans

Anglo & Hispanic
Americans

amount of overlap
(similarity)

The data of Figure 4 represent mean values; the considerable variations in psychocultural similarity across domains are shown in Table 4. In certain domains, such as 'money', Black and White groups show a great deal of agreement, while in other domains, such as 'society' and 'general problems', their views are much farther apart. The close parallel between White vs. Hispanic American and Black vs. Hispanic American differences offers further confirmation of the finding that Hispanic Americans differ markedly from U.S.-born Blacks and Whites.

Table 4. Mean similarity in perceptions between ethnic-racial groups in selected domains.

| Domain | Groups compared | | |
	Black/ White	White/Hispanic American	Black/Hispanic American
Family	.74	.40	.35
Friends	.70	.17	.19
Society, people	.58	.25	.25
Sex/love	.75	.31	.33
Money, economy	.80	.45	.46
Work, profession	.73	.31	.26
Education	.72	.27	.29
Health	.74	.35	.38
Religion	.71	.46	.43
Problems	.57	.23	.19
Mean	.69	.32	.32

The similarity coefficients presented here are means obtained by Z transformation over 16 stimulus themes. Each coefficient is based on approximately 1,000 pairs of observations.

Example 2. Distance between rich and poor. A comparison of groups of three different socioeconomic statuses (subsamples of the Black, White, and Hispanic Americans just discussed) is presented in Table 5.[4] The data reveal the extent to which differences in income level are associated with differences in perceptions and meanings. The coefficients show similarities between particular income groups and permit the comparison of groups in adjacent positions (low/middle or middle/high) and those in opposing positions (low/high). In all three cultural groups, the similarity is least between those in opposing positions (low/high). With the Hispanic group the difference between high- and low-income groups is somewhat greater than with Blacks or Whites. This is in agreement with the prevailing view that class differences in traditional societies are greater in both economic and social/psychological terms.

Table 5. Mean similarity in perceptions between high-, middle-, and low-income groups of the same ethnic-racial background.

| Group | Income groups compared | | |
	Low/Middle	Middle/High	Low/High
Black American	.73	.76	.69
White American	.76	.75	.70
Hispanic American	.71	.68	.61

The combined effects of income and culture are shown in Table 6. Again, the Black and White groups are more similar to each other at all income levels than either is to the Hispanic American group. Black and White high-income groups show less similarity than Blacks and Whites at lower income levels. Comparisons of Black and White groups with Hispanic Americans show that the high-income groups are most similar and the low-income groups the least so. The difference between high- and low-income Black and White groups is of the same order of magnitude as the overall difference between Blacks and Whites. However, the income-related differences are smaller than the differences found between groups with distinctly different cultural backgrounds.

Table 6. Mean similarity in perceptions between ethnic-racial groups compared in various income categories.

| Income level | Groups compared | | |
	Black/White	Black/Hispanic American	White/Hispanic American
Low	.70	.28	.28
Middle	.73	.31	.32
High	.62	.32	.36

Example 3. Distance between cultures. The psychocultural distances among Puerto Ricans, Slovenians, South Koreans, and Americans of comparable occupation, age, sex, and education (Szalay and Bryson 1975; Szalay and Pecjak 1979; Szalay, Moon, and Bryson 1971) are shown in Figure 5. Psychocultural distance is the inverse or logical opposite of psychocultural similarity ($d = 1.00 - r_{sim}$): the greater the similarity, the less the distance.[5] In this comparison, the Korean group shows the greatest distance from the American. When Korean and American occupational subsamples tested in their native countries are compared, students appear to be relatively close, while agriculturalists are the farthest apart. This suggests that education may have a potential to reduce psychocultural distance. The Slovenian students, tested in Ljubljana, Yugoslavia, show nearly the same distance from American students as the Puerto Ricans, but this does not necessarily mean that Slovenians and Puerto Ricans are closer to each other. The Puerto Rican data come from a student sample tested at the Inter-American University, San German, Puerto Rico, and the comparison of word-based and picture-based distance measures obtained here has important methodological implications. The small difference between them suggests that usage of words or pictures has little effect on the outcome of the assessment. The difference itself may be explained by the fact that pictures depict concrete scenes in which cultural similarities may be somewhat greater than in the more abstract domains represented by words.

Example 4. Reduction of distance. A recent study of Filipinos serving in the United States Navy offered an interesting opportunity to explore the reduction of psychocultural distance through continuous and intensive contact with another cultural group over a considerable length of time and within a military institution characterized by above-average homogeneity and pressure toward conformity (Szalay and Bryson 1977). We compared recruits who had recently arrived from the Philippines and Filipino Navy men who had served up to 25 years with U.S.-born Navy men of comparable rank and service time; three Filipino and three U.S.-born Navy samples were studied. Associations were elicited on high-priority issues and subjects involving such domains as service, interpersonal relations, personal motivations, and social values. Since English is the official language of education in the Philippines, the Filipino Navy men were truly bilingual and could be tested in English, though Tagalog themes were also used in the study.

The results (Figure 5) illustrate the acculturation process along as yet unexplored dimensions: the differential rate of change within various domains, changes in native perceptual

Figure 5. Psychocultural distances of foreign and domestic cultural samples from an Anglo American baseline. (For the calculation of U.S. baseline heterogeneity, see note 5.)

	r similarity
Korean agriculturalists	.01
Korean workers	.07
Korean students	.14
Slovenian students males	.21
Slovenian students females	.23
Puerto Rican students (word-based)	.26
Puerto Rican students (picture-based)	.32
Hispanic Americans low income	.28
Hispanic Americans middle income	.32
Hispanic Americans high income	.36
Black low income	.70
Black middle income	.73
Black high income	.62

Distance values (U.S. BASELINE HETEROGENEITY .16):
.83, .77, .70, .63, .61, .58, .52, .56, .52, .48, .14, .11, .22

and attitudinal dispositions, the rate of change in approximating host norms, and changes in self-image and in image of society and social institutions. The Filipino recruits start from a position of relatively close proximity to the U.S.-born group. Compared with distances shown in Figure 5, the Filipinos are closer (.40) than any other group tested (except Black Americans). After 10 years of service, the distance between Filipino and United States servicemen has dropped to .28; after 25 years, it has dropped to .20. The curve of adaptation is gradual and probably reflects such underlying changes as the erosion of inferiority complexes associated with Filipinos' below-average physical size when compared with Americans, the shift from stereotypical to more personal rapport with the environment, and the slow absorption of the salient values of the host environment (self-reliance, competitiveness, etc.).

Example 5. Distance on themes of practical importance. The psychocultural distance data presented earlier on Hispanic, Black, and White Americans were actually derived from a study concerned with mental health topics, and Figure 6 contrasts the

Figure 6. Changes in psychocultural distance between Filipino and U.S.-born Navy men with length of service. (For the calculation of U.S. baseline heterogeneity, see note 5.)

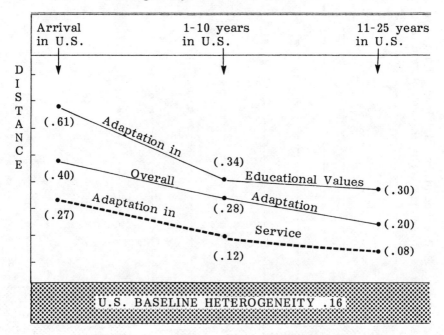

meanings of 'mental illness' for the Hispanic American and Anglo American samples. Hispanic Americans view mental illness as an extreme state of madness. Compared with Anglo Americans, Hispanic Americans show little awareness of the possibility of treatment and generally consider mental illness incurable (Szalay et al. 1978). Mental illness carries a heavy social stigma which dominates the meaning of 'mental health' as well. Stigma and shame have particularly heavy implications in the Hispanic cultures, where people are very much concerned about their reputations. [6]

Figure 7. Main meaning components of Mental Illness by Hispanic and Anglo-American groups.

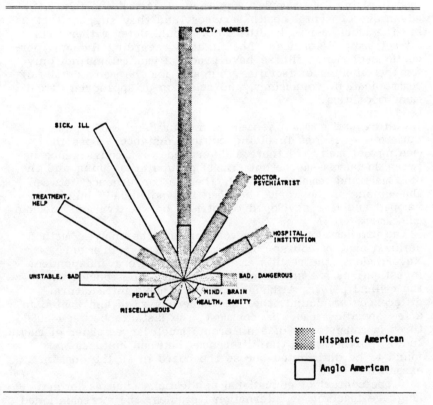

It may appear at first glance that the differences illustrated in Figure 7 result simply from language, from differences in terminology. Yet a closer look reveals that their roots go much deeper. An analysis of related themes ('mental health', 'psychiatrist') shows the same consistent trends. Anglo Americans view the psychiatrist more as a friend and helper, someone to

talk with and to consult about personal and interpersonal problems; they show an active interest in receiving advice and
treatment. 'Mental health' has a more or less positive meaning;
it refers to an ideal set of appropriate attitudes toward self
and the environment that is indispensable for success and
happiness. To Hispanic Americans, the psychiatrist is primarily a medical authority, a person to whom one turns only as a
last resort. The psychiatrist's role includes little of consultation or analysis, and the medical treatment sought from him
tends not to have cure as a realistic objective. To Hispanic
Americans, mental health is a logical opposite of mental illness
but has little positive meaning.

These insights help us to understand the people of a particular culture and to interact with them more effectively. They
help explain, for example, why Hispanic Americans take little
advantage of mental health services, and they suggest that using the label 'mental health center' would deter rather than
attract many Hispanics. The findings regarding Hispanic perceptions of mental illness have practical implications not only
for the labelling of facilities, but also for the many details of
communication, counseling, and selection of appropriate treatment modalities.

Culture and common sense. Our pluralistic world poses
numerous questions involving cultural distance: Does the
melting pot melt? Is there a divergence or a convergence between social classes, ethnic-racial groups, the young and the
old, male and female, etc.? Is there a convergence between
the nations of the world, between the industrially highly developed and less developed countries, between various ideological camps, etc.?

The problems at hand are complex and the analytic method
outlined can, of course, use a great deal of refinement.
Nevertheless, the results emerging from several independent
investigations are sufficiently consistent to be conclusive on
the critical point. Although some noticeable intracultural
differences are found, they are generally small and limited to
a few specific areas. In contrast, the distance between cultures is consistently of a different, much larger order of magnitude. Furthermore, the differences between cultures were
found to be distributed across the board in all the domains
examined.

In the context of educational applications such as foreign
language teaching or international studies, the aforementioned
findings on psychocultural distance bring the importance of
cultural factors into proper perspective. The predominantly
hidden influence of psychocultural factors creates a strong
need for empirical evidence to counteract the fallacy of cultural
parochialism. Without sufficient direct personal experience with
the rich diversity of cultural perspectives, it is frequently

argued that people's views and meanings are so diverse domestically that they could not be more diverse internationally.
This fallacious reasoning, resulting from narrow domestic perspectives, became so popular that it proved to be incorrigible without solid empirical evidence. This reasoning has been used in the past again and again in the context of diverse programs either to avoid the cultural dimension or to restrict its treatment to the teaching of such observables as style of dressing, diets, customs, etc.

Finding a way to show that domestically we share more than we may have thought and that we differ in deeper and more consistent ways than we may have assumed, requires that we pay more systematic attention to the realm of cultural differences. From the angle of intercultural communication or international education, it is not enough to stress the need for better understanding. As Hanvey (n.d.) urges, we have to learn the 'well-worn exhortations' to understand others; we have to learn the relevant specifics. These specifics must show in the particular ways in which perceptions and meanings of a foreign culture group agree and differ in comparison to ours in those specific themes and domains which fall into the sphere of our communicative or educational interest.

I have illustrated such insights in a few select contexts such as the meaning of ancestors or mental health. Our communication lexicons go further in this direction and offer extensive data on relevant specifics which go beyond the scope of the present study. A comparison of several volumes (U.S.-Korean, U.S.-Arabic, U.S.-Colombian, etc.) shows a rather consistent trend which underscores the changes associated with the fallacy of universal common sense. The findings show that the various traditional cultures forming the vast majority of the world population are more similar to each other, while they differ collectively in similar ways from our highly mobile postindustrial society. This sets us apart from the majority of the world population and suggests that considering the fast pace of our sociocultural development, we are going to need rather exceptional efforts to avoid losing touch with other nations and cultures. At the same time, these findings further remind us of the limited applicability of certain generalizations which, based on our domestic experiences, appear to be plain common sense.

NOTES

Major parts of these research investigations were supported by grants from the National Institute of Mental Health and the Office of Naval Research.

1. The Pearson product-moment correlation is calculated between the two scores (x,y) that a particular response obtained from two groups in the context of a given stimulus word.

2. The low psychocultural similarity found here between Anglo and Hispanic American samples is consistent with the

findings of a previous study of U.S. and Puerto Rican students (Szalay and Bryson 1975).

3. As a general rule, the word association task is administered in each group's native language. In comparisons of groups that speak different languages there is a possibility that language-based (translation) differences may increase the distance estimate, which is meant to have primarily a perceptual and motivational foundation. Szalay and Windle's (1968) comparative analysis of the associations of bilinguals provides an empirical basis for estimating this potential error factor. The associations produced by bilinguals in their native and in their second language were compared in order to assess the influence of language on associations. By eliciting associations, for instance, from fluent English-speaking Chinese subjects who have learned English in their native Chinese cultural environment, it is possible to obtain a measure of psychocultural distance relatively free of language-based influences.

4. In view of the large number of observations (in this case, 16,000), even the relatively small differences in correlation values shown in Table 5 are statistically significant.

5. Theoretically, in a case of maximal similarity our coefficient of similarity would show the theoretical maximum of 1.00. In reality, similarity between two groups is never perfect; intragroup heterogeneity sets practical limits to intergroup similarity. An adaptation of our distance formula would be to replace the theoretical maximum with $1.00 - r_{het}$, that is, make an adjustment for the heterogeneity of the group (r_{het}). Distance could then be expressed as $d = (1.00 - r_{het}) - r_{sim}$. Again, heterogeneity is the opposite of homogeneity ($1.00 - r_{het} = r_{hom}$), and the homogeneity coefficient (r_{hom}) can be measured empirically by randomly splitting a culture group into halves and calculating their coefficient of similarity. By using this procedure, we have obtained for White American groups $r_{hom} = .84$; this suggests a heterogeneity of $r_{het} = .16$. In the visual presentation of the United States baseline in Figures 3 and 4, accordingly, this $r_{het} = .16$ has been used as reference point from which the distances of other groups have been calculated.

6. Benedict (1946) has described this phenomenon in her discussion of 'shame' cultures, and Rotter (1966) has discussed it as characteristic of people with an external locus of control.

REFERENCES

Benedict, R. 1946. The chrysanthemum and the sword. Boston: Houghton-Mifflin.

Black, M. 1973. Belief systems. In: Handbook of social and cultural anthropology. Edited by J. J. Honigmann. Chicago: Rand McNally.

Campbell, D. T. 1963. Social attitudes and other acquired behavioral dispositions. In: Psychology: A study of a science. Edited by S. Koch. New York: McGraw-Hill.

D'Andrade, R., N. Quinn, S. B. Nerlove, and A. K. Romney. 1972. Categories of disease in American-English and Mexican-Spanish. In: Multidimensional scaling. Edited by A. K. Romney, N. Shepard, and S. B. Nerlove. New York: Academic Press. 9-54.

Deese, J. 1965. The structure of associations in language and thought. Baltimore: Johns Hopkins Press.

Hall, E. T. 1959. The silent language. New York: Doubleday.

Hall, E. T. 1966. The hidden dimension. Garden City, N.Y.: Doubleday.

Hanvey, R. G. (n.d.) An attainable global perspective. New York: Center for War/Peace Studies.

Miller, G. 1967. Psycholinguistic approaches to the study of communication. In: Journeys in science. Edited by D. Arm. Albuquerque: University of New Mexico Press.

Noble, C. E. 1952. An analysis of meaning. Psychological Review 421-431.

Osgood, C. E., G. Suci, and P. H. Tannenbaum. 1957. The measurement of meaning. Urbana: University of Illinois Press.

Pike, Kenneth. 1966. Etic and emic standpoints for the description of behavior. In: Communication and culture. Edited by Alfred Smith. New York: Holt, Rinehart and Winston. 152-163.

President's Commission on Foreign Language and International Studies [Perkins Commission]. 1979. Strength through wisdom. Washington, D.C.: Government Printing Office.

Rotter, J. B. 1966. Generalized expectancies for internal vs. external control of reinforcement. Psychological Monographs: General and Applied 13.169-175.

Szalay, L. B., and J. A. Bryson. 1973. Measurement of psychocultural distance: A comparison of American blacks and whites. Journal of Personality and Social Psychology 26.166-177.

Szalay, L. B., and J. A. Bryson. 1975. Subjective culture and communication: A Puerto Rican-U.S. comparison. Washington, D.C.: American Institutes for Research.

Szalay, L. B., and J. A. Bryson. 1977. Filipinos in the Navy: Service, interpersonal relations, and cultural adaptation. Washington, D.C.: American Institutes for Research.

Szalay, L. B., and J. Deese. 1978. Subjective meaning and culture: An assessment through word associations. Hillsdale, N.J.: Lawrence Erlbaum/Wiley and Sons.

Szalay, L. B., and B. C. Maday. 1973. Verbal associations
in the analysis of subjective culture. Current Anthropology
14.151-173.
Szalay, L. B., W. T. Moon, and J. A. Bryson. 1971. Com-
munication lexicon on three South Korean audiences: Social,
national, and motivational domains. Kensington, Md.:
American Institutes for Research.
Szalay, L. B., and V. Pecjak. 1979. Comparative analyses of
U.S. and Slovenian sociopolitical frames of reference. In:
Experience forms. Edited by G. Haydu. The Hague:
Mouton.
Szalay, L. B., P. Ruiz, R. Lopez, L. Turbyville, and J.
Bryson Strohl. 1978. The Hispanic American cultural frame
of reference: A communication guide for use in mental health,
education, and training. Washington, D.C.: Institute of
Comparative Social and Cultural Studies.
Szalay, L. B., R. E. Williams, J. A. Bryson, and G. West.
1976. Priorities, meanings, and psychocultural distance of
Black, White, and Spanish-American groups. Washington,
D.C.: American Institutes for Research.
Szalay, L. B., and C. Windle. 1968. Relative influence of
linguistic versus cultural factors on free verbal associations.
Psychological Reports 12.43-51.
Tolman, E. C. 1948. Cognitive maps in rats and men.
Psychological Review 55.189-208.
Triandis, H. C. 1964. Cultural influences upon cognitive
processes. In: Advances in experimental social psychology.
Edited by L. Berkovitz. New York: Academic Press.
Triandis, H., and V. A. Vassilou. 1967. A comparative
analysis of subjective culture. Urbana: Department of
Psychology, University of Illinois.
Wallace, A. F. C. 1956. Mazeway resynthesis: A bio-cultural
theory of religious inspiration. Transactions of the New York
Academy of Sciences 18.626-638.
Werner, O. 1969. The basic assumptions of ethnoscience.
Semiotica 1.329-338.
Whorf, B. L. 1956. Language, thought, and reality. New
York: Technological Press and John Wiley.

REMARKS ON THE NATURE OF
THE AUTOTELIC SIGN

Michael Shapiro
University of California, Los Angeles

The notion of the autotelic sign--a sign signifying itself--has
been implicit in the discussion of verbal art from at least the
time of the Prague School and the American New Critics. As
early as 1921, Jakobson had defined the principle that later
came to be called the poetic function in the following terms:
'Poetry is none other than an utterance with a focus on its
expression' (Jakobson 1921:10; translation mine--M.S.). I wish
to examine this received understanding of the poetic function
as defined by Jakobson and others, particularly in regard to
the status of the work of verbal art as a semeiotic entity. I
argue that the conception of poetry, in particular, as an autotelic or self-reflexive sign needs to be altered in order that
poetic theory and interpretative practice may both be advanced
in proportionate measure. My discussion relies in large part
on the theory of signs of the American philosopher-scientist
Charles Sanders Peirce, which constitutes the richest corpus
of knowledge and insight concerning the conceptual foundations
of semeiotic systems. Viewed in Peircean terms, the treatment
of language and poetry necessarily engages the notion of
teleology, without which the essential structure of genuine
semeiosis remains inexplicable (cf. Short 1981). To anticipate
the conclusion, the categorization of poetic semeiosis as predominantly autotelic is shown to be at odds with the nature of
poetry and the actual interpretations that works of verbal art
elicit from readers and critics alike.

For Peirce, 'a sign stands for something to the idea which it
produces or modifies' (1.339: such references are to Peirce
1965-1966 by volume and paragraph number), and in this formulation of the sign situation its three essential elements stand
out in relief. Peirce's 'sign' corresponds to the Augustinian
signans, his 'object' to signatum, and his 'idea' (or 'interpretant') to the Thomistic understanding of meaning as a mental

entity. A sign's status as a triadic relative is underscored by
Peirce when he terms the mutable components of a sign its
fundamenta relationis. A genuine, 'non-degenerate' sign necessarily partakes of this triadicity, and it is precisely the third
member of the triad--the so-called interpretant--that makes a
genuine sign what it is. What is more, the interpretant of a
sign proper is itself a sign (2.303).

Semeiosis consists in 'an action, or influence, which is, or
involves, a cooperation of *three* subjects, such as a sign, its
object, and its interpretant, this tri-relative influence not
being in any way resolvable into action between pairs' (5.484).
The interpretant, defined as 'the proper significate outcome of
a sign' (5.473) embraces triadicity as the only ontology that
does justice to the mental element of semeiosis.

Peirce's semeiotic is fundamentally embedded in his phenomenological categories--which he called Firstness, Secondness,
and Thirdness--and these must be discussed in any effort to
elucidate the nature of the autotelic sign, since they govern
the structure of all of his trichotomies, including the one most
pertinent to my topic, that of icon, index, and symbol. 'Firstness', writes Peirce, 'is the mode of being of that which is
such as it is, positively and without reference to anything
else' (Hardwick 1977:24). It is 'the unanalyzed total impression made by any manifold not thought of as actual fact, but
simply as a quality, as simple positive possibility' (Hardwick
1977:25). Firstness subsumes things that are termed Firsts,
but it is also implicit in Secondness, which Peirce defines as
'the mode of being that which is such as it is, with respect to
a second but regardless of any third' (Hardwick 1977:24).
Subsuming things that are Seconds, it is 'the experience of
effort, prescinded from the idea of a purpose' (Hardwick 1977:
25).

The most important category for this discussion is Thirdness,
'the mode of being of that which is such as it is, in bringing a
second and third into relation to each other' (Hardwick 1977:
24). This is the category that enables things to cohere, to
manifest system, to constitute structure. Peirce refers to it
as 'only a synonym for Representation' (5.105). To be a sign
is to represent; this formulaic statement imparts to Thirdness
the prominence it warrants in the sign situation. Thirdness
(into which category fall Thirds) Peirce describes as 'the
triadic relation existing between a sign, its object, and the
interpreting thought, itself a sign, considered as constituting
the mode of being a sign' (Hardwick 1977:31). Put in yet
another way, 'a sign *is* a sort of Third ... a Sign brings a
Second, its Object, into a *cognitive* relation to a Third ... a
Sign brings a Second into the same relation to a First in which
it stands itself to that First' (Hardwick 1977:31). There is,
then, a hierarchical relationship between the categories themselves, a relation of inclusion along a unidirectional gradient of
increasing complexity by which Thirdness encompasses

Secondness and Firstness, Secondness encompasses Firstness,
and Firstness remains in its unalloyed state a pure simplex.
   Peirce's best known triad of icon, index, and symbol is
determined by his conception of the categories. In this sign
division, what is at stake semeiotically is the relation between
the sign (or signans) and the object (or signatum). It must
be stressed from the outset that all linguistic elements are
symbols in the Peircean sense, albeit in varying degrees of
symbolicity. While the icon is defined as 'a sign of which the
character that fits it to become a sign of the sort that it is,
is simply inherent in it as a quality of it' (NE 4:242--such
references are to Peirce 1976 by volume and page number),
and an index is defined as 'a sign which is fit to serve as
such by virtue of being in a real relation with its object'
(loc. cit.), Peirce makes it clear that the essential function
of a sign is best fulfilled by the symbol. The crucial distinction between these sign types is that while icons and indexes
remain 'fitted to be signs' even if they go uninterpreted as
such, 'a symbol is *defined as a sign* [emphasis added--M.S.]
which becomes such by virtue of the fact that it is interpreted
as such' (NE 4:254). A symbol depends for its very being on
becoming determinate through interpretation: 'a symbol ...
that should not be interpreted, would either not be a sign at
all, or would only be a sign in an utterly different way' (NE
4:256). 'Now it is of the essential nature of a symbol',
Peirce continues, 'that it determines an interpretant, which
is itself a symbol. A symbol, therefore, produces an endless
series of interpretants' (NE 4:261). With respect to the particular kind of semeiosis involved in the action of symbolicity,
'a symbol is essentially a purpose, that is to say, it is a
representation that seeks to make itself definite, or seeks to
produce an interpretant more definite than itself. For its whole
signification consists in its determining an interpretant; so that
it is from its interpretant that it derives the actuality of its
signification' (NE 4:261).
   Thirdness, or symbolicity, is accorded functional prominence
in the Peircean concept of the interpretant. Since it is the
interpretant that is indispensable to the integrity of the sign
relation, semeiosis--and, consequently, meaning--are ineluctably
contingent on Thirdness via the role of the interpretant:
'Every genuine triadic relation involves meaning, as meaning
is obviously a triadic relation' (1.345). And 'the most characteristic aspect of a symbol' is precisely 'its aspect as related
to its interpretant; because a symbol is distinguished as a sign
which becomes such by virtue of determining its interpretant'
(NE 4:260).
   Despite their great utility and capacity to fulfill functions
that genuine signs cannot, icons and indices are degenerate,
in the mathematical (nonpejorative) sense. A pure icon is
independent of any purpose and is capable of asserting
nothing. 'If it conveys information', Peirce writes, 'it is only

in the sense in which the object that it is used to represent may be said to convey information. An *icon* can only be a fragment of a completer sign' (NE 4:242). A pure index is likewise incapable of asserting anything; it 'simply forces attention to the object with which it reacts and puts the interpreter into mediate reaction with that object, but conveys no information' (loc. cit.).

The perspective articulated by Peirce's semeiotic embraces symbols as the epitomical signs, an inherent dynamic, and a teleological movement toward symbolicity. Peirce understands this as the capacity of signs for growth, concomitant fundamentally with the very nature of symbols as generals. They are, indeed, incapable of signifying any particular thing directly, only kinds of things (2.301). His apothegm that 'a symbol alone is indeterminate' (NE 4:260) necessarily prefigures a historical trajectory, in which the indeterminacy becomes succeedingly attenuated over time and yields to graded increments of determinacy. 'The symbol represents itself to be represented; and that representedness is real being owing to its utter vagueness. For all that is represented must be thoroughly borne out...The very entelechy of being lies in being representable ... A symbol is an embryonic reality endowed with power of growth into the very truth, the very entelechy of reality' (NE 4:261).

What Peirce means in these difficult passages is the teleology inherent in all human semeiosis. The understanding of signs as entelechies is in accord with Peirce's definition of entelechy as 'the perfectionment of reality' (NE 4:300), and with the indeterminacy of the symbol: it is this crucial openness to interpretation that insures that the representation the symbol achieves never ceases to have its esse in futuro. This means, in turn, that the semeiotic values which inhere in symbolic sign complexes--that is to say, the interpretants--have their being, as Peirce notes, in 'causing the interpretation' of their objects (NE 4:297). Thirdness, with its definitional orientation toward the future, always teleologically transcends the limitations of Secondness, of the here and now.

It is now appropriate to consider the entire notion of the purely self-referential sign, in the context of certain assumptions concerning language that have emphasized iconicity and drawn attention away from the symbolic quotient in discourse. I concentrate my remarks here on the poetic symbol in particular.

Jakobson's definition of the poetic function in terms of the 'focus on the message for its own sake' (1960:356) stressed its place in relation to the speech event and the communicative situation as a whole, taking into account thereby the several basic tasks that language is called upon to discharge in its actual use (1960:357). Jakobson's subsequent refinement of his definition continues to underscore the simultaneous co-presence of the other functions besides the poetic in poetry (i.e. the emotive, metalinguistic, referential, phatic, and conative functions), the difference from nonpoetic language being in the 'dominance' of the poetic function. In evaluating this formulation, it is not enough, however, to speak, as Jakobson does, of 'the supremacy of poetic function over referential function' (1960:371). The actuality of this inadequacy is implicit in his own later discussion (1971:697-708), where he couches the problem in terms of the kinds of semeiosis involved.

Comparing the parallelistic syntax of equivalences in music to that of poetry, Jakobson perceives in this patterning what he calls 'introversive semeiosis' (1971:704). Introversive semeiosis is, for Jakobson, particularly characteristic not only of music but of all manifestations of the aesthetic function, such as glossolalic poetry or nonrepresentational art, where the referential function has been obliterated or scanted. But the mainstream of poetry and the bulk of art have a significant quotient of 'extroversive' semeiosis to complement the putatively superordinate presence of introversiveness or self-referentiality. What is central here--and Jakobson misses, as we shall see presently--is that the primary order of functions in language is reversed or inverted (whether or not the referential is ultimately effaced); that the poetic function, when dominant, effectuates a hierarchical reordering (reranking) of functions.

The affirmation and enlargement of this conception of hierarchy of function are of crucial importance to the understanding of the special status of the purely self-referential sign. The very fact that a hierarchization is involved whereby the relation of poetic to nonpoetic discourse is altered calls for greater and more precise scrutiny of the nature of hierarchy, its bearing on function, and the consequent kinds and degrees of semeiosis produced in works of verbal art.

However one construes the underlying system of metrical and semantic relations which a poetic text mirrors linearly, the system is a structure defined by patterns of oppositions. This principle was enunciated by Jakobson, who raised it, however, to an explanatory status it only partly deserves. This he did through his emphasis on parallelism as the characteristic constant of poetic discourse in general. Drawing from Gerard Manley Hopkins, who stated that 'all artifice ... reduces itself to the principle of parallelism' (1959:84), Jakobson postulates that 'the infallible belonging of the two poetic parallels to the same context' creates an 'atemporal interconnection of the two parallels' (1980:24).

Poetic analysis, which has to deal with the temporality inherent in all language, has nevertheless deviated little from this tendency to fix static resemblances by moving through patterned juxtapositions and recurrences to conceiving of resemblances as 'symmetries'. The spatial metaphor used to affirm a poem's self-reference has aided in the development of the notion of a verbal icon with unities disposed in certain

ways throughout its linguistic space--from the level of distinc-
tive features (and complexes of such phonological features) to
grammatical categories and tropes. But the reality of hierarchization means something quite different: an introduction of
'asymmetry' via ranking, or the establishment of dominance.
This dynamic (for that is what it is) effectively negates, or
subordinates, both the quotient of symmetry and the real
possibility of positing a static, atemporal iconicity at the core
of poetic language as such.

As in any functional relationship, the dominant asymmetry is
accompanied by a level of symmetry. In poetry, equivalence
relations at the paradigmatic level are transformed into equivalences at the syntagmatic level, establishing symmetries and
antisymmetries charted in profuse detail by Jakobson. At the
same time, however, representation, which addresses itself to
higher order (i.e. semantic) units, supersedes these equivalences and disequivalences by making reference to the
asymmetric values of the units involved.

It is important that the poetic situation, with regard to the
skewed projection of referential substance, is completely
parallel in fundamental respects to that obtaining generally in
language, due to the essential asymmetry within the communicative situation between encoder and decoder. Whereas encoding is fundamentally a reductive process, which takes
signs of a higher order of semeioticity--knowledge and experi-
ence--and transforms them into signs of the lowest order--
sounds or letters representing phonemes--decoding is what
Peirce would call 'abductive', a series of inferences whereby
information not contained in the signal or text is recovered by
means of the individual decoder's ability to supply a variety
of linguistic and extralinguistic premises.

For poetry, our interest centers on the decoding side of
these counterdirectional processes, on the complex chain of
'abductive semeioses' that constitutes interpretation. Now,
what differentiates decoding of poetic texts from that of ordinary speech is not asymmetry as such but the 'degree of
asymmetry' between encoder and decoder. In ordinary discourse the degree of asymmetry is normally not great enough
to impede communication, and the incidence of or necessity for
what can be termed hermeneutic intervention is thereby less.
It is in poetry, however, that the asymmetry between the encoder (here: the poet), as represented by the text, and the
reader or listener often does become most acute. Owing to
the relative absence of conventional meanings in poetry other
than in its most utilitarian examples (such as most folk genres),
the need for interpretation rises in direct proportion to the
semantic diffuseness of the text. Diffuseness can, in turn,
be gauged in inverse proportion to the codedness of the text's
semantics. The acute degrees of asymmetry possible and prevalent in many species of imaginative verse are related to the
semeiotic properties of the symbol (as conceived by Peirce).

All of this calls for a reexamination of Jakobson's reliance on parallelism as a 'characteristic feature of all artifice' (1980:23) and that feature which readily distinguishes poetic discourse from other discourse. The 'referral of a semiotic fact to an equivalent fact inside the same context' (loc. cit.), as Jakobson has it, forms the foundation of the view that the poetic sign--like the musical sign and that produced in the visual arts--is to be understood in spatial terms. In Jakobson's view (1980:23-24), although poetry and music are 'essentially temporal', their similarities (or parallelisms) are articulated spatially. Moreover, the artistic sign is situated nearest to the iconic pole (rather than the symbolic) in Jakobson's conception, with its claim that 'the factual similarity which typifies *icon* finds its logically foreseeable correlative in the imputed similarity which specifies the *artifice*' (1980:22). A host of other and lesser theorists have arrived at or acquiesced in this assessment, toward a definition of the poem as 'verbal icon'.

The rich lode of Peircean semeiotic, which Jakobson did so much to bring to the attention of language and literature scholars, allows us to see, however, that as in ordinary language there is a structural tendency for iconic relations to subordinate the symbolic, so in poetic discourse there is a marked tendency for the symbolic to reassert its primacy over the iconic. One of the reasons for this is the phenomenon of formal closure in poems. The reassertion of the predominance of the symbolic mode of semeiosis is counterbalanced in poetry by the ensuing need for hermeneutic intervention--in other words, by interpretation.

Among the arts, poetry appears on a continuum tending toward self-reflexiveness, well before music and after representational painting. Poems differ widely in the apportionment and frequency of self-referential recurrence, and for most verse it can be said that semantic and referential content supersedes self-reflexive content, rendering introversive semeiosis a decidedly subordinate aspect of the poem's totality of semeiotic values.

The hierarchical nature of the components of poetic discourse is mirrored in the diachronic dimension of semeiosis in poetry, which can be defined by the gradience (in their hierarchical interrelation) of the symmetrical and asymmetrical aspects of the poetic function. Practically speaking, with respect to known literary history, this gradience articulates a continuum of types of texts having its beginning in ordinary language-- more precisely, in expressive coded complexes like puns or irreversible binomials. The proper literary starting-point is miniature folk genres like proverbs and riddles, where the dominance of symmetric structures is especially clear and indubitable. As we move away from folklore, as indeed we must, the scale of poetic genres changes in congruity with the degrees of codedness of the texts constituting a given

genre, ultimately reaching the relatively uncoded genre of
imaginative verse. Lyric is intermediate in the continuum but
palpably closer to the asymmetric pole. Typologically, the
movement away from miniature folk genres to the imaginative
lyric and narrative verse of known poets is accompanied by a
regularly growing symbolicity, or imperative for hermeneutic
intervention.

The structure and development of poetic figures, or tropes,
is particularly well suited to an illustration of the dynamic,
teleological, and essentially symbolic nature of poetic language.
The life cycle of tropes typically involves the lexicalization of
an initially living metonymy or metaphor (Shapiro and Shapiro
1976). What is central to the relationship in a given context
of poetic and ordinary linguistic semeiosis--in figures--is that
their poetic quotient is defined not merely by the different
rank order of the poetic function vis-à-vis the referential, but
essentially by the hierarchical reordering that the poetic function effects when it dominates. The primary order of literal
and figural functions is reversed or inverted in the figural
syntagm versus the literal. It is this reversal that accounts
for the multidimensional meanings in poetry, and for the continuing possibility of interpretation which is part and parcel
of Peirce's delineation of the semeiotic properties of the symbol.

A close reading of Peirce allows access to yet another diacritic property of poetic and artistic semeiosis, one of ten
traditionally assigned to iconic or self-referential status: the
presence of style. For if Goodman is right, and 'style has to
do exclusively with the symbolic functioning of the work as
such' (1975:807), then the fundamental indeterminacy of
the embryonic symbol, the asymmetry between what it is and
what it tends to become through interpretation, helps to explain the true significate effects of style. Recurring to the
definition of style as 'a trope of meaning' (Shapiro 1980:246),
I can now clarify this conception by understanding style as
the superordinate ranking of the annexed, or stylistic, signata,
over the cognitive, or nonstylistic, signata. Style establishes
a hierarchy of interpretants in which the marked--emotive or
poetic--features (Jakobson 1972:77) are perceived to dominate
the neutral information conveyed by the text or artifact. It is
thus itself a result of troping, specifically a metonymization or
an instantiation of metonymy, the primary trope whose definiens
is the establishment of hierarchy among signata (Shapiro and
Shapiro 1976:7). Metonymy tends to be submerged in metaphor,
and metaphor in turn has a decided tendency toward lexicalization. The fully coded metaphor ('dead metaphor') is no trope
at all. Its demise, like the increasing codedness and resultant
evisceration of a particular 'style', is characterized by a concomitant dehierarchization, a collapse of dominance.

Peirce's idea of the symbol as the quintessential sign facili-
tates the assessment of other sign types and enables us to
distinguish objects from genuine interpretants. A pertinent
example of such an assessment is that of 'irony' as a

rhetorical strategy, since in ironic discourse the sign and its object are exactly the same. In discussing the nature of the autotelic sign, one may ask whether irony actually produces such a sign. Recent criticism has been tempted to regard irony as a value in itself, as a complete interpretant of a work of literature, and I return to this fundamentally wrong-headed enterprise in a moment.

Whereas in the case of the genuine tropes, metonymy and metaphor, there is a definitional hierarchization of two signata or meaning units, in irony (a nontrope) there is only the pragmatic understanding that a single signatum is not to be taken at face value. Irony essentially constitutes a mode of argumentation which raises a 'purely negative condition' on interpretation to a superordinate value. This external focus of irony encompasses its purely rhetorical elements which signal attitudes toward message, content, or addressee, sometimes through the smallest constituents of discourse, including diacritic signs. Irony is at best a stimulus to interpretation, a rhetorical means of commenting on a 'pre-text' leading toward meditation on the truth-value of a previous discourse. Since it is entirely context-bound, irony can never be a positive value. For that same reason, it can embrace a vast discourse without having to unmask any other signatum that differs from literal meaning. And because it is entirely context-bound, irony is at the opposite end of the continuum from true symbolic meaning (which is heavily metaphorical).

It is important to bear in mind that the necessary (and external) collateral experience or information utilized in the recognition of irony is not in the interpretant itself but in its object (cf. NE 3:841). An ironic utterance cannot be interpreted as such without that foreknowledge, but since the latter is not 'in' linguistic structure, it does not have to produce a secure ontological basis for interpretation. As a nonpresence, irony can never 'directly' address a system of values. As a purely negative condition on interpretation, it falls outside the pattern of interpretants that informs literary semeiosis. By not pointing beyond itself in the way that a symbol does--'a sign', as Peirce wrote, being 'something by knowing which we know something more' (Hardwick 1977:31-32)-- irony as strategy appeals to a prevailing tendency to regard verbal art as iconic rather than symbolic. Due to its final emphasis on the fact that poems do not assert anything in the conventional sense of assertion, an 'iconic fallacy' establishes a specious syllogism combining two premises: (1) literature does not assert anything; (2) icons do not assert anything; therefore, (3) literature is predominantly iconic, in a fundamental inversion of the semeiotic hierarchy and a subversion of the symbol.

The notion that irony is an ultimate interpretant has become a touchstone of the so-called Deconstructive critique of literature, whose practitioners include such names as Jacques

Derrida and Paul de Man (not to mention epigones). To the
Deconstructive critic, works of literature are to be read and
scrutinized for the ways in which they surreptitiously and
ironically refer to their own fictiveness. Those who would
confront the assumptions of this currently faddish school find
themselves faced with the utter naiveté of the mimetic straw
man it purports to destroy; he is scarcely a worthy target.
But a criticism that circumscribes the force of language and
literature to bad faith and ensuing pure rhetoric ultimately
reveals its own misapprehensions. A critique that seeks to
dereify language and succeeds only in reifying relations (such
as the assumptions about 'temporality' involved in the ironic
conception) coheres ultimately with the persistently external,
context-bound nature of irony. For it insistently disallows
the crucial connection between the interpretant and its antecedent sign on which symbolic representation depends.

It is noteworthy that the Deconstructive view which leads to
the notion of a literature endlessly commenting on itself comes
to join hands ideologically with Jakobson's view of introversive
semeiosis as the distinguishing characteristic of verbal art and
of the artistic sign in general. Both depart from an essentially
static assumption of the complementary distribution of rhetorical features and other structures in poetry. And 'structure'
still means to both essentially a standardized, exhaustive reduction of texts to those constitutive features which limit their
free play. While Deconstruction engages in a prolonged interrogation of language as such (invariably uninformed, curiously
enough, of so much as the rudiments of linguistic analysis or
the determinants of linguistic change), in an attempt to undermine its referential status, the Jakobsonian approach to poetry
deals with figurative language only to the extent of establishing symmetries within the poem's closed world. Figural language, in fact, thus becomes the focus of variously motivated
desires for an autotelic sign that would collapse the distinction
between signifier and signified (bringing to its logical culmi-
nation, on the Jakobsonian side, a programmatic manifesto on
the theory and practice of verse originating in Russian Futur-
ism). With its near-exclusive reliance on patterned juxtapositions and recurrences, the extreme degree of Jakobsonian
analysis arrives at the triumph of self-reference, much as the
Deconstructive critic does.

In fact, the accumulated tradition of reading and writing
poetry, and the recorded directionality of the development of
poetic canons throughout the historical period, argue for the
supersession of the autotelic sign in this variety of semeiosis.
The same asymmetry between encoder and decoder that informs
the ordinary use of language also constitutes the core of the
poetic situation, with its necessary and insistent elicitation of
a series of interpretants, in a teleological movement that
attempts to match interpretation with intentionality. The self-
referential component of the artistic sign, the one that accounts

for the measure of parallelism and recurrence--the Secondness--
to be found in a work of verbal art, is ultimately transcended
in the hierarchy of semeiosis by representation or Thirdness.
In going beyond the limits of iconicity or self-referentiality,
poetry remains foundationally true to its own nature as
symbolic art.

REFERENCES

Goodman, Nelson. 1975. The status of style. Critical In-
quiry 1.799-811.
Hardwick, Charles S., ed. 1977. Semiotic and significs: The
correspondence between Charles S. Peirce and Victoria Lady
Welby. Bloomington: Indiana University Press.
Hopkins, Gerard Manley. 1959. The journals and papers.
Edited by Humphry House. London: Oxford University
Press.
Jakobson, Roman. 1921. Novejšaja russkaja poèzija. Prague:
Politika.
Jakobson, Roman. 1960. Linguistics and poetics. In: Style
in language. Edited by Thomas A. Sebeok. Cambridge,
Mass.: MIT Press. 350-377.
Jakobson, Roman. 1971. Selected writings, II: Word and
language. The Hague: Mouton.
Jakobson, Roman. 1972. Verbal communication. Scientific
American 223/7.72-80.
Jakobson, Roman. 1980. The framework of language.
(Michigan studies in the humanities, 1). Ann Arbor:
Horace H. Rackham School of Graduate Studies, University
of Michigan.
Peirce, Charles Sanders. 1965-1966. Collected papers. 2nd
printing, 8 vols. in 4. Edited by Charles Hartshorne and
Paul Weiss (Vols. 1-6) and Arthur Burks (Vols. 7-8). Cam-
bridge, Mass.: Harvard University Press.
Peirce, Charles Sanders. 1976. The new elements of mathe-
matics. 4 vols. Edited by Carolyn Eisele. The Hague:
Mouton.
Shapiro, Michael. 1980. Toward a global theory of style (a
Peircean exposé). Ars semeiotica 3.241-247.
Shapiro, Michael, and Shapiro, Marianne. 1976. Hierarchy
and the structure of tropes. (Studies in semiotics, 8).
Bloomington: Indiana University.
Short, T. L. 1981. Semeiosis and intentionality. Transactions
of the Charles S. Peirce Society 17.197-223.

ARE FIGURES OF THOUGHT FIGURES OF SPEECH?

Samuel R. Levin
City University of New York

In the rhetorics of antiquity, the practice of verbal composition is treated under five heads: invention, disposition,
elocution, action, and memory. Under action was comprehended
the use of gesture, tone of voice, and general physical deport-
ment in the delivery of a speech. The cultivation of memory
was prescribed to insure that one could speak without notes or
a written text. Since action and memory pertain primarily to
oratory, the significance of those two capacities has steadily
diminished as rhetoric has been gradually transformed into a
theory concerned with written composition. In this new perspective the three other components of the classical program
continue to play significant roles--invention, or the starting
of ideas, and disposition, the arrangement and organization of
those ideas into a coherent whole, being just as important for
written as for spoken discourse. It is, however, the remaining component, elocution, or the artistic use of language,
which has emerged as the major focus of interest--to such an
extent as virtually to form a discipline of its own. Essentially,
this single division of the classical rhetoric constitutes the
field that we today call stylistics.

The matter of elocution was divided in the ancient handbooks
into three major categories: figures of speech, figures of
thought, and tropes. Concerning tropes a great deal has been
and continues to be written. But the figures have not evoked
a comparable degree of interest. One reason for this imbalance,
I think, is that whereas the tropes by their nature invite theoretical inquiry, the figures have seemed to offer less in the way
of intellectual interest. Thus even among the ancient treatises
one frequently finds extended discussions on the nature of the
tropes. When it comes to the figures, however, these same
treatises give the barest, most jejune explanatory accounts,
and then plunge immediately into an enumeration and exemplifi-
cation of the various types. The following statements are
typical of the theoretical grounding provided: Quintilian

tells us that figures of thought lie in the conception, figures
of speech in the expression (1953, III.357). Not less circular
is the version we find in the *Rhetorica ad Herennium*, whose
author tells us that 'it is a figure of speech if the adornment
is comprised in the fine polish of the language itself. [Whereas]
a figure of thought derives a certain distinction from the idea,
not from the words' (1964.275). The most suggestive remark is
made by Cicero in *de Oratore*, where he says, 'there is this
difference between the figurative character of speech and of
thought, that the figure suggested by the words disappears
if one alters the words, but that of the thought remains whatever words one chooses to employ' (1968:161). Compared to
the formulations of Quintilian and *ad Herennium*, Cicero's remark seems to contain an insight. If we ponder his observation, however, it yields little more than that a thought, once
conceived, can be given a figurative turn in more than one
way. What Cicero says about figures of speech, on the other
hand, implies that for him they are unproblematic.

For us, however, figures of speech, particularly as they relate to figures of thought, are not without theoretical interest.
For consider the phrase 'figure of speech'. It turns out that
the word 'speech' is one of a fairly large class infected with a
special kind of ambiguity. It is not that these words comprise
different meanings, like say 'bank' or 'light'; they comprise,
rather, different modes of the same meaning. In connection
with a somewhat similar problem, Bertrand Russell once said
(1952:172) it was a disgrace to the human race that it used
the one word 'is' to express both the copulative and the
equative relations (viz. 'Socrates is human' and 'Socrates is a
man'). If it is not a disgrace to the human race, it is at
least an embarrassment to the English language that it contains
words whose meaning applies sometimes to a mental or physical
process and sometimes to the result of that process. Consider,
for example, 'judgment', 'reflection', 'utterance', 'construction'. This is just a small sampling of the words that suffer
this type of ambiguity. Frege (1970:62), in the course of
working out his semantic theory, is at pains to point out that
by 'thought' he understands not the subjective act of thinking
but its objective content (actually, of course, his worry is
about 'Gedanke', which poses a similar problem). Husserl
(1967:passim) elaborates an entire vocabulary to pin down the
phenomenological components of intentional acts, separating the
noetic process from the noematic result, the act-phase from
the object-phase. These thoughts come to mind when, from the
standpoint of developments in modern speech act theory, one
reflects on the phrase 'figure of speech'. Having become
sensitized to the difference between the speaking and the
spoken aspects of the speech act, one is struck by the fact
that in the section of the handbooks devoted to figures of
speech the word 'speech' refers exclusively to the result of

the act, to what has been uttered, not the uttering of it, to the *énoncé,* not the *énonciation.* [1]

The figures of speech listed in the handbooks are numerous and varied. Nor is there always agreement as to the allocation of particular figures. Among the standard types, however, are the following: epanaphora, the beginning of successive clauses with the same word or group of words; antistrophe, the like repetition at the end of clauses; antithesis, the juxtaposition of contraries in balanced clauses; asyndeton, the combining of clauses without conjunctions; isocolon, a sequence of clauses containing the same number of syllables. Common to each of these types is the artistic manipulation of the syntactic space. To give one example: take the characterization of George Washington presented in a resolution to the House of Representatives in 1799: 'A citizen, first in war, first in peace, first in the hearts of his countrymen'. This is an instance of epanaphora and is typical of the genre. The art is on the surface, the effect situated entirely in the expression. In figures of speech one says what one is thinking, but encases it in a stylish frame. In terms of illocutionary strategy, therefore, figures of speech are routine. They are what they say they are. There is in them no art that derives from exploitation of the speech act.

But if the classical rhetoricians do not exploit the modern notion of the speech act in their treatment of figures of speech and if it in fact appears nowhere in the writings of the classical rhetoricians, it would be a mistake to conclude that they were ignorant of its implications. The rhetorics, after all, were handbooks for orators; they were designed to promote oratorical skill. And this skill, according to Quintilian, would be manifested to the degree that orators succeeded in instructing, moving, and delighting their audiences (1953, III.181). Now these are all perlocutionary effects--avenues toward persuasion--and since such effects are functions of illocutionary acts, the consideration of such acts must in some way have come into the calculations of the rhetoricians. I suggest that such a consideration can be inferred from the treatment accorded in the handbooks to figures of thought. We have to bear in mind that figures of thought (like figures of speech) are treated under the rubric elocution, i.e. the artistic use of language. We ought therefore not to expect the ordinary or straightforward acts of assertion, interrogation, or request to engage the interest of the rhetoricians. If the notion of speech acts were to emerge at all, it would be in some artful form, as some departure from the normal mode of speaking, as a type of verbal play.

Figures of thought, in other words, are acts of speech incorporating a devious intent. The deviousness, moreover, may be a function of either the illocutionary force of the utterance, its propositional content, or some interplay between the two. [2] Austin, when he first broached the problem of performative

utterances, referred to them as masqueraders. A sentence
like 'I name this ship the *Queen Mary*' is of the declarative
form and appears to make a statement. But as Austin says
(1962:4f.), such sentences do not 'describe' or 'report' anything, nor do they tolerate judgments of truth or falsity in
the normal way. They thus merely masquerade as statements.
Ross has extended the notion of masquerade to take in rhetorical questions. A question like 'I ask you how any decent
citizen can give his vote again to Governor Schamlos?' (Ross's
example) only masquerades as a question. The illocutionary
act that it (derivatively) performs is more nearly that of an
assertion (in this case negative), so that the speech act is
indirect (Ross 1975:233f.). Given this artful property of
rhetorical questions, it should occasion no surprise to find
that the ancient rhetoricians included them among the classical
figures of thought. The ancients, of course, did not limit
themselves to questions in which the performative verb explicitly appears (as in Ross's example), since even without it the
illocutionary diversion which gives point to such questions
would still be operative. Thus we have Cicero's reminder of
long suffering expressed in the question 'How long, O Cataline,
will you abuse our patience?' As Quintilian says of this
formulation, 'How much greater is the fire of his words as
they stand than if he had said "You have abused our patience
a long time"' (1953, III.379). Pausing over Quintilian's own
formulation, we in our turn might say, 'How much greater is
the fire of *his* words than if he had said...?'

It is characteristic of rhetorical questions that they serve
as conveyances for their own answers. This is a corollary of
the fact that they function indirectly as assertions. The
answer to Cicero's question is that Cataline will no longer
abuse the patience of his Roman compatriots. This answer is
presupposed and preemptive. Any attempt by Cataline to provide his own answer to Cicero's question--to say, for example,
'Well, for perhaps two or three more months'--would be regarded as at best a desperate joke. In another of Cicero's
questions to Cataline, 'Do you not see that your plots are all
laid bare?', Cicero takes for granted that Cataline indeed does
see. We might say that in rhetorical questions an act of subversion is committed on the illocutionary force of the utterance
by foreclosing the possibility of an answer. We shall see a
different kind of subversion in the figure of thought to which
I now turn.

Consider the figure of thought known as antiphrasis or
preterition. In this figure one disclaims the intention to say
something which is said in the very disclaimer. An antiphrasis
may be put in the form of a question, as in 'Why should I
mention my opponent's lust for power?' This is not a rhetorical
question, such as would be 'Why should I reward my opponent's
lust for power?' The latter is a rhetorical question in that it
presupposes a particular answer by way of an assertion that it

indirectly makes. In the antiphrastic question, on the other hand, the point is not to suggest a particular answer, but to implicate someone in the assertion that it indirectly makes.

Although antiphrases may be expressed in the form of questions, that is not their customary mode. As a rule they appear in the form of negative statements, viz. 'I will not speak of my opponent's unsavoury reputation or his well-known criminal record'. It is not obvious how to analyze such sentences in speech act terms. They seem to be merely negative sentences that make an assertion. Since, however, the negative occurs in the illocutionary force indicating part of the sentence, I think they might more properly be called disavowals. In antiphrases, then, we have a structure in which what is disavowed in the illocutionary force is delivered by the propositional content. Consider by way of comparison a (performative) sentence like 'I deny that my opponent's record entitles him to a second term'. This is a direct speech act; there is a consistency between the illocutionary force and the propositional content. In a disavowal, on the other hand, the relation is inconsistent; what is presupposed by the illocutionary force is subverted by the propositional content. In antiphrases this subversion is effected in that their main verb is typically one of mentioning, like 'say' or 'speak'. These verbs have a kind of reflexive or autological property, so that even when negated they go right on talking, as it were.

The next topic that I take up is that of irony, a device that according to Quintilian may function either as a trope or a figure of thought. The distinction is not all that easy to bear out; here is what Quintilian says about it (1953, III.401):

Irony involving a figure does not differ from the irony which is a trope, as far as its genus is concerned, since in both cases we understand something which is the opposite of what is actually said; on the other hand, a careful consideration of the species of irony will soon reveal the fact that they differ. In the first place, the trope is franker in its meaning, and, despite the fact that it implies something other than what it says, makes no pretence about it. For the context as a rule is perfectly clear, as, for example, in the following passage from the Catalinarian orations. 'Rejected by him, you migrated to your boon-companion, that excellent gentleman Metellus'. In this case the irony lies in two words, and is therefore a specially concise form of trope. But in the figurative form of irony the speaker disguises his entire meaning, the disguise being apparent rather than confessed. For in the trope the conflict is purely verbal, while in the figure the meaning, and sometimes the whole aspect of the case, conflicts with the language and the tone of voice adopted.

Among the examples that Quintilian gives for irony as a
figure of thought are two passages from the *Aeneid*. In the
first one the speaker is Turnus, the noble king of the
Rutulians. Provoked by Drances' argument that he meet
Aeneas in single combat and so spare Drances and the other
Latins the need to continue fighting, he says, 'Brand *me* as
coward, Drances, since thy sword has slain such heaps of
Trojans'. In the second example the speaker is Juno: 'It was
I that led the Dardan gallant on, To storm the bridal bed of
Sparta's queen!'

Irony, of course, consists in saying the opposite of what is
meant--or meaning the opposite of what is said. This opposition, however, can take one of two basic forms: it may focus
on the word or on the proposition. It appears to be Quintilian's
position that if the opposition is focused on a word, the irony
is a trope; if focused on the proposition, it is a figure of
thought. Thus in the example he gives of irony as a trope,
we are to take 'excellent gentleman' as meaning 'low-life' or
something similar. An example of Searle's (1979:112f.), 'That
was a brilliant thing to do', uttered when someone has just
broken your priceless Chinese vase, would also be a trope on
this account, the irony consisting in the substitution of
'brilliant' for 'stupid'. In the examples in which irony is a
figure of thought, on the other hand, the irony requires us
to read an opposition into the entire proposition. Turnus, who
utters the lines of the first example, is not a coward--Drances
is the coward, and it was not Drances but he, Turnus, who
had slain heaps of Trojans; in the second example it was not
Juno who led Paris to Helen--it was Venus.

Irony is a figure of thought, therefore, when a speaker in
asserting a proposition means to be understood as asserting its
diametric opposite. In this process the reversal of meaning
usually depends heavily upon context and background information. Irony as a figure of thought thus involves a pragmatic dimension. This dimension is, of course, also relevant
for lexical irony, i.e. when it is a trope. However, as a
figure of thought irony typically requires negating the proposition expressed, and this negation entails reversing the roles
of propositional elements like names, personal pronouns, or
other deictics. It is this fact, I believe, that justifies the
claim that irony as a figure of thought involves an opposition
that focuses on the proposition. Thus compare the sentence
'Yes, you've always been a *true* conservative' with 'All along
I was (supposed to be) the *liberal*', the first to represent
irony as a trope, the second as a figure of thought. In the
first sentence the ironic meaning is arrived at by inverting
the word 'true' to yield 'You've always been a false conservative'. In the second it is arrived at by negating the proposition and implicitly affirming the original proposition of someone
else, thus, '*I* was not the liberal, *you* were'.[3] From this we
can see that irony as a trope is based on antonymy, an

opposition involving the meaning of words, whereas irony as a figure of thought is based on negation, an opposition involving the content of propositions.

In each of the three figures of thought discussed so far, we have a type of masquerade. In rhetorical questions an assertion masquerades as a question. In antiphrases an assertion masquerades as a disavowal to make that assertion. In irony an assertion masquerades as its opposite. The figures of thought that I now discuss, while also duplicitous, are not masqueraders; they accomplish their devious designs in a different way.

Consider first the figure known as apostrophe. Quintilian says that this figure consists in the diversion of the address from the judge to another party, and instances 'What was that sword of yours doing, Tubero, in the field of Pharsalus' (1953, III.397). Passing over the rhetorical question in which the apostrophe is embedded, we see that Cicero (who is here speaking for the defense) has shifted his address from the judge to Tubero, the prosecutor in the case. In the part of the figure that is relevant for my purposes, i.e. the apostrophe, no conflict is set up between the illocutionary force and the propositional content. Rather, an act of dissembling is performed on a term of the speech act setting. By terms of the setting I mean the roles played by the speaker, the addressee, and the contextual background. In the example at hand Cicero addresses Tubero, but he intends the force of his remark to be registered with the judge.

Nor is it necessary for the execution of apostrophe that a third party be present; it may be employed just as readily in a simple interlocution. Thus, in hearing from a speaker a wrong or silly remark about the moon's gravitational pull, an interlocutor might respond, 'Newton, did you ever hear such foolishness?' Further, in cases where an absent party is addressed, that party need not be a human being. Thus another of Quintilian's examples is 'I appeal to you, hills and groves of Alba', where the appeal is intended for members of the immediate audience. Again, the point of the figure is to have whatever is expressed registered with an addressee other than the one to whom it is purportedly directed.

Accepting this misdirection as its point, apostrophe may be distinguished from invocation, a device with which it is sometimes conflated. Thus in Wordsworth's poem which begins 'Milton, thou should'st be living at this hour', the address or invocation, although to someone not present in the audience, is direct. The entire sonnet is addressed to Milton; there is no diversion from or reversion to a different, local addressee, as there would be in an apostrophe. Apostrophe is therefore a special type of indirect speech act, the indirectness involving not the expression of one illocutionary act through the medium of another, but the appeal to one addressee through the address to another.

I turn now to the figure known as prosopopoeia or personification. In modern studies personification is frequently
treated as a form of metaphor, one in which something nonhuman is endowed with human characteristics, this endowment
being achieved through the application to nonhuman or abstract entities of predicates that normally apply to humans.
If we read 'Virtue jumped on her horse and rode away', we
take 'virtue' to be designating something that is both human
and abstract. If virtue continues to be a principal in the
narrative development, we are dealing with an allegory. Now
among the predicates normally applied to humans are those
signifying the use of language. In the rhetorical figure of
personification the personified entities are made to speak; in
fact, this is the sole purpose for which they are introduced.
Quintilian (1953,III.393) cites an example of Cicero's: 'For if
my country, which is far dearer to me than life itself, if all
Italy, if the whole commonwealth, were to address me thus,
"Marcus Tullius, what dost thou?"'. The author of ad
Herennium says that 'Personification consists in representing
an absent person as present, or in making a mute thing or one
lacking form articulate, and attributing to it a definite form
and a language...' He then provides this example: 'But if
this invincible city should now give utterance to her voice,
would she not speak as follows, "I, city of reason,..."'.
In these examples, which are typical, the personification is
not metaphoric. The abstraction (the city) is not 'instilled
with life', it does not become a character speaking in its own
voice and playing a role in the narrative development; it
serves, rather, as a surrogate voice, a mouthpiece for the
views of the speaker. In apostrophes, as has been seen, an
absent addressee is made to stand in for another--the one
present; in personification, an absent speaker stands in for
another--the one actually speaking. We might label such
figures masks. Between masks and masquerades there is the
following difference: in a masquerade the speech act belies
its purpose, in a mask a propositional element belies its character. Thus, in the former the dissimulation is one of behavior, in the latter it is one of appearance. This difference
is a correlation of the fact that a masquerade involves the
proposition, a mask merely a term.
Another figure functioning as a mask is hypophora or suggestion. In this figure a speaker puts a question to an
addressee or audience and then provides for it his own
answer; the same person thus assumes the roles of both
speaker and addressee. Here is an example from ad Herennium:
'Your enemy, whom you assume to be guilty, you doubtless
summoned him to trial? No, for you slew him while he was yet
unconvicted. Did you respect the laws which forbid this act?
On the contrary, you decided that they did not even exist in
the books. When he reminded you of your old friendship,
were you moved? No, you killed him...' (1964.313).[4] The

speaker, in asking the questions, ostensibly wishes the
addressee to vouchsafe the answers. Instead, he provides
them himself. In answering the questions the speaker thus
functions as a mask for the addressee. The difference between
hypophora and our other two types of masking is that in
hypophora the speaker and addressee are both present; in
the other two types one or the other was absent. [5]

Another form of the same figure is effected when the speaker
puts the questions to himself and then provides the answers.
Again from ad Herennium: 'Now what should I have done when
I was surrounded by so great a force of Gauls? Fight? But
then our advance would have been with a small force...Remain
in camp? But we neither had reinforcements to look for, nor
the wherewithal to keep alive. Abandon the camp? But we
were blocked...' Here we might say that the speaker, in asking the questions, is functioning as a mask for another speaker.

The six figures of thought that I have dealt with here represent but a fraction of the dozens that one may find listed in
the handbooks, and I do not wish to suggest that the remaining types could be comprehended by the two categories masqueraders and masks. In fact, I am quite certain that they
cannot be. What I am confident of, however, is that whatever
other categories may be required, they will evince a quality
of deviousness or misdirection. This is made clear by the
ancient rhetoricians. In the following passage, for example,
Quintilian (1953,III.359) compares figures of thought with the
use of feints in swordplay:

For although it may seem that proof is infinitesimally affected
by the figures employed, none the less those same figures
lend credibility to our arguments and steal their way
secretly into the minds of the judges. For just as in swordplay it is easy to see, parry, and ward off direct blows and
simple straightforward thrusts, while side-strokes and feints
are less easy to observe and the task of the skillful swords-
man is to give the impression that his design is quite other
than it actually is, even so the oratory in which there is no
guile fights by sheer weight and impetus alone; on the other
hand, the fighter who feints and varies his assault is able
to attack flank or back as he will, to lure his opponent's
weapons from their guard and to outwit him by a slight
inclination of the body. Further, there is no more effective method of exciting the emotions than an apt use of
figures. For if the expression of brow, eyes and hands
has a powerful effect in stirring the passions, how much
more effective must be the aspect of our style itself when
composed to produce the result at which we aim?

I remarked earlier that the operative dimension in figures of
thought is pragmatic rather than semantic. This follows from
the fact that figures of thought make perfect sense taken

literally. Their figurativeness is a function of their use, not
their meaning. It is in this respect that figures of thought
differ from tropes. For the ancients a trope involved the use
of a word or phrase in an unaccustomed meaning. The author
of *ad Herennium* says (1964:333) that tropes have this in common, 'that the language departs from the ordinary meaning of
the words'. Quintilian says (1953, III.301), 'By a trope is
meant the artistic alteration of a word or phrase from its proper
meaning to another'. These characterizations are quite general.
They do not make clear how the 'departure' or 'alteration' of
meaning is accomplished in tropes. The point is that 'alteration' of meaning may take one of two basic forms: it may be
located in the expression itself, or it may be established in
the relation between the expression and its context of use.
The first type of 'alteration' is semantic, the second pragmatic.
In Keats's line 'Thou still unravished bride of quietness', there
is a clash between the meanings of 'bride' and '(of) quietness'.
Descriptively, this condition is referred to as semantic deviance. In figures of thought, as we have seen, there is no
semantic deviance; there is illocutionary deviousness. Instead
of art in the expression, there is guile in the expression of it.
What obtains as a consequence is pragmatic incongruity.

These considerations suggest that a more general revamping
of the classical analysis might be in order. Recall that lexical
irony counted as a trope for the ancients, and that such
'tropes' are like figures of thought in having a literal sense.
We might therefore wish to range both types of irony under
figures of thought, distinguishing them merely as lexical and
propositional. On this approach, also, a certain class of
expressions sometimes advanced as metaphors might also be
allocated to figures of thought. Thus, the argument that
semantic deviance is not a necessary condition for metaphor
is usually urged with examples like 'Edison discovered gold in
his laboratory', intended to mean that he grew rich from his
inventions. Searle's example (1979:105) is 'I have climbed to
the top of the greasy pole', uttered by Disraeli on becoming
Prime Minister. Such 'metaphors' are equivocal at best. Their
operative dimension is pragmatic, not semantic, thus qualifying
them as figures of thought.

But these problems are outside the concerns of this paper.
Here I have tried to show that figures of thought make their
point through some deviousness in the performance of the
speech act. In view of this fact, and recalling the ambiguous
nature of the word 'speech', I conclude that the question posed
in the title of this paper should be answered in the affirmative.

NOTES

I wish to thank D. Terence Langendoen for discussing this
paper with me and causing me to see more clearly some of the
issues involved.

1. The ancient handbooks were, of course, written in Latin or Greek, so that the phrase 'figure of speech' (or 'figure of thought') does not occur in them. In the translations of those handbooks into English, however, and in the English critical tradition, it is that phrase that we have to deal with. Moreover, the general question of what relation obtains between the two types of figures remains, no matter what phrases are employed by way of designation.
2. The fundamental analysis of the speech act into its illocutionary force and propositional content is given in Searle (1969).
3. The sentence 'All along I was the liberal' can be uttered, with a different intonation, to affirm its content as true. On this reading, which is factual, not ironic, the speaker, in making a positive assertion about himself, implies that the addressee was not a liberal, thus 'you were not'. In the ironic utterance of this sentence the actual assertion is to be taken as false. I owe this observation to Langendoen.
4. The author of ad Herennium lists this as a figure of speech, but Quintilian (1953,III.503) quite properly counts it a figure of thought.
5. This is not strictly true; in the first example of apostrophe given earlier, the speaker and addressee were both present.

REFERENCES

Austin, J. L. 1962. How to do things with words. Cambridge, Mass.: Harvard University Press.
Cicero. 1968. De Oratore. Translated by H. Rackham. Cambridge, Mass.: Harvard University Press.
Frege, Gottlob. 1970. On sense and reference. In: Philosophical writings of Gottlob Frege. Translated by Peter Geach and Max Black. Oxford: Basil Blackwell.
Husserl, Edmund. 1967. Ideas. Translated by W. R. Boyce Gibson. London: George Allen and Unwin.
Quintilian. 1953. Institutio Oratoria. Vol. III. Translated by H. E. Butler. Cambridge, Mass.: Harvard University Press.
Rhetorica ad Herennium. 1964. Translated by Harry Caplan. Cambridge, Mass.: Harvard University Press.
Ross, John Robert. 1975. Where to do things with words. In: Syntax and semantics III: Speech acts. Edited by Peter Cole and Jerry L. Morgan. New York: Academic Press.
Russell, Bertrand. 1952. Descriptions. In: Semantics and the philosophy of language. Edited by Leonard Linsky. Urbana: University of Illinois Press.
Searle, John R. 1969. Speech acts. Cambridge: Cambridge University Press.

Searle, John R. 1979. Expression and meaning. New York: Cambridge University Press.

BEYOND TRANSLATION:
ESTHETICS AND LANGUAGE DESCRIPTION

A. L. Becker
Institute for Advanced Study and
University of Michigan

> *'Art and the equipment to grasp it are made in the same shop'*
> *Clifford Geertz*

This essay is put together as a main plot plus several asides, meant to give some support to the main plot. The main plot is an answer to the question: how does one describe a language in order not to exclude esthetic--one might even say moral-- values?

1. **Language as paradox.** In the fifties, the Spanish Heideg- gerian philologist, José Ortega y Gasset (1959) began a seminar on Plato's *Symposium* with a discussion of 'the difficulty of reading'. To read a distant text--distant in space, time, or conceptual world--is a utopian task, he wrote, a task whose 'initial intention cannot be fulfilled in the development of its activity and which has to be satisfied with approximations essentially contradictory to the purpose which had started it' (1959:1). In that sense, the activity of language is in many particular ways utopian: one can never convey just what one wants to convey, for others will interpret what they hear, and their interpretation will be both exuberant and deficient. As Ortega (1959:2) put it:

1. Every utterance is deficient--it says less than it wishes to say.
2. Every utterance is exuberant--it says more than it plans.

He called these 'Axioms for a New Philology'. (I think we can substitute 'linguistics' for 'philology', since Ortega himself

appears to use the terms interchangeably.)[1] It may seem
strange to found something on a paradox--the successful
resolution of which is utopian--yet Ortega is not the first to
find matters lingual in some basic way paradoxical. Bateson
(1972:271-278) gave us the notion of the double bind, as a
condition necessary for higher learning. A double bind is a
situation in which one receives two simultaneous and contradictory messages plus the further condition that one may not
or cannot leave the situation. Such a bind impels one to
examine the context of the whole situation and, in some way
or other, try to correct or reshape it. Scollon (1981:344-345)
has argued that 'all communication must...depend on some form
of double bind':

> In any communication, the participants are faced with the
> dilemma of respecting the other's right to be left alone
> (negative face) and the other's right to be accepted as a
> participating member of society (positive face)...I believe
> the temporal bond of ensemble completes the picture...it is
> ensemble which holds participants together in a mutual atten-
> tion to the ongoing situation, and it is the polarity of posi-
> tive and negative face that forces the attention to the com-
> munication of relationship. These in consort produce a
> double bind which is the mechanism by which conversants
> learn to learn.

And so conversation, like philology, is a matter of continual
self-correction between exuberance (i.e. friendliness: you are
like me) and deficiency (i.e. respect: you are not me). In
reading a text from Java or Burma, my understanding is
exuberant because of all that I read into the text and
deficient because of all that I am blind to.

Of course, this is true too between even the closest of
friends. However, across great lingual distance one can seldom distinguish cultural stereotype from personal deviation.
The hardest thing for me to do in Southeast Asia is to hear,
authentically, the individual voice. The differences of culture,
in their freshness and strangeness, cannot at first be--as they
are to an insider--part of the background. Across distant
languages, the hardest thing to hear is the individual voice,
i.e. the deviation from stereotypes. A deviation is the way
prior text is shaped to the situation at hand.

Everything I observed about Javanese puppet theatre--which
made me aware of new possibilities for drama--was heard by
Javanese friends with an ultra-polite version of 'So what else
is new?' My esthetic enjoyment in coming to terms with
Javanese theatre was at the level of the genre itself: I never
heard the individual voices until I was able to background the
newness of the whole tradition (Becker 1979).

Perhaps this can be made clear with a story about birds.
There are several varieties of white-crowned sparrows. Those

in Ann Arbor sound slightly different from those in Berkeley or Princeton, though the major contours of the song are recognizable. The bird book (Peterson 1961:237) gives it this way:[2]

> Voice: --song begins with a clear plaintive whistle...but ends with a husky trilled whistle.

However, that is not all that there is to a white-crowned sparrow song. The general contours are constrained by the species--white-crowned universals, maybe; some variation is dialectical, but part of what a white-crown is singing is his own song, his own deviations--so that other birds know not only that there is a white-crowned over there, but that it is the same white-crowned who was there yesterday. Each song is to some extent shaped by the particularity of the living being and the environment.

Language, too, can be seen as a hierarchy of constraints, from the species-wide constraints on all humans (and perhaps birds and whales, too), to the particular constraints that make me sound like me--and work out of my memory, shape as I shape, relate to others as I do, and live in my world with some kind of coherence. One can study this continuum at any level, but language is not reducible to just one level. Certain phenomena--like esthetic understanding--appear only at the level of the particular. If we are interested in language in full context--real language--we must take care not to exclude the individual voice, which is the only place where self-correction, i.e. change, happens--where the living organism interacts with the environment.

2. **Dewey's vernacular esthetics.** In order to see what we miss if we exclude esthetic values in studying a language, we must first confront that difficult term, esthetics. As a term it is laden with problems--mainly from an exuberance of prior context.[3] One way to cut through all that context is to follow John Dewey and vernacularize the term: bring it back to everyday experience.[4]

> The sights that hold the crowd--the fire engine rushing by...the men perched high in the air on girders, throwing and catching red-hot bolts. The sources of art in human experience will be learned by him who sees how the tense grace of the ball player infects the onlooking crowd (Dewey 1934:5).

In all these experiences, one does not remain a cold spectator, but--in Ricoeur's terms (1981:182)--we are 'appropriated' by an event, integrated with it. In a famous passage, Dewey (1934:16) says that experience

comes from nature and man interacting with each other.
In this interaction, human energy gathers, is released,
dammed up, frustrated and victorious. There are
rhythmic beats of want and fulfillment, pulses of doing
and being withheld from doing.

As he says repeatedly, a live being recurrently loses and re-
establishes equilibrium with his surroundings. Imagine walking in the woods, and suddenly realizing you are lost. Emotion, says, Dewey, is the conscious sign of a break--actual
or impending--in the equilibrium of a person with his or her
surroundings. But the break--realizing you are lost--'induces
reflection' as well as emotion. One forms an idea of where one
is, and as the idea is acted upon, one may come gradually to
feel it is correct, and a new integration with the world seems
more and more possible, and emotion more and more intense.
As Dewey (1934:17), writes, 'the moment of passage from
disturbance into harmony is that of intensest life'. At that
moment an idea--a plan to find one's way in the forest--becomes
incorporated in the world. This is a successful experience, for
Dewey 'art in germ'.
   'The thinker', writes Dewey (1934:16), 'has his esthetic
moment when his ideas cease to be mere ideas and become cor-
porate meanings of objects'.
   There is a difference--no matter how difficult it may be to
place it--between being lost in the woods and seeing a new
play. The difference does not lie so much in the experiences
themselves as in the cultural frames in which we think about
them, as ethnologists and conceptual artists have taught us.
It is a game in forest service training to be left in the woods,
with a compass and a map, and no food. The task is called
orienteering. Here the artifice--the make-believe (Walton 1978)--
is only in the circumstances leading up to being lost and the
human safety net they insure. One is intentionally lost, like
a philologist with a new text.
   Successful interaction with the environment--nowadays we
would say context--is mediated for humans (and cetaceans?
and birds?) by language. And because there is language con-
stantly between us and the world (except, I am told, after long
meditation) we lose our animal grace, our unself-consciousness.
Language gives rise to lying, deceit, and self-deception (Bateson 1972:128). Or, at least, it adds a whole new dimension to
these sins. Make-believe--for good or bad, or both at once--
becomes possible. In a language-encrusted world, the situation
at hand is hard to get at.
   The problem is not only that there is language, but that it is
so complex. Using language involves doing several things at
once, any one of which can go wrong. That is, in using language I am making sounds (or inscribing them), shaping structures, interacting with people, remembering and evoking prior
text, and referring to the world--all at once. [5]

Successful interaction with one's context involves harmonizing
constraints from all those sources:

Successfully making sounds (or inscribing them)
Successfully building structures
Successfully evoking prior text (or scripts)
Successfully interacting with other people
Successfully referring to a world

Of course, one may be unsuccessful in any of these ways,
too, and language can get pathological, because of, say,

A speech impediment
Structural confusion
Unshared prior text
Interpersonal animosity
Lying about the world

These are potential varieties of unsuccessful language experience, ways by which a person can lose integration with context. Successful language experiences imply the successful
integration of all these acts involved in uttering. It is at best
an unstable integration. Sometimes and with some people we
are fluent, sometimes utterly clumsy and inarticulate.
An esthetic experience, then, in this Deweyan sense, is one
which begins in disequilibrium (or call it noise or incoherence)
and moves toward equilibrium (or harmony or coherence). In
art, a special kind of esthetic experience, the disequilibrium--
the *ostranenie* (defamiliarization)--is intentional, and there is
make-believe in one of the dimensions of meaning.
In another language--distant or close--one has to learn (by
self-correction) new ways of interacting in all five dimensions:

New ways of sounding--(and new ways to make your face
   look as you sound)
New ways of shaping words, phrases, sentences, discourse
New ways of interacting--new speech acts
New traditions of prior texts (new scripts)
New perceived, natural worlds

3. Biography of a sentence. To illustrate these things, I
would like to think about a sentence I have liked for a long
time. Dewey (1934:28) quotes it as an example of the intense
emotion of the integration of a live being and its context. It
is by Emerson, from his long essay, *Nature* (in which he
examines all the different ways a person can relate to nature):

Crossing a bare common in snow puddles at twilight
under a clouded sky, without having in my thought
any occurrence of special good fortune, I have enjoyed
a perfect exhilaration. (1934:28)

The first thing to do when studying a sentence like that is to memorize it, just as a pianist studying someone else's music begins by memorizing it, and then comes slowly to understand it. One experiences the sentence by slow self-correction of the exuberance and deficiency with which one begins. (One such exuberance in reading Emerson--an exuberance which makes his writing difficult, even painful, to many of my friends--is the speed at which you read him. He must be read slowly, and sounded. He wrote slowly, with a quill pen, for the lecture hall. In order to be appropriated by the work, one must read slowly.)

As you repeat the sentence, bleached, backgrounded things come to the foreground. For instance, it takes a while to hear the sentence, and when one does hear it, to see pattern in the sounding. There are sound metaphors, vocal gestures that enact part of the meaning. I think that what will stand out, in repeating the Emerson sentence, is the k--s sequence, the lingual motion from the back to the front of the mouth. It is there, at the beginning and ending and repeated in the key words:

Crossing...common...snow...clouded sky...occurrence of special...exhilaration.

There appears a kind of dimly perceived, submorphemic mean-ing in articulation itself, including the way one's face looks when making the sounds. In order to see and feel the ges-tural metaphor of k--s (i.e. motion outward) more clearly, reverse it and sound a list of s--k works (i.e. motion inward.)[6]

The correspondence of the sound metaphor and the other meanings of the sentence create what Peirce called iconicity: motion outward and feeling integrated with the world outside. Someone is sure to ask, could Emerson have known all this? The answer, I think, is yes. He did not know it as we have known it just now, but surely the sounds of key words echo through a sentence in the process of composing it, and they are a source of coherence in that sentence, and sometimes something more, a sound metaphor, there in the words. (In this way, words seem more culturally determined and a priori than sentences, which are more shapable to context; that is, the sequence k--s was there in *crossing* before Emerson wrote, but probably not the sequence from *crossing* to *exhilaration.*) We might now define an iconicity as an 'integration' across two or more of the multiple acts of using language. In this case it was an integration between sounding and referring.

There is another powerful integration, in this second case, across syntactic shaping and referring. We would all probably divide the sentence into two parts, between *fortune* and *I*. Something rather strange happens at that point in the sentence-- as a Javanese linguist put it, it is like a shift in the flow of electricity. Up to *I* the phrases one by one seem to relate backward (i.e. leftward) to the verb, *crossing.* They context-ualize *crossing:* i.e. crossing what? (a bare common), what kind of common? (*in snow puddles*), when? (*at twilight under a clouded sky*) how? (*without having in my thought any occur-rence of special good fortune*). The subject of *crossing* is not given, which creates the dependency of this participial phrase on the second part of the sentence. Its nonfiniteness creates a further dependency. But with the finite main clause (*I have enjoyed a perfect exhilaration*), all those backward-looking phrases reverse polarity, and all become context for the experience of enjoying perfect exhilaration.

This reversal of polarity gives each of the phrases something new to relate to. We might play with the sentence in order to see this more clearly. First, I number the parts:

1. Crossing a bare common,
2. in snow puddles,
3. at twilight,
4. under a clouded sky,
5. without having in my thought any occurrence of special good fortune,
6. I have enjoyed a perfect exhilaration.

Try any combination of numbers--say 162534. For my taste, every combination seems possible. However, the change of polarity is lost if 1 is not first and 6 last.

A parsing problem arises over whether we treat 2-5 as modi-fiers of 1, each more distant, and the whole 1-5 as a modifier of 6 (I saw it that way at first) or, on the other hand, con-sider that the structure is tight up to the *I* and then the modification shifts and the phrases relate separately to 6, as the separate conditions of *exhilaration.* My feeling is that the sentence is dynamic, and that its structure changes. That change of polarity is what gives it rhetorical power, what Gertrude Stein (1931) called its 'emotion'--the grammatical ground on which exhilaration means.

These are but two ways that the sentence performs what it says. Crudely put, the sounding enacts 'motion outward' and the syntactic shaping says something like, 'reorient things'. These are two instances of particular iconicity. [7]

I am unclear what prior text Emerson's sentence evokes--perhaps a sermon--but the language act he performs is clear. Burke (1966:5) has called it pontification:

pontificate; that is, to 'make a bridge'. Viewed as sheerly terministic, or symbolic, function, that's what transcendence is: the building of a terministic bridge whereby one realm is transcended by being viewed in terms of a realm 'beyond' it.

Having got about that far in thinking about the sentence and using it a while (and wondering about things like the odd deviation of *in snow puddles*--was that use of *in* a norm for Emerson?), I got a notion to try to translate that sentence into Kawi, an ancient written literary language of Java, still alive in Bali. In the process I learned a great deal more about how the sentence is integrated to a context. There are many things which won't translate. The k--s sequence wouldn't work. The change of syntactic polarity was not possible either. In fact, as a rhetorical figure (a language game, a coherence system) this sentence was not possible. Since I had thought some of the meanings of the sentence might appeal to them, I sent a copy of it, in English, to several Kawi scholars in Indonesia. Then, while I was there for ten weeks, working on something else, I talked with each of them about how to translate it into Kawi. The oddest thing about the experience was that none of my friends thought it was at all odd to translate from Old American to Old Javanese. [8]

By the kind of double coincidence one learns to expect in Java and Bali, two of my friends were working on dictionaries going from modern Indonesian to Old Javanese (Kawi). It would be like a dictionary from Modern American English to Anglo-Saxon. Everyone had told these lexicographers that such a dictionary was useless. But no. For my task it was useful. Word by word we went from English to Bahasa Indonesia to Kawi. The result was a bizarre English sentence with Kawi words. And, of course, the untranslatable words were little words, like *I, have, a, of*--the little words that supply cohesion within a sentence. Each requires pages of interpretation --for example, a whole set of choices about 'I' which is not relevant to us in English.

In Java, another of my friends began the translation by imagining he was a shadow puppeteer, and he asked, where in a shadow play might that statement (Emerson's) appear, and who could say it? Until that was decided there was no basis for grammatical choices. 'Who is speaking?' I was asked, 'Is it the puppeteer himself? Impossible, the play is not ever about him. Is it the audience? Impossible, no reason to utter that sentence. If it is in the play, who? to whom? Only a wise god, like Siva or Krishna, talking to other gods, could be so personal. The pronoun must be *nghulun* (see Becker and Oka 1974). At that point, lexical and grammatical choices were constrained. Already, in the single term 'I' there is a Javanese exuberance, an unavoidable excess of meaning.

Notice here that there are two modes of translation, lexical and pragmatic (or rhetorical). Another friend approached the task a third way. He searched old texts for a similar figure; he found parts of it but no figure like the Emerson sentence. However, by trial and error we all came to a consensus translation.

Lumampah ta nghulun i harahara asepi
walk (topic) I at field empty/lonely

Ikang sangku ringkā liniputing hima
that pool there covered snow

ri wayah ning sandyākāla
at time of evening

kasongan ikang ākāsa sök denikang nilajalada
under the sky full of-the blue clouds

tanpangen ta nghulun ri wṛtta ning waralabha
not-recall (topic) I at event of good fortune

paripūrna suka ta manah ni nghulun
perfect liking (topic) heart of I

There is a great deal more exuberance to the Old Javanese
sentence and, at the same time, great deficiencies; for example, there is no equivalent of the English 'have' strategies in
Kawi. But, when I asked my friends if the Kawi version of
Emerson were a good sentence, if it were beautiful in Kawi,
they all said no. How could such a strange sentence be
beautiful? It is unique. There is no Javanese context for it
to be a part of, no family for it to have resemblance to.
   To make a point, I have been going backwards--translating
out of English instead of into it--defamiliarizing Emerson to
show how far the Kawi experience is from Emerson, at the
most backgrounded or unself-conscious of levels. If 'art and
the equipment to grasp it are made in the same shop' (Geertz
1976:1497), then how can esthetic values--the successful integration of person and context--be understood across cultures
and languages? We are back to the original question, how does
one describe a language in order not to exclude those esthetic
values?

4. **Description as self-correction.** The experience of the
Kawi figure, in all its multiple modes of meaning, is different
from the Emerson sentence. We usually experience it the other
way around, when literature, music, mythology, or grammar or
any other cultural artifact is brought into English and appears
too exotic in some ways, too bland in others; but we interact
with it and get meaning, seldom bothering to look too closely
at the sources of that meaning. But mostly those distant texts
seem like the distant god that the Javanese first personal pronoun evoked: far from the vernacular, particular world we
know. My point is not just the impossibility of translation--
which we all know and immediately forget about, but rather its
incompleteness as a source of understanding another language,
as a particular means by which an individual interacts with his

environment--as a possible form of life. It seems to me an interesting task for a linguist to try, in description, to go beyond translation. That is, I think we can use translation as a starting point and--by cutting back exuberancies and filling in deficiencies in all dimensions of meaning--move back toward the original. And as the original emerges, like a slowly developing photograph--there is an esthetic experience very special to the philologist--a newly achieved integration within a new world.

But there is an immediate protest. This task is utopian. How can we ever exhaust the manifold exuberancies and deficiencies of even a single sentence, to say nothing of a whole literary work? The answer, it seems to me, is that constraints on description are rhetorical and not logical, or as Grimes put it (1975:257-258), 'the speaker quits elaborating what he has to say at the point where he has reason to believe that the hearer knows what he is talking about'.

Imagine a grammar which begins with a detailed description of a single rich utterance (i.e. a lebensform, an episteme, a language game, a coherence system)--minimally a sentence, since that is the smallest lingual unit for which all the modes of meaning are staged (see Ricoeur 1981a). We might think of it as a biography of a sentence, a particular sentence. What the reader might see from that is how to make important corrections of exuberancy and deficiency in approaching that language. Translation is the beginning point, necessarily, and the end point is when the particularity of the sentence slowly emerges, enough so that it evokes an authentic environment, a context. Dewey (1934:15-16) put it, somewhat cryptically, this way:

> The thinker has his esthetic moment when his ideas cease to be mere ideas and become the corporate meanings of objects.

That means, I think, when a 'plan' to find one's way out of the woods becomes a successful 'way' to get out of woods, or when an interpretation of a distant text makes it appear a successful means of being in the world. [9]

I am not attempting to replace those in linguistics who seek formal representations of a speaker's abstract lingual competence, but rather to suggest that not all we need to know about languages can be seen that way, and that our methodology in seeking generalization has its own exuberancy and deficiency and needs the self-correction of understanding in a new mode of particularity, new language games, new ways of being in the world, successfully. In fact, I am merely elaborating on Wittgenstein's (1958:81) somewhat puzzling statement: 'To understand a sentence means to understand a language'. To understand a sentence is to hear it or see it in a situation where all of its relations to context--all of its meanings--are

active and somehow interacting. At the heart of esthetics is
that complex interaction. Bateson and others have explored
its disharmonies--those pathological effects of contradictory
messages in different 'channels' of meaning. (For example,
saying 'I love you' but conveying a metamessage of annoyance,
even hatred.) Is the opposite of contradictory messages--the
harmony or coherence of meanings our understanding seeks--
just a lack of contradiction, or something more: a kind of
moiré effect across systems, like the exhilaration Emerson
experienced?

5. **Summary.** Several friends have suggested that a summary of the argument in this essay would be helpful, although
the assumption that an essay (unlike an article) is coherent
around an argument need not always hold, since an essay is
predominantly a genre of description and exploration of describing and exploring a particularity rather than supporting a
generality. Yet one might shape a general argument here, as
follows.

(1) Esthetics, in a Deweyan sense, is about emergent attunement of a live being with its context.

(2) Particular language--as a mode of being in the world (à
la Wittgenstein or Heidegger)--is attuned to context in at least
five different ways, depending on the mode of context:
medium, interpersonal use, lingual structure, evoked prior
text, and the extralingual world (Nature) that the text presupposes.

(3) In any of these modes, esthetic attunement (or lack of
attunement) is possible, giving rise to different definitions of
esthetics (see note 3).

(4) Attunements across modes (i.e. homologies between
medium, use, structure, prior text, and Nature) give a text
a kind of esthetic depth which is quite particular.

(5) Esthetic depth is in most cases impossible to translate,
so that fuller understanding of a distant text requires a step
beyond translation, a deconstruction of the translation and a
reconstruction of the context of its source, mode by mode, so
as to describe and explore its particularity.

NOTES

Several people have helped me in articulating these thoughts:
D. Tannen, J. Becker, S. Tyma, D. Tyma, J. Verhaar, T.
Givon, H. Byrnes, C. Geertz, and R. Isaac; and, in Indonesia,
I Gusti Ngurah Oka, Soewojo Wojowasito, L. Mardiwarsito, H.
Bambang Kaswanti Purwo, and I Gusti Ngurah Bagus. Special
thanks are due Anneliese Kramer for helping me to see that
language description is also esthetic.

1. In several places in his work (1950, 1957, 1959), Ortega
mentions his 'principios de una Nueva Filología'. The earliest

such mention I know of is in his *Papeles sobre Velazquez y Goya* (1950):

Dos leyes de apariencia antagónica, que se complen en toda enunciación. Una suena así: <<Todo decir es deficiente>> --esto es, nunca logramos decir plenamente lo que nos proponemos decir. La otra ley, de aspecto inverso, declara: <<Todo decir es exuberantes>> esto es, que nuestro decir manifesta siempre muchas más casas de las que nos proponemos e incluso no pocas que queremos silenciar.

Later, in *Man and People* (1957:242) he writes:

...precisely the splendid intellectual achievement repre-sented by linguistics as it is constituted today obliges it (noblesse oblige) to attain a second and more precise and forceful approximation in its knowledge of the reality, 'language'. And this it can do only if it studies language not as an accomplished fact, as a thing made and finished, but as in the process of being made, hence *in statu nas-cendi*, in the very roots that engender it.

Here and elsewhere, Ortega projects a comparative phenomeno-logy of language which he calls 'una Nueva Filología'. As far as I know, he did not go beyond the two axioms quoted here before he died in 1955.
    2.   Charles Pyle once remarked on how interesting a meta-language for sounds one finds in birdbooks. Why is the whistle 'plaintive', then 'husky'? Here is a purely metaphoric metalanguage, in which birds are quite usefully humanized.
    3.   One can describe the history of esthetics as a shifting emphasis on one or more of the various ways in which a sym-bolic system relates to a context. For instance, emphasis on part-whole relations in a hierarchy (structure) leads to an esthetics of proportion--the relation of parts to each other (e.g. the *congruentia partium* of Augustine or the elegance of mathematicians and formalists). Emphasis on interpersonal relations leads to an esthetics of emotion or powerful feeling: pity, fear, eros, the sublime, or the *rasas* of Indic esthetics. Emphasis on prior text leads to an esthetics or recognition or the reenactment of Jungian archetypes, or perhaps the working out of a genre, e.g. the novel or the sonata allegro form. Emphasis on the medium leads to an esthetics of sound itself (in language or music), or 'the line', or the human voice. (For a study of the Chinese philosophy of sound, see DeWoskin 1982.) Emphasis on the world leads to an esthetics of imitation or mimesis--the imitation or representation of 'reality' (from Aristotle to Marx). One can see the shifting emphases on these different perspectives, and their combination, in a work like Beardsley (1966) (see also Philipson 1961). The advantage

of an approach like Dewey's (1934) is that it encourages a
multiple view in which all these sources of esthetic experience
are possible.

4. I am using the term 'vernacular' in the sense recently
developed by Illich (1980:41):

> *Vernacular* comes from an Indo-Germanic root that implies
> 'rootedness' and 'abode'. *Vernaculum* as a Latin word was
> used for whatever was homebred, homespun, homegrown,
> homemade, as opposed to what was obtained in formal ex-
> change...*Vernacular* was used in this general sense from
> preclassical times down to the technical formulations found
> in the *Codex of Theodosius*. It was Varro who picked the
> term to introduce the same distinction in language. For
> him, *vernacular speech* is made up of the words and pat-
> terns grown on the speaker's own ground, as opposed to
> what is grown elsewhere and then transported. And
> since Varro's authority was widely recognized, his defini-
> tion stuck. He was the librarian of both Caesar and
> Augustus and the first Roman to attempt a thorough and
> critical study of the Latin language.

In his very enlightening article (now, I am told, a book)
Illich describes the first attempt in Europe to grammaticize
the vernacular as a mode of political control, with the
Gramática Castellana of Elio Antonio de Nebrija, in 1492.

5. For the general notion of language as interlocking
actions, I am indebted to Pike (although he formulates it somewhat differently, as in Pike 1978). If one defines meaning as
relation to context, then these acts can be considered five
epistemologically different contexts in which a text has meaning. Coherence then is possible between a text and one source
of meaning (e.g. a sentence and its structural context--the
larger discourse of which it is a part), or between one kind of
context and another (e.g. between structural and interpersonal
context, or between prior text and present reference, etc.).
These latter coherences are what Peirce termed 'iconicities'.
For an earlier version of this approach, see Becker (1979).
Cf. Ricoeur (1981) for a different formulation of context.

6. The notion of 'sound metaphor', along with the term, is
taken from Fonagy (1971), which includes a bibliography of
earlier work.

7. One of the more intriguing questions which occurs to
one studying iconicities (or coherence across two or more dimensions of meaning) is whether there may not be some resultant
phenomenon (or epiphenomenon) like the moiré effect, a kind
of Peircean 'third'.

8. It must be pointed out, however, that in Java, and
particularly Bali, Kawi or Old Javanese is still alive. Kawi is
reshaped in the Shadow Theatre. Almost everyone has heard
it sounded and understands a bit. Consequently, it is not so

much a prior stage of language as a specialized current register. Furthermore, each of my informants knows at least five
languages, and is quite accustomed to regular code-switching.
   9. The connection between esthetic experience and morality
for Dewey is that both involve, in a rather Buddhist way,
harmony with the situation at hand. Dewey writes (1972:94):

> What, then, is moral theory? It is all one with moral
> *insight*, and moral insight is the recognition of the
> relationships at hand. This is a very tame and prosaic
> conception.

For the development of Dewey's conception as the basis for a
critique of the social sciences (which is quite applicable to current linguistics), see Rorty (1981). One might substitute
linguistics for social sciences in the following passage:

> What we hope from the social sciences is that they will
> act as interpreters for those with whom we have difficulty
> in talking. (Rorty 1981)

See also Rorty (1978) for a detailed argument against the
rationalist foundations of much current linguistics.

REFERENCES

Bateson, Gregory. 1972. Style, grace, and information in
   primitive art. In: Steps to an ecology of mind. New York:
   Ballantine.
Beardsley, Monroe C. 1966. Aesthetics from Classical Greece
   to the present. New York: Macmillan.
Becker, A. L. 1979. Text-building, epistemology, and
   aesthetics in Javanese shadow theatre. In: The imagination
   of reality: Essays in Southeast Asian coherence systems.
   Edited by A. L. Becker and Aram A. Yengoyan. Norwood,
   N.J.: Ablex.
Becker, A. L., and I Gusti Ngurah Oka. 1974. Person in
   Kawi: Exploration of an elementary semantic dimension.
   Oceanic Linguistics XIII.229-255.
Burke, Kenneth. 1966. I, eye, aye--Emerson's early essay
   'Nature': Thoughts on the machinery of transcendence. In:
   Transcendentalism and its legacy. Edited by Myron Simon
   and Thornton H. Parsons. Ann Arbor: University of
   Michigan Press.
Dewey, John. 1934. Art as experience. New York: Minton
   Balch.
Dewey, John. 1972. Moral theory and practice. In: Early
   works of John Dewey. Vol. 3. Carbondale: Southern
   Illinois University Press.
DeWoskin, Kenneth. 1982. A song for one or two: Music
   and the concept of art in early China. Ann Arbor, Mich.:
   Center for Chinese Studies.

Fonagy, Ivan. 1971. Double coding in speech. Semiotica III.189-222.

Geertz, Clifford. 1976. Art as a cultural system. MLN 91. 1473-1499.

Grimes, Joseph. 1975. The thread of discourse. The Hague: Mouton.

Illich, Ivan. 1980. Vernacular values. The Co-Evolution Quarterly Summer.22-49.

Ortega y Gasset, José. 1950. Papeles sobre Velázquez y Goya. Madrid: Revista de Occidente.

Ortega y Gasset, José. 1959. The difficulty of reading. Diogenes 28.1-17.

Peterson, Roger Tory. 1961. A field guide to the birds. Boston: Houghton Mifflin.

Philipson, Morris, ed. 1961. Aesthetics today. New York: Meridan.

Pike, Kenneth L. 1978. Here we stand--creative observers of language. In: Approches du langage: Actes du colloque interdisciplinaire tenu à Paris. Sorbonne, Serie 'Etudes' 16.9-45.

Ricoeur, Paul. 1981. The model of the text: Meaningful action considered as a text. In: Hermeneutics and the human sciences. Edited by John B. Thompson. New York: Cambridge University Press.

Rorty, Richard. 1978. Philosophy and the mirror of nature. Princeton: Princeton University Press.

Rorty, Richard. 1981. Method and morality. In: Values and the social sciences. Edited by N. Hahn, R. Bellah, and P. Rabinow.

Scollon, Ron. 1981. The rhythmic integration of ordinary talk. In: Georgetown University Round Table on Languages and Linguistics 1981. Edited by Deborah Tannen. Washington, D.C.: Georgetown University Press. 335-349.

Stein, Gertrude. 1975 [1931]. How to write. New York: Dover.

Walton, Kendall. 1978. Fearing fictions. Journal of Philosophy LXXV.5-27.

Wittgenstein, Ludwig. 1968. Philosophical investigations. Trans. by G. E. N. Anscombe. New York: Macmillan.

CONVENTIONS OF REPRESENTATION: WHERE DISCOURSE AND IDEOLOGY MEET

Mary Louise Pratt
Stanford University

Consider the following passage, the opening paragraphs of Defoe's *Robinson Crusoe*, first published in 1719:

I was born in the year 1632, in the city of York, of a good family, tho' not of that country, my father being a foreigner of Bremen, who settled first at Hull. He got a good estate by merchandise, and leaving off his trade lived afterward at York, from whence he married my mother, whose relations were named Robinson, a very good name in that country, and from whom I was called Robinson Kreutznaer; but by the usual corruption of words in England, we are now called, nay, we call ourselves and write our name, Crusoe, and so my companions always called me.

I had two elder brothers, one of them was lieutenant collonel to an English regiment of foot in Flanders, formerly commanded by the famous Coll. Lockhart, and was killed at the battle near Dunkirk against the Spaniards. What became of my second brother I never knew any more than my father or mother did know what was become of me.

Being the third son of the family, and not bred to any trade, my head began to be filled very early with rambling thoughts. My father, who was very ancient, had given me a competent share of learning, as far as house-education and a country free-school generally goes, and designed me for the law; but I would be satisfied with nothing but going to sea, and my inclination to this led me so strongly against the will, nay, the commands of my father, and against all the entreaties and perswasions of my mother and other friends, that there seemed to be something fatal in that propension of nature tending directly to the life of misery that was to befal me. [1]

This text deploys a set of conventions of representation readily recognizable to any reader of eighteenth century novels or the picaresque tradition. There is the opening statement of pedigree, and even some outright arbitrariness in the acquisition of one's name. There is the early emergence of wanderlust in the redundant middle child, the abandonment of family and community against all entreaties, and the life of supposed misery and misfortune which results. Many of these same conventions are used in the following passage as well. This text is the opening of Richard Lemon Lander's book *Records of Captain Clapperton's Last Expedition to Africa*, published in 1830:

Many allusions to my earlier history occurring in the following pages, it may not, perhaps, be deemed impertinent on my part, if I should attempt to give a short and hasty sketch of my life, devoted as it has been to perpetual wanderings and chequered by a thousand misfortunes.

My family is as ancient, I dare say, as that of any upon the face of the earth, although, notwithstanding the profoundest research, I have been unable to trace its descent, with genealogical accuracy and precision, to a more remote era than the period of my grandfather's nonage; the history of all my ancestors previous to him being either mixed with fable, or involved in doubt and uncertainty...

I am the fourth of six children, and was born at Truro, in Cornwall, in 1804, on the very day on which Colonel Lemon was elected Member of Parliament for the Borough. Owing to this striking coincidence, singular as it may seem, my father, who was fond of sounding appelations, at the simple suggestion of the doctor who attended the family, added Lemon to my baptismal name of Richard: an example of the trivial means by which people are oftentimes accommodated with an extra name. As nothing remarkable occurred for the first five or six years after I came into the world, I shall pass them over in silence, simply observing that when yet in infancy, whilst I was in the act of gazing one morning at something attached to the ceiling of my father's stable, a piece of iron, having a sharpened edge, fell and entered my forehead; which accident was of so serious a nature that I was ill for several weeks, and narrowly escaped with life.

My rambling inclinations began to display themselves in early youth. I was never easy a great while together in one place, and used to be delighted to play truant and

stroll from town to town, from village to village whenever
I could steal an opportunity...[2]

Here again we find the comic lack of pedigree, the arbitrariness of name, the reference to a life of misery resulting from
the passion-driven individualism of the wanderer. Lander
here invokes another commonplace of eighteenth century narrative, that of the childhood accident, made most memorable for
us by Tristram Shandy's excruciating encounter with a window
sash. The childhood accident is a comic device whose function
is, among other things, to overexplain or overdetermine the
eccentricities and immoderacies of the protagonist's character
in adulthood.

The point I want to examine in these texts is the very
obvious one that they use many of the same conventions of
representation--one might even say they are instances of the
same discourse--though one is from a fictional novel and the
other from a nonfictional travel account. Now we might want
to account for these similarities by saying that Richard Lander
is 'novelizing' his travel acount, that he is borrowing or imitating, or redeploying the novelistic discourse exemplified by
the *Robinson Crusoe* passage. At the same time, however, we
would probably also want to say that Defoe is borrowing or
imitating or redeploying in his novel the discourse of nonfictional autobiography. We are left with what looks like a
chicken and egg problem. Are the conventions of representation which these texts share primarily novelistic or primarily
autobiographical? Are they primarily associated with fiction
or with nonfiction? The answer I'd like to consider is that
they are not primarily one or the other. They exist as conventions of representation relatively independently of both
genre distinctions and the fiction-nonfiction distinction. They
can--and indeed should--be studied across those categories.

The next four passages quoted here exemplify another case
of the kind of convention of representation I am talking about,
and again the examples come from novels as well as nonfictional
travel accounts. These four passages are all versions of what
I have called the 'woe-is-me' scene. Here, after a peak experience, whether of triumph or defeat, the speaker-protagonist
pauses in solitude to assess his or her situation. There follows
an enumeration of misfortunes and woes, then a plunge into the
pits of despair, from which the protagonist is rescued by some
new hopeful thought, often religious in character. This self-
generated consolation mobilizes the protagonist again physically,
and the narrative action proceeds. Again, I think most novel
readers will find this device a familiar one. The four examples
here include: (1) Sir James Bruce the night after discovering
what he believed to be the source of the Nile (1770); (2)
Robinson Crusoe after completing his first house (1719); (3)
Mungo Park in Africa having been robbed of all his possessions
by Moorish bandits (1802); and (4) Samuel Richardson's

Pamela having failed in a nocturnal attempt to escape from a country house where she is being held (1740). There is no need to work through these examples individually here--the conventions are clear. Some of the common surface linguistic features of the woe-is-me scene are indicated in these quotations, notably the introductory time phrase that suspends the narrative sequence, the enumeration of troubles and woes, and the *but*-clause that introduces the ray of hope:

> *The night of the 4th*, that very night of my arrival, melancholy reflections upon my present state, the doubtfulness of my return in safety, were I permitted to make the attempt, and the fears that even this would be refused, acording to the rule observed in Abyssinia with all travellers who have once entered the kingdom; the consciousness of the pain that I was then occasioning to many worthy individuals, expecting daily that information concerning my situation which it was not in my power to give them; some other thoughts, perhaps, still nearer to the heart than those, crowded upon my mind, and forbad all approach of sleep...
>
> I went to the door of my tent; everything was still; the Nile at whose head I stood, was not capable either to promote or to interrupt my slumbers, *but* the coolness and serenity of the night braced my nerves, and chased away those phantoms that, while in bed, had oppressed and tormented me.
>
> It was true, that numerous dangers, hardships, and sorrows, had beset me through this half of my excursion; *but* it was still as true that *another Guide*, more powerful than my own courage, health or understanding, if any of these can be called man's own, had uniformly protected me in all that tedious half; I found my confidence not abated, that still the same Guide was able to conduct me to my now wished for home...[3]

> *Having now fixed my habitation*, I found it absolutely necessary to provide a place to make a fire in, and fewel to burn; and what I did for that, as also how I enlarged my cave, and what conveniences I made, I shall give a full account of it in its place. But I must first give some little account of my self, and of my thoughts about living, which it may well be supposed were not a few.
>
> I had a dismal prospect of my condition, for as I was not cast away upon that island without being driven, as is said, by a violent storm, quite out of the course of our intended voyage, and a great way, viz. some hundreds of leagues out of the ordinary course of the trade of mankind, I had great reason to consider it as a determination of Heaven, that in this desolate place and in this desolate manner I should end my life; the tears would run plentifully down my face when I made these reflections, and sometimes

I would expostulate with my self, why Providence should
thus compleately ruine its creatures, and render them so
absolutely miserable, without help abandoned, so entirely
depressed, that it could hardly be rational to be thankful
for such a life.

But something always returned swift upon me to check
these thoughts, and to reprove me...[4]

After they were gone I sat for some time looking around
me with amazement and terror. Whichever way I turned,
nothing appeared but danger and difficulty. I saw myself
in the midst of a vast wilderness, in the depths of the
rainy season, naked and alone; surrounded by savage
animals, and men still more savage. I was five hundred
miles from the nearest European settlement. All these circumstances crowded at once on my recollection, and I con-
fess that my spirits began to fail me...*The influence of
religion, however,* aided and supported me. I reflected
that no human prudence or foresight could possibly have
averted my present sufferings. I was indeed a stranger
in a strange land, *yet* I was still under the protecting eye
of that Providence who has condescended to call himself
the stranger's friend.[5]

...and so when I came to the pond side, I sat myself down
on the sloping bank, and began to ponder my wretched
condition; and thus I reasoned with myself.

Pause here a little, Pamela, on what thou art about,
before thou takest the dreadful leap; and consider whether
there be no way yet left, no hope, if not to escape from
this wicked house, yet from the mischiefs threatened thee
in it.

I then considered; and after I had cast about in my mind
everything that could make me hope, and saw no probability;
a wicked woman, devoid of all compassion! A horrid helper,
just arrived in this dreadful Colbrans! An angry and re-
senting master, who now hated me, and threatened the most
afflicting evils!...

I was once rising, so indulgent was I to this sad way
of thinking, to throw myself in: *but* again, my bruises
made me slow; and I thought, What art thou about to do,
wretched Pamela? How knowest thou, though the prospect
be all dark to thy short-sighted eye, *what God may do for
thee,* even when all human means fail?[6]

Again, the claim I would make is that we should resist the im-
pulse to view the woe-is-me scene as primarily associated with
the novel or with fiction, and see it rather as unmarked with
respect to fictionality or genre.

Within poetics, formal narrative analysis has for a long time
been making generalizations at the level I am talking about.

That is, it has long been agreed that 'narrative' and 'story'
as formal constructs are not specific to literature nor to fiction, but are highly generalized discourse structures that
operate even outside verbal representation. This same highly
generalized perspective can be extended beyond rudimentary
narrative sequencing to other aspects of discourse structure
and content. Such an undertaking, however, requires going
beyond the tendency in at least some sectors of linguistics, to
treat representative or assertive discourse primarily in terms
of the presence or absence of truth claims. This has been a
limitation, for instance, in speech act theory, where the analysis of representative speech acts scarcely gets beyond simply
defining nonfictional representatives by the presence of a truth
claim, and defining fictional negatively by the suspension of
such claims. Clearly, there is a great deal more to say about
the ways people represent the world to themselves linguistically.
Poetics has as a rule had more to say about fictional utterances,
but its treatment of nonfictional linguistic representations has
been impoverished. There seems to be a tendency in poetics
to assume that conventions found to be operating in literature
must by definition be literary conventions, that is, conventions
primarily associated with literature and constitutive of 'literari-
ness'. This judgment usually means in turn that such conventions are taken to be primarily associated with fictionality, and
are studied primarily from an esthetic viewpoint. Their historical, social, and ideological dimensions are not explored,
though these dimensions are as germane to the study of discourse as esthetics. Indeed, an understanding of the social,
historical, and ideological dimensions of discourse can contribute
a great deal to the interests of esthetics. There is much to be
gained, then, from an analysis of linguistic representation which
decenters the questions of truth versus falsehood, fiction versus nonfiction, literary genre versus nonliterary genre, and
focuses instead on generalized strategies of representation.
At Stanford my colleague Rina Benmayor and I have been
examining such strategies in novels and nonfictional travel
accounts, such as those I have been citing here. These two
genres provide extremely fruitful terrain in which to examine
shared conventions of representation. From at least the six-
teenth century on, the two have completely interpenetrated and
mutually determined each other. This is a fact that gets
obscured by a literary theory centered on fiction and committed
to a radical distinction between fictional and nonfictional
representation.
   Using some further examples from these two genres, I propose
in the rest of this paper to exemplify a kind of stylistic analysis
that (a) works across the fiction-nonfiction line and (b) deals
simultaneously with esthetic, social, and ideological dimensions
of discourse. The case I have chosen to focus on is landscape
description in the context of colonial and neocolonial relationships. What I want to illustrate is how landscape descriptions,

in some cases, embody esthetically and ideologically a kind of 'discourse of empire', while in others the representation is designed to undermine or replace such a discourse. Landscape description has, of course, long been recognized as an exceedingly fruitful case for studying the interaction of esthetics and ideology. This interaction is particularly conspicuous in the context I am dealing with here.

I begin with a convention that I like to call the 'monarch-of-all-I-survey' scene, in which a speaker-protagonist stands up on a high place of some kind and describes the panorama below, producing a simultaneously verbal and visual 'picture in words'. This device is a commonplace of European romanticism in particular, and is found widely in nineteenth century poetry and narrative alike. In travel accounts, the monarch-of-all-I-survey scene is typically used by Victorian explorers to render moments of discovery of geographically important phenomena such as lakes, river sources, islands, and so on. Here, for example, is Sir Richard Burton's rendering in 1860 of his discovery of Lake Tanganyika in Central Africa (emphasis mine):

Nothing, in sooth, could be more picturesque than this first view of the Tanganyika Lake, as it lay in the lap of the mountains, basking in the gorgeous tropical sunshine. Below and beyond a short foreground of rugged and precipitous hillfold, down which the foot-path zigzags painfully, a narrow strip of *emerald green*, never sere and marvellously fertile, shelves towards a ribbon of glistening yellow sand, here bordered by sedgy rushes, there cleanly and clearly cut by the breaking wavelets. Further in front stretch the waters, an expanse of the lightest and softest blue, in breadth varying from thirty to thirty-five miles, and sprinkled by the crisp east-wind with tiny crescents of *snowy foam*. The background in front is a high and broken wall of *steel-coloured* mountain, here flecked and capped with *pearly mist*, there standing pencilled against the azure air; its yawning chasms, marked by a deeper *plum-colour*, fall towards dwarf hills of mound-like proportions, which apparently dip their feet in the wave. To the south, and opposite the long, low point, behind which the Malagarazi River discharges the red loam suspended in its violent stream, lie the bluff headlands and capes of Uguhha, and, as the eye dilates, it falls upon a cluster of outlying islets, speckling a sea-horizon. Villages, cultivated lands, the frequent canoes of the fishermen on the waters, and on a nearer approach the murmurs of the waves breaking upon the shore, give a something of variety, of movement, of life to the landscape, which, like all the fairest prospects in these regions, wants but a little of the neatness and finish of Art,--mosques and kiosks, palaces and villas, gardens and orchards--contrasting with the profuse lavishness and magnificence of nature, and diversifying the unbroken coup d'oeil of excessive vegetation to rival if not to excel, the

most admired scenery of the classic regions....Truly it was
a revel for soul and sight! Forgetting toils, dangers, and
the doubtfulness of return, I felt willing to endure double
what I had endured; and all the party seemed to join with
me in joy.[7]

A stylistic analysis of this passage requires, among other
things, identifying the convention of representation being invoked, specifying which aspects of the discourse are determined
by it and which are not, and establishing what sort of meaning-
making task the convention is being called upon to accomplish
in the particular context in which it has been invoked. In
Burton's case, and in nineteenth century discovery narrative
in general, the monarch-of-all-I-survey scene is invoked to
render momentously meaningful the act of discovery, itself
practically a nonevent. The 'discovery' of Lake Tanganyika,
for example, involved going to the region and asking the natives
if they knew of any big lakes in the vicinity, then paying them
to take the explorers there, whereupon the explorers 'discovered'
what the natives had already told them. We are all familiar with
the contradictions that the term 'discovery' holds in this context. In Burton's situation, the contradictions are particularly
acute, since he has been so ill he has had to be carried to the
site, again by native assistants, while his companion John Speke,
though able to walk, has been blinded by fever and is therefore unable properly to discover anything. The discovery itself consists of what in our culture counts as a purely passive
experience, that of seeing something. At this point in history
there is, for example, no taking of possession for England or
for God, no sacking of cities, no bringing home of spoils. At
most, an English name might be given. In short, the explorer's
achievement can exist almost exclusively through language--a
name on a map or a tree trunk, a report to the Royal Geo-
graphic Society, a lecture, a travel book.
    In the Burton passage, one can identify at least three con-
ventional means by which Burton creates qualitative and quanti-
tative value for his achievement. First, the landscape is
estheticized. The sight is seen as a painting and the description is ordered in terms of background, foreground, symmetries
between foam-flecked water and mist-flecked hills, and so forth.
Notice that the esthetic pleasure of the sight is here declared
to constitute singlehandedly the value and significance of the
journey--he would do it twice over for the same thrill. Second,
density of meaning in the passage is sought. The landscape is
represented as extremely rich in material and semantic substance.
This density is achieved especially through the huge number of
adjectival modifiers. Scarcely a noun in the text is unmodified.
Notice too that many of the modifiers are derived from nouns
(such as *sedgy, capped, mound-like*), and thus add density by
introducing whole new material referents into the discourse. Of
particular interest in this respect are nominal color expressions:

emerald green, snowy foam, steel-coloured mountains, pearly mist, plum-colour. Unlike plain color adjectives, these terms introduce new material referents into the landscape, referents which all, from steel to snow, tie the landscape explicitly to the speaker's (and the reader's) home culture, infiltrating it with 'a little bit of England'.

Thirdly, a relation of dominance is predicated in the passage between the seer and the seen. This relation is expressed most clearly by the metaphor of the painting. If the scene is a painting, then Burton is both the viewer-critic there to appreciate it, and the verbal painter who produces it for us. The scene, in other words, is produced by and for Burton. From the painting analogy it also follows that what Burton sees is all there is, and that the landscape was intended to be seen from precisely where Burton has emerged upon it. Thus the whole scene is deictically ordered with reference to his vantage point. The viewer-painting relation also implies that Burton has the power if not to own, then at least to judge this scene. And it is quite revealing that his judgment is that what is lacking here is more Art, where Art is defined, surprisingly, as the presence of mosque and kiosks, palaces, gardens, and so forth. Art, that is, is equated with a Mediterranean concept of civilization, and the conclusion is that the villages and cultivations already present in the scene are not enough esthetically. This depiction of the 'civilizing mission' as an esthetic project is an old and familiar strategy in Western imperialism. It is a way of interpreting the Other as not only available for, but actually in need of intervention from the outside. (We will be looking shortly at some contemporary versions of this strategy.)

The point I want to stress here is that in this example, and in any other, of the monarch-of-all-I-survey scene, the conventional estheticization of the landscape simultaneously articulates a particular social meaning, an ideology. In Burton's discourse, on the one hand the esthetic impact of the landscape is made to constitute the social value of his discovery, and on the other hand a judgment of esthetic deficiency is used to articulate a relation of dominance of the (civilized) West over (barbarous) Africa. This same set of connections operates in almost reverse fashion in the following description, produced by Burton's partner and rival, John Speke. Accompanying Burton further, Speke became convinced he knew where the coveted source of the Nile was located. Upon their return to England, Speke immediately mounted a second expedition to return to Africa to prove himself right and the skeptical Burton wrong. With his new partner, Grant, Speke arrived at the lake he was looking for--the Victoria N'yanza--but was prevented by a number of circumstances from trekking all the way around it to prove absolutely his hypothesis, which ultimately did turn out to be correct. Many readers will be familiar with the deadly polemic which ensued back in England between Burton and Speke, and which resulted in Speke's apparent suicide. What is of interest

here is the way in which Speke's retrospective description of
his discovery translates his disappointment as an explorer into
esthetic disappointment at the landscape (emphasis mine):

> We were well rewarded; for the 'stones' as the Waganda call
> the falls, was by far the *most interesting sight* I had seen
> in Africa. Everybody ran to see them at once, though the
> march had been long and fatiguing, and *even* my sketchbook
> was called into play. *Though beautiful,* the scene was *not
> exactly what I had expected*; for the broad surface of the
> lake was shut out from view by a spur of hill, and the falls,
> about 12 feet deep, and 400 to 500 feet broad, were broken
> by rocks. *Still* it was a sight that attracted one to it for
> hours--the roar of the waters, the thousands of passenger-
> fish...hippopotami and crocodiles lying sleepily on the water,
> the ferry at work above the falls, and cattle driven down to
> drink at the margin of the lake--made all in all, with the
> *pretty nature* of the country--small hills, grassy-tipped, with
> trees in the folds, and gardens on the lower slopes--as
> *interesting* a picture as one could wish to see.
> The expedition had now performed its functions. I saw
> that old father Nile without any doubt rises in the Victoria
> N'yanza, and as I foretold, that lake is the great source of
> the holy river which cradled the first expounder of our
> religious belief. I mourned, however, when I thought of
> how much I had lost by the delays in the journey which had
> *deprived me of the pleasure of going to look* at the north-
> east corner. [8]

Here again we see the language of esthetics being used to
encode--and mystify--the significance of the event. Speke's
disappointment is expressed as the loss of a personal esthetic
pleasure rather than the loss of a social triumph or a piece of
geographical knowledge. Likewise, the sight/site he does get
to see is evaluated in purely esthetic terms, and found acceptable but wanting. It is surely not a coincidence that the particular esthetic defects the frustrated Speke finds are first a
barrier to the visibility of the lake, and second, an interruption
of the forward movement of the falls.
   In twentieth century travel accounts, the monarch-of-all-I-
survey scene is repeated all the time, but now from the balconies
of hotels, where again we find our cultural mediators perched,
assigning significance and value to what they see. Here are
two typical examples, the first by the Italian novelist Alberto
Moravia, writing about a trip to Africa in 1972, and the second
by the American Paul Theroux, also a novelist, writing about a
train journey through Latin America:

> From the balcony of my room I had a panoramic view over
> Accra, capital of Ghana. Beneath a sky of hazy blue, filled
> with mists and ragged yellow and grey clouds, the town

looked like a huge pan of thick, dark cabbage soup in which
numerous pieces of white pasta were on the boil. The cab-
bages were the tropical trees with rich, trailing, heavy
foliage of dark green speckled with black shadows; the
pieces of pasta the brand-new buildings of reinforced concrete, numbers of which were now rising all over the town. [9]

Guatemala City, an extremely horizontal place, is like a city
on its back. Its ugliness, which is a threatened look (the
low morose houses have earthquake cracks in their facades;
the buildings wince at you with bright lines) is ugliest on
those streets where, just past the last toppling house, a blue
volcano's cone bulges. I could see the volcanoes from the
window of my hotel room. I was on the third floor, which
was also the top floor. They were tall volcanoes and looked
capable of spewing lava. Their beauty was undeniable; but
it was the beauty of witches. The rumbles from their fires
had heaved this city down. [10]

The contrast between these grotesque and joyless cityscapes
and the gorgeous, sparkling panorama depicted by Richard Burton could hardly be greater. And yet upon inspection, it becomes clear that the three strategies operating in Burton's dis-
course--estheticization, density of meaning, and dominance of
seer over seen--are also at work here. The difference is that
they are being invoked at a different historical moment to make
a very different sort of meaning. A different, historically
later ideology is being expressed. Density of meaning was
created in Burton's discourse through the plentiful use of
adjectival modifiers, and a general proliferation of concrete,
material referents introduced either literally or as metaphors.
The Theroux and Moravia texts clearly share these properties.
In Burton, the speaker positioned himself in a relation of dominance over the landscape and the Other, particularly through
the extended metaphor of the painting. Like Burton, both
Moravia and Theroux situate themselves in the position of judge
over what they see. Despite the fact that they are on unfamiliar
terrain, like Burton, they both claim complete authority for
their vision: what they see is all there is. No sense of limitation on their knowledge or authority is suggested. And perhaps less explicitly than in Burton, relations of dominance and
possession are articulated through metaphors.
     For Theroux, Guatemala is a city on its back, in a position of
submission or defeat before him, and with a threatened look.
Moravia sees Accra as a plate of soup, that is, a dish Ghana
has prepared--pasta and all--for him to eat. Estheticization we
also have in these texts, except that where Burton found beauty,
symmetry, order, and the sublime, Theroux and Moravia find
the precise esthetic opposites: ugliness (ragged clouds, morose
houses), incongruity (the beauty of witches, bits of pasta in
the cabbage soup), disorder, and triviality. It is striking that
in both descriptions, the landscape is represented as violating

the conventions on colors so central to landscape description:
Moravia sees yellow clouds, Theroux a blue volcano. And as
with Burton's description, the esthetic vision expresses and at
the same time mystifies a social and political vision. On reading
beauty, order, and grandeur in his landscape, Burton makes it
a worthy prize for the explorer and his country. His is the
heady optimism of incipient empire. Moravia and Theroux, on
the other hand, are voicing the era of neocolonial dependency,
when historical reality, and most conspicuously the reality of
Third World cities, has long since belied the myth of the
civilizing mission. For them, the meaning to be produced, the
task to be accomplished, is a negative one of rejection, dissoci-
ation, and dismissal. It is a quite different but historically
related strategy for authenticating the self through the mediation
of the Other.

As with Burton's concept of 'discovery', this strategy too has
its contradictions. It is impossible for Westerners to dissociate
themselves fully from the manifestations of Western intervention
and exploitation, whether in the form of concrete skyscrapers
or crumbling slums. Perhaps this contradiction explains why
both writers express a fear of violence on the part of the landscapes they are describing. Theroux is threatened by the
volcanoes, which could bring down the city, including the hotel
in which he is perched. Moravia sees the Western style buildings, including the one he is standing in, as on the boil in a
pot of otherwise African soup, like the cartoon missionaries in
the cannibals' pot. The absence of such paranoia in Burton
and Speke is striking by contrast.

The Theroux and Moravia texts exemplify a discourse of
negation and devaluation which has become in the late twentieth
century the predominant strategy constituting the West's consciousness of the Other. No longer a cornucopia of resources
inviting the artful hand of development, the Other is represented
negatively as a conglomeration either of incongruities and
asymmetries or of absences and scarcities. One thing that
stays constant, however, is the relation of dominance embodied
in the monarch-of-all-I-survey convention.

Conventions can, of course, be undermined and changed.
Consider, for instance, what is done with the monarch-of-all-I-
survey convention in the following passage from an account of
another trip to Ghana, by Afro-American novelist Richard
Wright:

I wanted to push on and look more, but the sun was too
much. I spent the afternoon fretting; I was impatient to
see more of this Africa. My bungalow was clean, quiet,
mosquito-proof, but it had not been for that I'd come to
Africa. Already my mind was casting about for other
accommodations. I stood on my balcony and saw clouds of
black buzzards circling slowly in the hazy blue sky. In the
distance I caught a glimpse of the cloudy, grayish Atlantic.[11]

On the one hand, Wright produces what is a very reduced instance of the conventional scene. He gives us a 'glimpse' of a landscape which does have the negative connotations found in Moravia and Theroux. At the same time, however, Wright explicitly documents his discomfort with the vantage point of the balcony, from which, he feels, one can see almost nothing. He acknowledges, in other words, the limitations on his perception and on his position. To see, he says, one must be walking in the streets, not immobilized above the scene. At one and the same time, then, we find Wright reproducing the dominant discourse and undermining its authority.

The modern ideology of negation I have been discussing takes a somewhat different form in descriptions of rural landscape, and the contrasts are instructive. In the following two descriptions of rural landscape, again from Theroux and Moravia, what is found is not ugliness (as in the cityscapes), but scarcity of any kind of meaning, a kind of esthetic and semantic underdevelopment which both writers connect with the prehistoric. First Theroux, who by now is in Patagonia:

The landscape had a prehistoric look, the sort that forms a painted backdrop for a dinosaur skeleton in a museum: simple terrible hills and gullies; thorn bushes and rocks; and everything smoothed by the wind and looking as if a great flood had denuded it, washed it of all its particular features. Still the wind worked on it, kept the trees from growing, blew the soil west, uncovered more rock, and even uprooted those ugly bushes.

The people in the train did not look out the window, except at the stations and only then to buy grapes or bread. One of the beauties of train travel is that you know where you are by looking out the window. No signboards are necessary. A hill, a river, a meadow--the landmarks tell you how far you have come. But this place had no landmarks, or rather it was all landmarks, one indistinguishable from the other-- thousands of hills and dry riverbeds, and a billion bushes, all the same. I dozed and woke: hours passed; the scenery at the window did not alter. And the stations were interchangeable--a shed, a concrete platform, staring men, boys with baskets, the dogs, the battered pickup trucks.

I looked for guanacos. I had nothing better to do. There were no guanacos.[12]

Then Moravia, generalizing on the African landscape:

Thus a journey to Africa, when it is not a mere full excursion from one to another of those big hotels that the inhabitants of the Western world have strewn across the Black Continent, is a veritable dive into prehistory.

But what is this prehistory that so fascinates Europeans? First of all, it should be said, it is the actual conformation

of the African landscape. The chief characteristic of this
landscape is not diversity, as in Europe, but rather its
terrifying monotony. The face of Africa bears a greater
resemblance to that of an infant, with few barely indicated
features, than to that of a man, upon which life has
imprinted innumerable significant lines; in other words, it
bears a greater resemblance to the face of the earth in prehistoric times, when there were no seasons and humanity had
not yet made its appearance, than to the face of the earth
as it is today, with the innumberable changes brought about
both by time and man. This monotony, furthermore, displays
two truly prehistoric aspects: reiteration, that is, repetition
of a single theme or motif to the point of obsession, to the
point of terror; and shapelessness, that is, the complete lack
of limitation, of the finite, of pattern and form, in fact. [13]

Again, the contrast with Burton's description could hardly be
more pronounced. But this time the contrast is not between
positive and negative esthetic judgments, but between density
and scarcity of meaning. One need hardly comment on the
ideological significance of representing parts of the world as
having no history and therefore in need of being given one by
us. What is of interest here is the association of the prehistoric with absence of differentiation. One of the most conspicuous hallmarks of high-technology, industrialized societies,
especially capitalist ones, is precisely the endless creation of
differentiations, specializations, subdivisions. In a rather
different way, then, these two texts say, as Burton did, that
what is needed is more of 'us'. And again, in both texts we
find that no limitations on the speakers' interpretive authority
are suggested, despite the fact that they are in a completely
alien environment. What they see is all there is. Here the
authority of the home culture is incorporated in the form of
generalized assertions, such as Theroux's statement that 'one
of the beauties of train travel is that you know where you are
by looking out the window'. Here a statement that obviously
could have meaning only with reference to a specific cultural
and material context is asserted as a context-free norm from
which the Other is then seen to deviate. Semantically, the
natives of Patagonia are failing to travel correctly on their own
trains, and Patagonia itself is failing to provide the right kind
of landscape for the train to go through.
　　Again, the point to be stressed is that it is not necessary to
claim this kind of interpretive authority. The following text by
Albert Camus illustrates one writer's effort to work against
both the rural commonplace (landscape as undifferentiated and
ahistoric) and the urban commonplace (cityscape as ugly and
trivial), and against the overall authoritative stance of this
discourse. The excerpt is from Camus' story *The Adulterous
Woman*, about a French-Algerian woman making a trip into the
interior on a sales trip with her husband. The trip turns into

an existential crisis for her. Here we have her at an oasis in
the desert, standing at the top of the southernmost French
fort, looking out over the Sahara. It is an obvious invocation
of the monarch-of-all-I-survey convention. Notice in this passage the way the stereotypical prehistoric, lifeless landscape is
successively postulated, then rejected or qualified. Notice,
too, the severe limitations postulated on the completeness and
reliability of the outsider's perceptions--what she sees is very
far indeed from being all that is there.

> From east to west, in fact, her gaze swept slowly, without
> encountering a single obstacle, along a perfect curve. Be-
> neath her, the blue-and-white terraces of the Arab town
> overlapped one another, splattered with the dark red spots
> of peppers drying in the sun. Not a soul could be seen,
> but from the inner courts, together with the aroma of roast-
> ing coffee, there rose laughing voices or incomprehensible
> stamping of feet. Farther off, the palm grove, divided into
> uneven squares by clay walls, rustled its upper foliage in a
> wind that could not be felt up on the terrace. Still farther
> off, and all the way to the horizon extended the ocher-and-
> gray realm of stones, in which no life was visible. At some
> distance from the oasis, however, near the wadi that
> bordered the palm grove on the west could be seen broad
> black tents. All around them a flock of motionless dromedaries,
> tiny at that distance, formed against the gray ground the
> black signs of a strange handwriting, the meaning of which
> had to be deciphered. Above the desert, the silence was as
> vast as the space.[14]

No sooner is the perfect undifferentiated curve of the horizon
postulated than the eye shifts to the multicolored irregular
shapes of the terraces and the uneven squares of the palm
groves. Everywhere there are signs of things going on that
the observer can perceive only partially. The undifferentiated
landscape is invoked a second time ('the ocher-and-gray realm
of stones'), and again immediately complicated by the presence
of the tents and dromedaries. And again, the protagonist's
authority is limited--she cannot decipher the handwriting which
is nevertheless in need of decipherment. In short, what is produced here is a drastic qualification of the monarch-of-all-I-
survey scene. What is not produced here, or anywhere else in
Camus' work, is a new or more acceptable vantage point. In
the final passage I propose to discuss, again from Richard
Wright, we do see an attempt to establish a different, non-
dominating position from which he, like Camus, produces a discourse that rejects the roles of interpretive authority and judge
in favor of representing the very experience of one's own
ignorance, disorientation, and limitation. It is no accident that
Wright here portrays himself at night, when you know that what
you perceive is not all that is there:

Night comes suddenly, like wet black velvet. The air,
charged with too much oxygen, drugs the blood. The
scream of some wild birds cuts through the dark and stops
abruptly, leaving a suspenseful void. A foul smell rises
from somewhere. A distant drumming is heard and dies, as
though ashamed of itself. An inexplicable gust of wind
flutters the window curtain, making it billow and then fall
limp. A bird chirps sleepily in the listless night. Fragments
of African voices sound in the darkness and fade. The
flame of my candle burns straight up, burns minutes on end
without a single flicker or tremor. The sound of a lorry
whose motor is whining as it strains to climb the steep hill
brings back to me the world I know. [15]

Wright is representing an experience of incomprehension and
self-dissolution that does not give rise to terror or madness,
but rather to a serene receptivity and intense sensuality.
Notice how the fragmentation and abruptness of impressions are
counteracted by a strong, continuous rhythm. As impressions
flow in and out, the subject's consciousness--here symbolically
represented as *my candle* (the *my* is significant, since there is
no *I* previously in the passage) burns peacefully in the heart
of the unknown, without a tremor of fear--a steadiness that
seems to surprise Wright himself. In this context the arriving
lorry does not have its usual meaning of the nick-of-time
rescuer. Wright feels no need to move at all--he stays exactly
where he is. The lorry does not bring him back to the known
world, it brings that world back to him.

The foregoing discussion will doubtless have communicated a
set of ideological commitments of my own--a criticism of discourses that implicitly or explicitly dehumanize, trivialize, and
devalue other realities in the name of Western superiority, and
an appreciation of discourses that do not do these things, and
instead acknowledge the limitations on the West's ability to
make sense of other peoples and places (especially those it
seeks to hold in subjugation). Some may wish to argue that
such commitments have no place in academic investigations, or
in linguistics, but I think they are wrong. To begin with, that
argument is obviously as ideologically committed as my own.
More generally, any discourse has ideological dimensions--values--
just as it has esthetic and sociological ones. Poetics and sociolinguistics are equipping us with a stylistics that can deal with
these latter two dimensions. Ultimately, we will need a stylistics
that can deal with the first one too.

NOTES

1. Daniel Defoe, The Life and Adventures of Robinson
Crusoe. Harmondsworth: Penguin Books, 1965, p. 27.
2. Richard Lander, Records of Captain Clapperton's Last
Expedition to Africa. London: Henry Colburn and Richard
Bentley, 1830, pp. 1-3.

3. James Bruce, Travels to Discover the Source of the Nile. Edited by C. F. Beckingham. Edinburgh: University Press, 1964, p. 163.
4. Daniel Defoe, Robinson Crusoe, op. cit., p. 80.
5. Mungo Park, Travels in the Interior of Africa. Edinburgh: Adam and Charles Black, 1878, p. 225.
6. Samuel Richardson, Pamela. London: J. M. Dent and Sons, 1914, Vol. I, pp. 150-151.
7. Reprinted from The Lake Regions of Central Africa, by Richard Burton. Copyright 1961, by permission of the publisher, Horizon Press, New York.
8. John Speke, Journal of the Discovery of the Source of the Nile. London: Blackwood and Sons, 1863, pp. 466-467.
9. Alberto Moravia, Which Tribe Do You Belong To? Trans. Angus Davidson. New York: Farrar, Straus, and Giroux, 1972, p. 1.
10. Paul Theroux, The Old Patagonian Express. Boston: Houghton Mifflin, 1978, p. 123.
11. Richard Wright, Black Power. New York: Harper, 1954, p. 154.
12. Paul Theroux, op. cit., p. 397.
13. Alberto Moravia, op. cit., p. 8.
14. Albert Camus, 'The Adulterous Woman'. In: Exile and the Kingdom. Trans. Justin O'Brien. New York: Vintage Books, 1957, pp. 22-23.
15. Richard Wright, op. cit., p. 263.

INTEGRATIONAL SEMANTICS:
AN UNDERSTANDER'S THEORY OF MEANING IN CONTEXT

Benjamin Hrushovski
National Humanities Center and
Tel-Aviv University

To the memory of a great teacher, friend, and example,
Roman Jakobson--a phenomenologist in the observation of
language facts, a structuralist in their analysis, and a
positivist in his belief in the possibility of a science of
language.

1. Introduction

1.0 The following remarks intend to present an outline and several concrete examples for a new, comprehensive theory of semantics.[1] If semantics is the theory and study of meaning, and if meaning is all the information an understander may obtain while perceiving (reading or hearing) a text, then it must be clear that semantics cannot be limited to the study of isolated units: words (as 'signs'), sentences, speech acts, or their combinations. The meanings, meaning-complexes, and meaning-chains, which understanders obtain from texts, result from processes of integrating (discontinuous) semantic materials located in a given text as well as outside of it.

1.1 The 'understander's' point of departure is merely a methodological device, intended to illuminate components of meaning not always accounted for in 'objectivist' semantic analyses of texts. Speakers, writers, and other producers of texts are aware of the same mechanisms and invest meanings in the text they produce accordingly (though there may not always be an identity between the speaker's and the understander's meaning).

1.2   Granted, texts are made, on the whole, of words and
sentences.   Yet the units of meaning are not words and sentences but patterns combining semantic elements, which, indeed,
reside in--and are constructed from--these words and sentences.
The older stages of semantics--the study of the meaning of
words (as summarized, e.g. by Ullman and Weinreich), syntactic
semantics, even various new approaches to the theory of texts
and discourse--all contributed essential data for the understanding of meaning-units and meaning-forms.   I do not wish to dis-
count the value of such studies, but to point out that in actual
communication they provide merely potential values in an understander's constructs.   I believe that they must all be subsumed
under a wider framework which would observe meanings as they
really occur: as open-ended networks of constructs, forming
bridges between given pieces of language and the world (or language) outside of it.

1.3   The proposed 'Integrational Semantics' is the theory of
meanings resulting from processes of integration of semantic
material, within a text and outside of it.   I prefer this name to
such more widely accepted titles as 'text grammar', 'text theory',
or 'discourse analysis' for two major reasons.   (a) If words or
sentences are not the ultimate independent units of meaning,
neither is a text.   A text cannot be produced or 'generated'
from one 'theme' or one core; a text often provides a multitude
of 'themes', meanings, and meaning-patterns; it cannot be ex-
hausted in one summary or even in one interpretation.   (b) Elements within a text may be linked semantically not only to their
immediate context or not even to other elements in the same text
but to relevant elements elsewhere--either verbal or verbalizable.
Thus, the fifth sentence in a news item in today's paper may be
linked to the third sentence in yesterday's paper more than to
its own neighbors.
     In short, though a text is the vehicle in which meanings are
conveyed, it is both more and less than any independent complex unit of meaning.

1.4   In recent years, a considerable body of work from different directions confronted the study of discourse and its comprehension.[2]   Some contributions are parallel to work done here,
or may be accounted for in this framework.   Others are more
limited or weak for reasons that should become clear from the
proposed theory.   However, the space of an article does not
allow for a proper consideration and critical assessment of the
work in this field.   My goal is, rather, to provide an independent general theoretical framework, to propose an outline
of a model which may accommodate the disparate concerns in
one perspective.   Instead of basing each step on accepted
theories and terminologies (which become ambiguous and interpretation-dependent when carried from one theoretical system to
another), I shall propose my own terms, explained as simply as

possible, and based on the assumption that 'in the area of philosophy of language perhaps as much as in any other philosophical field, chaos reigns, little is agreed on, new methods are to be eagerly seized upon, and we have hardly begun' (Caton 1971:3).

1.4.1 In what follows, I shall try to show how the model works and how it can account for various observable phenomena of meaning in language texts. A more careful, technical working out of detailed descriptive procedures must be left for another occasion.

Moreover, I shall not propose an abstract framework in its logical order, but rather work up to it, 'showing what I mean' through specific examples and particular aspects, combining interpretations with generalizations.

Needless to say, I am indebted to numerous studies in this wide area, as well as in the study of literature and interpretation.

1.5 This approach involves several basic assumptions about language, some of which seem obvious to many contemporaries, but are not fully realized in theory.

(a) The problem of communication is not 'how to do things with words' but 'how to convey things with language': meanings, requests, emotions, attitudes, ambiguities, information, etc. (abbreviated 'Meaning').

(b) Language is not an independent vehicle for conveying meaning. It is rather used to (re-)orient the understander in a 'network of information' ('World', which includes all previous texts as well).

Utterances often do not carry (merely) new information but send the understander to available stores of information (either observable or mediated through language), zeroing in on specific elements and reshuffling, reinterpreting, or adding on to them.

In other words, a speaker of language uses language as well as the 'World' to convey his intentions, guiding the understander by means of his words (as well as gestures, etc.). This is true even for such highly abstract texts as philosophy, which cannot be understood without previous philosophical texts or such notions as 'time', 'space', etc. And it is certainly true for newspapers, which cannot be understood without newspapers (or newscasts) of previous days.

(c) Semantic theory must overcome the 'First-Sentence Fallacy'--the analysis of a sentence as if it stood alone. There are no first sentences in language. The 'first sentences' of children are highly embedded in their (nonverbal) context.

(d) We must abandon the inherited notion that sentences are the units of meaning. 'The logical form of a sentence is identical with its meaning as determined compositionally from the senses of its lexical items and the grammatical relations between its syntactic constituents' (Katz 1972:xxiv). Whether we convey something through combinations of words within a sentence or dispersed in several sentences makes no difference. *I see red brick houses* may be conveyed either in one sentence (as here) or in parts of several, discontinuous sentences: *red houses* in one, *brick houses* in another--to be integrated by an understander (see Sections 4.12-4.13). Such dispersed elements are not connected formally in language but are available for patterning, in a kind of 'semantic syntax' of interpretive constructs, which, in turn, may be analyzed, as sentences in a syntactical semantics would.

I am stressing this point because even many discourse analysis theories that declare their wish to go 'beyond the sentence' actually see discourse as a combination of sentences rather than a restructuring of semantic stuff.

(e) This may be generalized: there is a fallacy assuming that semantics lies in discrete, static units, rather than (possible or potential) constructs, sometimes based on diffuse bodies of text.

(f) Another limitation lies in the widespread restriction of linguistics to the study of codified forms and expressions. Indeed, *my friend* in English does not indicate my friend's sex, whereas in other languages such information would be codified in grammar. But English can express it lexically: in *boy-friend* and *girl-friend*. Similarly, many semantic categories may be expressed either, or both, in codified and noncodified ways; a semantic integration will decide on the nature of the category (time, embedded speaker, etc.).

Furthermore, even codified forms may be misleading. The grammatical third person may be used in literature for expressing the semantic first person, and the grammatical second person in poetry may do the same. On the other hand, first person poems may represent a voice different from the author's. A confrontation of such grammatical forms with the contents and genre of the text will provide the correct 'semantic person'.

(g) Interpretations of literary texts involve primarily 'understanding of language'. A theory of language must be able to account for the modes in which meanings are conveyed in literary texts. This is true not only for 'interpretable deviance', e.g. metaphor (Weinreich),[3] but also for the more basic 'mimetic' aspect of language, its 'world-constructing' capacity.

Applications of linguistics to literary texts were often of limited value not because they did not understand 'literature' but because existing linguistic methods do not account for central aspects of language. We should reverse the order of investigation: use literary texts for the observation of language phenomena and the construction of a more adequate theory of language.

(h) Theory must not shy away from the diffuse, ambivalent, multidirectional, imprecise, potentials-filled nature of language--which is its great strength in interacting with a multifarious and changing 'World'. One should not confuse method with ontology, the neatness of a theoretical apparatus with a

schematic neatness in language. Perhaps not everything may
be said precisely or translated into logical formulas; it may be
observed nevertheless.

2. A three-story construct of meaning

2.0 Meanings are conveyed in language through texts. To
be sure, there are many nonlinguistic modes of conveying meaning, either independently or combined with linguistic utterances.
I do not discuss those here, although I believe that they, too,
can be explained within this general framework.

2.0.1 However, the structure of meaning and meaning-
complexes is not identical with the structure of texts. On the
one hand, the establishment of meanings obtained from a text
requires the involvement of material outside the given text.
And on the other hand, texts often have semantic material not
directly relevant to a given meaning-complex as well as important
nonsemantic aspects. Also, the composition of a text is not
identical with the composition of its meanings.
For this reason, the description of meaning requires a separate model from the description of texts, though the two are
interdependent and intertwined in reality.

2.1 Meaning is a result of a three-story construction, which
may be represented by the following diagram.

RP   RP = Regulating Principles
|
sense
|
FR   FR = Frame of Reference

The middle level--the level of 'sense'--represents both the
senses of words and those aspects of meaning which result from
syntactic operations.

2.1.1 For utterances to become meaningful, they must be
applied to specific 'Frames of Reference' (FR). A Frame of
Reference is any continuum of referents to which utterances,
texts, or their interpretations may refer.

2.1.2 These FRs may be 'real': a certain situation in time
and space, e.g. a room, a city, a street, etc.; or 'ideal', e.g.
a certain theoretical system, a science, an ideology, etc. Any
'theme' or 'state of affairs', any abstracted relationship may
constitute an FR, e.g. the relationship between John and Mary,
the war in Vietnam, slave-owner mentality, etc. An FR that
occupies a specific area in space within the grasp of a human
observer and usually tied to a specific point in time is called
a 'scene'.

2.1.3 Thus, FRs may actually exist in the world or be imaginary, fictional, hypothetical. Their ontological status need not concern the semanticist; as long as some information about an FR is provided, we can adjudge further utterances relating to it.

2.1.4 FRs may be 'present' or 'absent' in the speech situation. If I say in a classroom: *Please close the door*, the FR provides information additional to my words, e.g. it is noisy outside, the wind is blowing, the door was too heavy for me to move, or somebody just opened it. If, however, I tell a story about an 'absent FR', I cannot simply say that I asked someone to close the door without explaining the reasons or circumstances.

In works of fiction, the characters behave as if they speak in 'present FRs', but since the reader is not actually present, the text must provide him with additional information about the fictional FRs. The problem becomes especially acute in 'scenic' fiction, in passages presented from a character's point of view or through his stream of consciousness, since a character would not normally tell or think to himself all the background for his reactions or emotions.

2.1.5 Absent FRs may be 'known' to the hearer or 'unknown', in varying degrees. It makes a difference if we say something about an object in the living room, known to the hearer, or if we tell him about an object in a foreign city, which he has not seen.

2.1.6 Regulating Principles (RP) derive from the authorities standing behind an utterance: the speaker, the narrator, any represented position of a character or any producer of a text. Point of view, irony, the 'tone' of a text, attitudes deriving from the genre of a text--tell us 'in what sense' to take the senses of the words.

2.1.7 The three stories of a meaning construct are much more interdependent than we might assume. In daily life situations, it seems that only the middle story is given in language. Somebody who came running, panting and excited, telling us in confusion of an accident he saw, provides the Regulating Principles; we know how to 'read' his evidence, his intonations and exaggerations seem to be located not in language but in real life. And so is the Frame of Reference--the accident--about which he is telling.

In literary texts, on the other hand, all three stories must be present in the text and given in language. However, in non-literary texts, too, important parts of the RP and FR are given in language: we don't hear the intonations of a journalist's report, but we have clues to reconstruct them from the text;

we don't see the FR in Beirut, to which he refers, but some information about it is provided in his text.

2.1.8 In any case, the competence of using language is based on such an interaction in a three-story construct, and even if only the level of sense is provided in words, it cannot be understood properly and precisely without assumptions about the other two stories.
In what follows I do not devote much attention to the RPs.

2.2 The construction of an FR

2.2.0 The concept of 'Frame of Reference' becomes necessary when we observe the constructs of meaning in interpretations of literary texts. Though less obvious, the concept is needed for the explanation of any understanding of meaning in language use.

2.2.1 This may be demonstrated by example (1a).[4]

(1a) He opened the door. A few pieces of clothing were strewn about. He caught the fish in his net.

The first two sentences are not connected by any syntactic or logical means. There is no relation of coreference between them. They talk about different referents (r_1;r_2). Nevertheless, a reader will automatically see the description as coherent. The reader constructs a hypothetical FR: a room, in which both sentences may be accommodated (i.e. a hypothetical continuum in which r_1 and r_2 are both located). Thus we obtain a two-story semantic structure.

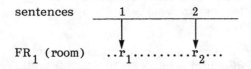

2.2.2 The concept of FR explains how readers perceive or assume things that have not been explicitly stated in language. A room clearly must have a floor, walls, windows, furniture, and so on. We need not specify all such details when a frame of any 'standard' nature is given. The establishment of an FR implies the existence of many 'indeterminacies', which were described in Ingarden's phenomenology but are not taken into account in 'objective' theories of linguistics or semantics.

2.2.3 Thus, two sentences may be connected if their referents are not coreferential but are 'co-FR', i.e. may be accommodated in one FR.

2.2.4 The third sentence in this example, however, cannot reasonably be accommodated in the same FR: we do not normally catch fish in a net in a room. Indeed, the sentence, though in itself a literal sentence, is automatically perceived by understanders as a metaphor (be it a girl or a culprit in a detective story, according to various readers). The mechanism is simple: since the sentence could not be accommodated in its literal meaning within the constructed FR, and *he* in the third sentence seems to be coreferential with *he* in the first, we must transform the new sentence in order to make the text coherent. In this case, the transformation was metaphorical, based on a conventional idiom. Without the notion of FR and the two-story structure of meaning, we could not account for this metaphor, since the sentence in itself has nothing metaphorical about it. (To be sure, a fuller analysis would account for the third story, of RP as well. Thus, the third sentence may be seen as presented from 'his' point of view, conveying something like 'He thought to himself: ...').

2.2.5 In another reading, the third sentence may be accepted literally. In that case, however, we must change our 'standard' notion of a room and assume some California eccentric who has a pool with fish and a net in his own room or backyard. Such a hypothesis about the FR is possible, but will enforce constraints on any unfolding of the story. Since the hypothetical FR was a construct, it may have to be changed or reconstructed, as often happens in fiction. In this case, instead of changing the sentence to accommodate it to an assumed FR, we changed the FR itself.

2.2.6 Consider now a different version of the same opening.

(1b) He opened the door. A few pieces of clothing were
strewn about. The beach was beautiful in the light of
the early morning. To his satisfaction he saw that he
caught the fish in his net. She was not to be seen
anywhere. He attended to his business of pulling the
net out of the water.

We now see that, in our previous reading, the easy assumption of a 'room' accommodating the first two sentences, made us assume automatically that he opened the door and looked inside. One can, of course, open a door to the outside and accommodate the fish and the net by placing the house at a seashore. In the second version, one FR accepts plausibly both the woman and the fishing in their literal meaning.

2.2.7 In this version, no metaphoric reading is necessary to justify any sentence. However, not only a negation of literal meaning may create metaphors, as many theories of metaphor assume. By placing the description of fish-catching in close

proximity with the description of the girl who apparently un-
dressed (and went swimming?), the text encourages a metaphorical transfer between the two. (In this case, the reader is encouraged even more, by the metonymy of the alliterated *beautiful beach*). The one FR, based on a continuum in space, was
split in two thematically distinguished sub-FRs, which, in turn
entered into a metaphorical relationship.

2.2.8 In this example, in both versions (1a) and (1b) there
was no FR known in advance, out there in the world, to which
the words might refer. The FR was constructed by the same
sentences which expressed things about it. It is--to use a
famous simile--like sailing on a sea while building (and rebuild-
ing) the boat under your own feet. The interdependence between the two stories, of sense and FR, is a characteristic
feature of literary texts, as seen in the so-called hermeneutic
'circularity' of interpretation. It is found, however, in nonfictional texts as well. For example, though the war in
Lebanon is an objectively given FR, opinions about it are
interdependent with assertions about various specific 'facts'
or properties of that FR.

2.3 Relating senses to FRs

2.3.0 Consider the sentence in example (2).

(2) This is a filthy hotel.

This sentence has no definite meaning unless it is related to a
specific frame of reference. There are several possible cases.
 (a) If the sentence is used in a rundown hotel where the
floors or furniture are clearly filthy, the literal sense of the
words is accepted.
 (b) If the floors are clean, the worse for the hotel: to
accommodate the word *filthy*, for this FR, we must turn it
into a metaphor.
 (c) A hotel may be *filthy* in both the literal and metaphorical
senses. The proper meaning may be ascertained only by check-
ing the actual FR, and may be contested, in whole or in part,
by any observer.

2.3.1 As we see, it is not only that senses of words are
related to referents, but the referents in turn may influence
the meaning in which the 'senses' are to be perceived. It is a
two-way operation. We need a frame of reference to ascertain
the truth-value of sentences or the literal value of words.

2.3.2 (d) If, however, the same sentence is used by a man
staying in his girlfriend's apartment, neither *filthy* nor *hotel*
can preserve their literal meaning. The whole sentence cannot
be accepted as such, because the referent 'apartment' cannot

accept the pointer 'this hotel'. The 'understander' must process the sentence for a possible meaning in the given frame of reference, e.g.: 'To me, this place is filthy: I see it as a hotel, a temporary residence; I am leaving'. Instead of saying *I am leaving you*, the speaker used the utterance (2) which became metaphorical in the given FR.

2.3.3 Literary texts as well as everyday language are replete with such transfers of sentences from their habitual FRs, where their literal meanings obtain, to 'alien' FRs, requiring various kinds of understanders' transformations for their acceptance.

2.3.4 A further point must be made (though I cannot discuss it in detail here). When speaking of 'truth-value' we must not see it narrowly as an either-or question: true or false. Evaluating the truth-status of utterances involves a wide range of possibilities: observations may be true 'in a sense', exaggerated, ideologically biased, partial, or may merely map a 'horizon' from which the speaker himself dissociates his position.

I am not going to tell you that actors and directors are crazy, because that would be either libelous or unnecessary. (Walter Kerr, 'Does the Actor Do Everything--Or Nothing at All?' *The New York Times*, Sept. 23, 1979)

Truth-evaluation is made by comparing a given utterance with other sources of information on the same FR (and/or by comparing the speaker's position with other speakers' positions).

2.4 Consider another example. Coming home, I said to my wife:

(3) Why don't you wear your blue dress?

My wife understood what I meant. It was not the color blue I was interested in, but rather the formality of the dress, which fit the party to which we were invited. My wife's understanding was due to her zeroing-in on two FRs: (1) the possible purpose for changing her dress, namely, the party to which we were invited (FR$_1$); (2) her wardrobe, of which her blue dress was part (FR$_2$). My sentence sent her to these two stores of information, from which she could easily retrieve the property 'formal', justifying my request. Though I did not refer directly to the referent 'formal', it was retrieved from the store of information (FR$_2$) as a possible bridge between the two FRs.

2.4.1 My wife, however, answered: *It is not cold*. This means that, from all the available information about her blue

dress, she selected another property: its being warm, and
related it not to the party but to another FR: the cold evening
(FR$_3$).

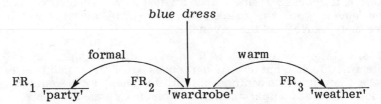

2.4.2 Of course, such misunderstandings which arise con-
stantly in human communication may be corrected--either immediately or at a later time.

The distinction between the meaning of a given sentence and
the speaker's intended meaning is usually described as 'utterance meaning' versus 'speaker's meaning'. It is important to
note, however, that such 'speaker's meaning', as well as the
not necessarily equivalent 'understander's meaning', can be obtained by specifically relating the utterance to concrete FRs
and to available information about them.

2.4.3 Speakers do not usually convey new information in
their utterances but rather manipulate information known before-
hand. Instead of saying to my wife:

Turn back, move three steps to the right, open a door, go
to the left wall, there is a closet, open the door, you'll see
dresses hanging, ... etc.

and then explaining exactly where we are going, what is the
character of our hosts, and why I suggest that she wear her
blue dress, I merely used the last clause. One might say that
one advantage of a marriage is the acquisition of a common store
of information which enables humanly possible brevity of speech.

2.4.4 One might argue that, in this analysis, I have gone
beyond language. But we cannot understand language unless
we recognize that it always goes 'beyond language', i.e. sentences rely on previous information, whether obtained through
language or otherwise.

2.4.5 There seems to be a difference between brief utterances,
connected directly to situations in reality, on the one hand, and
long texts, especially in literature, which first create such situations by means of language. In both cases, however, a sentence will draw upon what is assumed to be 'known' about a
given situation, whether provided in the language of the 'same'
text or not.

In other words, in daily usage, between one utterance and another there are pieces of a 'real' world, creating an illusion that individual utterances may be independent, that language is separate from reality; whereas in literature there is no such excuse: the 'real' world is given in a verbalized form, and the mechanism is easily observable.

2.5 One day I opened the French newspaper, *Le Monde*. The first sentences of the newspaper, opening the front page lead article were:

(4) Une Nouvelle Allemagne

La brutalité avec laquelle le chancelier allemand cherche à 'mettre au pas' ses partenaires européens annonce-t-elle que la 'nouvelle Allemagne' retrouve par une pente naturelle certains charactères de la 'mauvaise Allemagne' de naguère? M. Schmidt se veut-il un nouveau 'chancelier de fer'? (*Le Monde*, Sept. 27, 1974)

2.5.1 The language of this article sends the reader to retrieve information from several frames of reference of European history. To understand the sentences, the reader has to know, or find out, about the European partnership to which the German chancellor belongs; the arguments after World War II as to whether a 'New Germany' was possible; the dictatorial tendencies of the 'Iron Chancellor', Bismarck. Then, the reader has to know the circumstances of the present FR to which the sentences refer. Clearly, *Le Monde* could not have meant that Germany returned literally to Nazi tactics or even to Bismarck's rule. (After all, Schmidt ruled at the time by a shaky majority of one vote.)

2.5.2 Indeed, from other articles in the same issue of *Le Monde* and from other news media of the day, it turned out that Germany vetoed a rise of 5 percent in agricultural products suggested by other members of the European Common Market at the commission in Brussels. Only with that knowledge can we understand the meaning of the word, *brutality*, in this text. Mr. Schmidt did not punch anybody in the nose, he was not even there when the vote was taken. *Brutality* here means something like 'being inconsiderate, forcing of others' hands'.
In communicating through language, what we are interested in are not the general concepts which words cover, but their specific meaning in a given utterance. The meaning of a word such as *brutality* becomes specified from the FR to which it is applied.

2.5.3 The same word, *brutality*, is specified in a different direction in the following sentence:

... will *The Times* now advocate that the U.S. public school textbooks reveal the full brutality of the westward 'advance' through North America which swept aside hundreds of American Indian nations? (Letter to *The New York Times*, Sept. 8, 1982)

2.5.4 Thus, senses of words are not 'given' or fixed, and then applied to specific referents. It is from what we know about the referent, and often from a complex state of affairs in a specific FR, that the sense of the word becomes specified in its meaning.

2.6 A telling example of an interpretation of an expression based on this mechanism can be found in Stewart Alsop's *Newsweek* article 'The Serious Man', written after Nixon's second inauguration (*Newsweek*, Jan. 22, 1973). Alsop claims that Nixon is *un homme serieux*, something that Nixon felt was lacking in his opponent, George McGovern. The article revolves around an analysis of this expression.

The literal meaning is, of course, 'a serious man'. Less literally, but more accurately, it means a man who has to be taken seriously. Less literally still, but still more accurately in terms of the President's thinking, it means a tough man, a hard man, a man not be pushed around.

Alsop distinguishes here three degrees of meaning: the literal, the 'more accurate', and the real meaning as defined in terms of the President's position and idiolect. This third meaning is the one that really counts in communication and would be perceived as such by any TV viewer at the time. Understanders may arrive intuitively at such a correct meaning; when they have to account for it, however, they will resort to a technique so clearly demonstrated in Alsop's article.

2.6.1 The process of accounting for the 'accurate' meaning may be described as follows. We first try to apply literally the expression *serious man* to Nixon's personality and activities. This cannot work, especially if we keep in mind that McGovern had a Ph.D. and could be considered more serious in that respect. As in the case of some previous examples (hotel, the fish in the net), we will try to find such a transformation of the expression which would make it acceptable in relevant FRs.
Indeed, while scanning the field of Nixon's activities, Alsop found a number of FRs to which the expression could be applied: '... he has been behaving like the grim reaper', firing officials in his administration; pushing the Europeans around in the economics talks; and resuming the bombing of

North Vietnam. *The serious man* can apply to these FRs if we transform it into 'a man to be taken seriously'; and even here, the word *seriously* can be accepted only in a special, metaphorical sense.

2.6.2 Thus Alsop established a 'patterned relationship' between the expression and a number of relevant FRs within a 'network of information'.
We do not have a case of a direct reference to a given referent, but rather a matching of certain abstractions from possibly relevant FRs with a fitting transformation of an expression.

2.6.3 The interpolated phrase, *a man to be taken seriously*, has no direct referent in the FRs to which it applies (Vietnam, the administration, etc.). It is merely possible to apply it, as one possible generalization. We feel that such an expression is true for a given FR when we feel that it is plausible to abstract from the mass of information (e.g. about Vietnam) a generalized pattern which would justify the given label.

2.6.4 To support his hypothesis, Alsop does not stop at the interaction between the two stories, of sense and FR, but resorts to the third story of RP as well. He observes Nixon's use of French, though 'his French is not even vestigial', and explains it by Nixon's meeting with that aloof loner, DeGaulle, giving an additional twist to the image of 'a serious man'.

2.6.5 We may represent it in the following diagram.

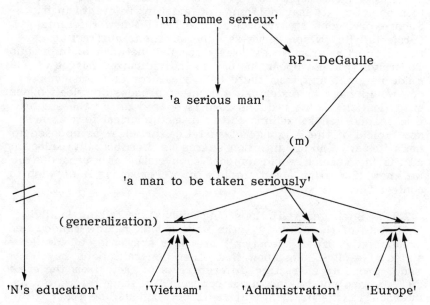

2.6.6 To sum up: it is not the immediate context which specifies the meaning of an expression. It is rather a 'patterned relationship' which has to be established between an utterance and specific FRs selected from a wide network of information. An understanding hypothesis will always require: (1) the establishment of such a patterned relationship between an expression and (hypothetically) relevant FRs to which it may apply; (2) the adjustment (metaphorization, transformation, specification, etc.) of the expression to the assumed FRs, or interpolation of additional expressions between the two. Clearly, the two activities are simultaneous and interdependent; arguments against the one will usually undermine the other. Such seems to me to be a major point of contention in literary interpretations.

2.7 Consider example (5).

(5) Raymond Aron says that the French today behave like 'the caricature of Europeans'. But in fact all parties to the argument are behaving like caricatures of themselves: the Americans are talking as loudly as the bad Americans of political fiction; the British are trying hard to look as narrow-minded and isolationist as the John Bull of legend; and the French are clamoring about 'honor and dignity' as if they still were at the court of Louis XIV. (Arrigo Levi, 'The Silent Europeans', *Newsweek*, April 15, 1974)

2.7.1 This example shows that utterances, though referring to a specific FR, may not hinge on existing referents in it. Such expressions rather project onto the FR new referents (projected Rs) which serve as generalizations abstracting certain properties from an extremely complex network of information. To arrive from European history to individualized images of the major nations, and from there to 'caricatures of themselves', one would have to undertake a complex process of selection and simplification. This arduous road is spared us by the suggestive pseudo-generalizations (often in metaphorical form) which are typical of the language of analytical articles--as opposed to news items. Though intuition spares us from actually collecting all the facts which would support such claims as Raymond Aron's, we know how to go about finding counterexamples if we wish to contest them.

2.7.2 Such generalizations ('Americans are talking loudly', 'bad state of the economy', 'the British look narrow-minded and isolationist', 'urban alienation') are false summaries of complex states of affairs. We know that other generalizations may be made, probably extracting different sets of facts from the same FR. We are not talking about concrete, existing referents, but interpolating generalizing referents between us and the world.

Sometimes it is done on a level which became an FR in its own
right (e.g. economic theory), sometimes it is an ad hoc interpolation (as in Raymond Aron's metaphoric expressions).

2.7.3 Such generalizations take on the form of 'localized
universals'. They serve as semantic abbreviations. No matter
how well we know that 'love', 'Natasha's love', 'Andrej's conver-
sion', 'ambivalence', 'he is nice', etc. do not convey the complexity and individuality of the situation--and cannot really
stand alone, without the detailed information about the given
FR--we need such 'abbreviations' in everyday life as in the
reading of novels.

2.7.4 Another class of abbreviation is that of personal names.
Though considered semantically empty, in integrational semantics
they serve as convenient 'accumulators' of masses of heterogeneous meanings. If 'Kissinger' or 'Haig' said something on
the Middle East, their names carry a whole history of negotiations, attitudes, etc. The same holds not only for names of
people but of individual situations: 'the depression of 1929',
'D-day', etc.

2.8 A text is not necessarily a description of a 'given' frame.
Consider example (6).

(6) Yesterday, at a conference of shop stewards of a team-
    sters union local representing city employees, Mr. Koch
    was told that municipal workers expected 'real' pay in-
    creases beyond cost-of-living adjustments in the round
    of bargaining talks for new contracts in the first year
    of the next mayoral term. (*The New York Times*, Oct.
    23, 1977)

In this case, a new FR is constructed: a meeting between
the mayor of New York, Mr. Koch, and representatives of the
Teamsters Union. This passage is an intersection of elements
from a number of heterogeneous FRs. The reader must bring
knowledge about those separate FRs to understand the given
passage. The reader must know (or find out) about: the
role of labor unions, the special nature of the Teamsters Union,
the state of the American economy, as well as the politics of
mayoral elections.
The understander, as well as the writer, operates here not
only with meanings of words and concepts, but with complex
patches of information (known FRs) which he does not have to
detail but merely indicate their availability.
Of course, such disparate FRs are not merely separate
'worlds', but belong together in a wider universe, a Field of
Reference (FiR): the USA today.

2.9 Another case of intersecting FRs in the same utterance is their metaphorical use, as in the opening of an article in *The New York Times* 'Week in Review', shown in (7).

(7) Administration's Doughboys Draw Fire on the Hill

> With the President toughing it out in the bully pulpit, the Administration's good soldiers were left to slog up Capitol Hill last week, defending the virtues of his economic program and explaining the vagaries of the economy. (*The New York Times*, March 7, 1982)

To the description of President Reagan's defense of his economic program, the author brought allusions to Teddy Roosevelt (*the bully pulpit, slogging up* San Juan Hill); as well as to the American foot soldiers of World War I (who turned out to be the President's budget director, David Stockman; his chief economic advisor, Murray Weidenbaum; and Federal Reserve Board Chairman Paul Volcker).

The writer uses such remote FRs to reflect vividly and succinctly on the given situation as well as to open a store of possible parallels and contrasts.

3. Frames of Reference and Fields of Reference

3.1 Frames of Reference (FR) combine into larger wholes, Fields of Reference (FiR). An FiR is a vast hypothetical 'universe' for which a number of (discontinuous) FRs are given.

3.1.1 For example, in a novel, a character is presented in certain situations (FRs) at the age of 2, 13, 23, but not during all the years in between. We nevertheless assume that, being a human character in a realistic world, he lived during the nonpresented years as well. The FiR encompasses the whole span. In the same way, a number of countries mentioned in a newspaper on a given day are perceived as parts of a vaster FiR, the earth. Or: the separate FRs, connected by Mayor Koch's meeting with the teamsters (example (6)) are connected somewhere in one FiR: contemporary USA.

3.2 Individual FRs may intersect and criss-cross an FiR in any number of ways. For example, if we conceive of the war in Vietnam as one FiR, we can recognize that it is composed in our mind of many FRs: descriptions of battles, individual human destinies, fictional stories in books and films, political and ideological arguments in the United States, the behavior of General Westmoreland, relations between American soldiers and Asian women, etc.

3.3 Individual referents do not 'belong' to fixed FRs (as concepts would belong to a 'frame'), but rather may be organized and reorganized in various FRs.

This fact is widely used by literary and nonliterary texts. For example, the description of a party necessarily includes the appearance of individual persons. The party is an FR in one time continuum and one place. A person appearing within it belongs to another FR as well: his own biography, which is not fixed in time and space. Indeed, mention of a character in a party scene serves often as an occasion to move through his biography (or his consciousness) to other times and places in the past or in the future (either through the character's recollections or the narrator's remarks).

3.3.1 The same technique is used in newspapers. Though relying in part on the reader's previous knowledge of any given FR to which new information is added, newspapers do not rely on it fully. They tend to flashback or fill in some of that previous information. Thus, in a description of the death of Haile Selassie, *The New York Times*, after first mentioning his name, deviated to tell the biography of the man and his country. In graphic terms, we might say that, within a horizontal FR_1 of the emperor's death and funeral, the article inserted a vertical FR_2 of his biography. Many other FRs--ideology, opinion, the person's adversaries, questions about the future--may crisscross the same base.

$$FR_1 \text{ (time = 0)} \quad \begin{array}{c|c|c|c} FR_2 & FR_3 & FR_4 & FR_5 \\ \hline \text{'party'} & & & \end{array}$$

3.3.2 Indeed, writers as well as journalists favor the establishment of a 'basic FR' in the form of a concrete scene, in which other FRs (characters, political views, abstract arguments) are easily embedded.

3.4 Most communication, except for literature, relates to FRs that exist 'out there'. We either had or ideally could have additional information on the same FR, which may qualify, enrich, explain the meanings in the given text or provide a basis for their truth evaluation. This is true not only for things which exist in nature or history, but also for such constructs as myths (to which a number of texts contribute), scientific theories, ideologies, philosophical systems or superstitions.

3.4.1 A literary text (or as some would prefer to call it, a text of fiction, provided we include drama and poetry in the same category) is a text which creates at least one 'Internal Field of Reference' (IFiR). That means that at least some of the referents are given only in this text and no outside information may be valid for the truth evaluation of statements about such referents. Clearly, fictional characters in a novel as well as many actions and situations in which they appear are of this nature. Furthermore, they must be not just isolated referents but pertain to a coherent continuum, modeled upon some external FiR.

3.4.2 The concept of an 'Internal FiR' is necessary also to overcome claims such as that statements in literature are 'pseudo-statements' (I. A. Richards), 'quasi-judgments' (R. Ingarden), or that 'fictional' statements are the opposite of 'serious' (J. Searle). Within the internal FiR, all statements are 'serious' and are processed by the reader as in 'real' FRs: they may be true or false, and variously specified, with, of course, the one limitation: this is done only with available information for the given FiR.[5]

3.4.3 The problem of interpreting literature is largely due to the fact that a literary text both creates its own unique Field of Reference and at the same time provides semantic material for referring to it. This 'circularity', or interdependence, is especially difficult ('obscure') in poetry, notably in modernist poetry, where the FR is a state of mind rather than an objective scene, and an ambivalent state of mind at that.

3.5 By saying that a literary text creates an Internal FiR, I do not imply any absolute separation of a 'fictional world' from reality. Indeed, the reader of a work of fiction must 'imagine' an 'intentional' field or 'imaginary space' into which he projects the reconstructed characters, events, meanings. At the same time, however, semantic material within a literary text may refer or relate to External Fields of Reference (ExFiR).

3.5.1 ExFiRs are FiRs outside of an IFiR, i.e. Fields for which additional information may be obtained outside the given work of fiction. Such are names of cities and streets, historical characters, as well as generalizations about human nature, discussions of ideas, existentialism, psychoanalysis, etc. Such means, linking the IFiR with the external world, provide channels for the transfer of additional information into the IFiR. For example, *Paris, 1830* open up for the reader a store of information from outside the novel or story. They may also throw light on the status of the internal presentation: whether it is grotesque, ahistorical, socialist, etc.

3.5.2 An IFiR is parallel to an ExFiR as parallel lines that never meet would be. For example, the fictional characters live and act in New York in the 1970s but they can never meet people in New York outside of the novel nor can one move from the last day of the novel to a real day in time.

Yet, those are two parallel planes which have a number of points in common: 'shared referents' and 'shared FRs' (such as a New Year's Eve celebration in Times Square).

For the same reason, the characters may speak of events in the past or in the future which are shared by the IFiR and the ExFiR (e.g. *the Eisenhower years*). The relationship between the Internal and External FiR may be represented in the following diagram.

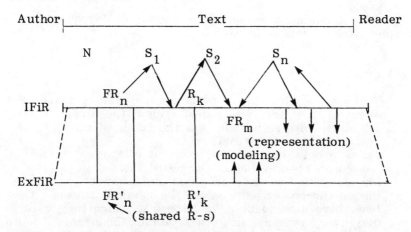

N: narrator   FR: Frame of Reference
S: speaker   IFiR: Internal Field of Reference
R: referent   ExFiR: External Field of Reference

3.5.3 The 'shared Rs' serve ᴜ; channels between the two parallel fields. To what extent semantic material should be transferred from one to the other depends on the specific components of both sides, is changing with different readers, and is a matter for an interpretation to argue.

3.5.4 In addition to the specific, direct referential relations between the two, there is a more cardinal relationship: IFiRs are 'modeled' upon ExFiRs (not necessarily realistic ones), and, in reverse, 'represent' them. But this is made through complex constructs of mutually adjusting abstractions, depending on conventions, historical poetics, etc.

3.6 Nevertheless, many texts that are not fictional, though claiming to have an External FiR, tend to create some autonomous FRs of their own. This is the function of a news 'story'. Though it claims to describe something in the real world, it often presents an individual scene, characters, intonations, voices, dialogue, which have an autonomous existence even if cut off from their factual background. Thus the reader does not really have to supply his own imaginary situations onto which new items of information would be added.

4. Integration of semantic material in a text

4.0 So far we have analyzed primarily short expressions, discussing the various uses of FRs and FiRs to which they relate. Speakers, however, tend to develop what they have to say about an FR throughout an unfolding text. The integration of material within texts will be demonstrated through some examples, leading up to a discussion of the structure of texts.

4.1 The following passage is the opening of Joyce's story, 'Eveline', from *The Dubliners*. [6]

(8) Eveline

> She sat at the window watching the evening invade the avenue. Her head was leaned against the window curtains, and in her nostrils was the odour of dusty cretonne. She was tired.
>
> Few people passed. The man out of the last house passed on his way home; she heard his footsteps clacking along the concrete pavement and afterwards crunching on the cinder path before the new red houses. One time there used to be a field there in which they used to play every evening with other people's children. Then a man from Belfast bought the field and built houses in it-- not like their little brown houses, but bright brick houses with shining roofs. The children of the avenue used to play together in that field--the Devines, the Waters, the Dunns, little Keogh the cripple, she and her brothers and sisters. Ernest, however, never played; he was too grown up. Her father used often to hunt them in out of the field with his blackthorn stick; but usually little Keogh used to keep nix and call out when he saw her father coming. Still they seemed to have been rather happy then. Her father was not so bad then; and besides, her mother was alive. That was a long time ago; she and her brothers and sisters were all grown up; her mother was dead. Tizzie Dunn was dead, too, and the Waters had gone back to England. Everything changes. Now she was going to go away like the others, to leave her home.
>
> Home! She looked round the room, reviewing all its familiar objects which she had dusted once a week for so many years, wondering where on earth all the dust came from.

4.1.1 In this passage, the writer presents us with a wealth of information and opens up quite a few patterns for possible development in the story: characters, relationships, times, etc.

Let us observe the presentation of one referent: the *new houses*. Bits of information about this referent are scattered throughout the passage, both directly and indirectly describing the new houses.

(8a) The new houses

Direct information:	Indirect information:
the last house	avenue
his home	
the new red houses	cinder path before [them] [◄ ► concrete pavement]
	there used to be a field [they played, children]
	a man from Belfast built [them]
bright brick houses with shining roofs	not like their little brown houses

4.1.2 For a full perception of what the houses are like, the reader has to collect the scattered elements in one pattern and integrate them with one another. The various attributes do not merely specify the house but qualify each other as well. For example, in the expression, *the new red houses*, the redness attains a particular tint and material quality characteristic of bricks, which is quite different, let us say, from the redness of wood. Furthermore, it is a bright redness, though both *bright* and *brick* are given in a later sentence (and it is only by a process of inference that we may assume that the *houses* are the same as in that previous sentence).

In a real life situation, pointing to the *new red houses* would provide the hearer with the additional information, namely, that it is the redness of bright bricks. Here the text is presented from the point of view of Eveline, an observer within such a situation for whom it is enough to note something known to her: *the new red houses*. The reader, however, does not know what Eveline can see and must obtain it from additional information scattered throughout the text.

One cannot convey in language the full particularity of objects. An illusion of particularity and specificity is created through the qualifying of category concepts. All we can say in this text is that *red* is qualified by *brick* and *bright*. The integration may be represented as in (8b).

(8b) red |brick |
         |bright |

Similarly, *new* is qualified in several ways: (1) the houses are new as opposed to what was there in the past--a field; (2) they are new houses as opposed to the old type of housing represented by her *little home*; (3) they are very new since only a cinder path rather than the concrete pavement leads to them.

The qualifications of the various properties can be represented in the (8c) diagram.

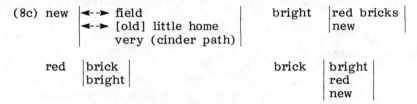

(8c) new   ◄--► field   bright | red bricks |
             ◄--► [old] little home | new |
             very (cinder path) |

red | brick   brick | bright |
       | bright | | red |
                                         | new |

4.1.3 A further interesting point: *red* and *brick*, though scattered in two sentences, when integrated create an image of 'redbrick housing'. 'Redbrick housing' conveys a whole social-cultural concept, reinforced in its 'foreignness' by such remarks in the text as that it was built by a man from Belfast and (in a later passage) is inhabited by Italian workers.

A further interpretation, integrating the redbrick housing with additional elements in the text, will present it as a 'new' and 'shining' intruder, 'invading' Eveline's world and representing her feeling that 'everything changes'.

4.1.4 The construct of the houses is, furthermore, used in the text for the construction of other semantic materials. Thus, the opposition, *houses* (in the present)--*field* (in the past) provides a motivation for the introduction of two extensions and the resultant opposition between Eveline's own present and past.

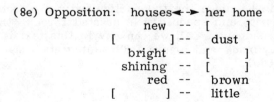

(8d) house   --► she, in home, today

      field   --► she in childhood

4.1.5 A further opposition is constructed between the 'houses' and Eveline's 'home'. (Only on one occasion is the word *home* used to designate the man's house.) Note the sparing use of attributes: almost no counterparts are given for any attributes, though they are obviously implied.

(8e) Opposition: houses◄--► her home
                      new   --   [   ]
              [   ] --   dust
             bright   --   [   ]
          shining   --   [   ]
              red   --   brown
        [   ] --   little

4.1.6 The carefully constructed house in this passage does not reappear in the story. It merely serves to make the concept of 'home' concrete by opposition. Indeed, *home*--the last word of the long second paragraph and the first word of the third--becomes the locus of the story and its symbolic center. The opposition of the 'positive' attributes of the 'shining' external world to the 'negative' attributes of the 'little' and dusty home is overturned in the course of the story, *home* being a more intimate place than *house*.

4.1.7 In the opening of this story, the house serves a function of 'referential grounding'. A secondary referent ('house') is established in the beginning of a text to develop on its basis a more central referent ('home'), continuing in the same FR, much as a secondary character is introduced at the beginning of a novel as a basis for the unfolding of the major characters.

4.1.8 Though some of the specific techniques as observed here may be conventions of literature, and the close and exhaustive attention to the details may be borrowed from literary interpretation, there is nothing literary about the semantic integration itself. We merely attended to a 'maximal reading' of the text. The technique of this very elementary example of semantic integration is valid for any text containing scattered elements for the presentation of one referent or one FR--be it stories, newspaper articles, or conversations into the night.

4.2 A less direct mode of integration may be observed in the pattern of repetition of the word *dust*. When it first appears, in the second sentence of the story, it is not part of any statement that the sentence makes; it is merely 'irrelevant' semantic material, emphasizing the concreteness of the description. However, when *dust* here is connected with the repetition of *dust* in the last sentence of the quoted passage, we understand the first *dust*, realizing that it expresses Eveline's revolt (apparently, she did not dust the house as she should have), as well as her helplessness vis-à-vis the decaying house (dust being both a symbol of disintegration and a Biblical allusion, reinforced by *where on earth all the dust came from*, alluding to 'from dust you come, and to dust you shall return').

4.2.1 Such reevaluation of former material from later material is well known in the structure of detective stories. It is true, however, for any semantic material dispersed throughout a text. This case is a typical instance of interpretation as practiced in readings of literature. It is however not a 'literary' form but a matter of 'understanding' literary texts as bodies of language. Such phenomena are to be found in everyday language as well, though less intensively. Thus, the use (or omission) of expressions in Soviet documents may be interpreted by Sovietologists

as indicating shifts in Soviet policies or attitudes, i.e. judged
in comparison with other texts.

4.3 As we see from these examples, elements in a text may
be linked discontinuously; this is true for semantic as well as
nonsemantic (e.g. sound) patterns. Indeed, the patterning of
any text is done on two levels: the Level of the Text-Continuum
and the Reconstructed Level. On the latter level we link up and
rearrange discontinuous elements in a text, according to their
inherent logic: time--in a chronological order, person--in a
psychological structure, and so on.

4.3.1 In this short opening of a story, a very complex state
of affairs is conveyed to the reader. On the Reconstructed
Level, we obtain a network of relationships, including: relations
in space, time, people, binary oppositions, point of view (combining the narrator's and Eveline's positions), as well as such
nonsemantic aspects as sound patterns:

Reconstructed level

Binary oppositions: People:
inside vs. outside   hostile father
dusty vs. shining   mother dead
home vs. house   brothers and sisters
present vs. past   neighborhood children (left)
grown-up vs. childhood
staying vs. leaving   Point of view:
                                   Eveline, embedded in Narrator
Space:
Dublin vs. Belfast   Referential grounding:
old homes vs. red-brick   House, E. sitting at window
    housing
                                   Sound-patterns
Time:
past vs. present vs. future

Rhetorical oppositions

This network of relationships as presented on the Reconstructed Level will be further filled in and enlarged in the
course of the story.

4.4 We may observe that neither the motif of dust nor the
house were introduced as subjects or topics of any sentence.
They may nevertheless become important, or even merely
thematized, on the Reconstructed Level.
We may observe how the text continuum led us to the
'houses'. The first sentence introduces 'evening'. This becomes a generalization (G_1) for which a detail (D_1) is provided:

'Few people passed'. Then a detail of this description ($D_1 = G_2$) is given: one man (D_2).

However, in a concrete description, if Eveline is observing the man, she must see or hear him in some concrete space: she hears his footsteps on the pavement, then on the path. Thus, we are led through a chain of concatenations: evening--few people--one man--walking--path, and the path leads to the houses. Thus, 'houses' are introduced not as a theme of any sentence or passage, but as a sixth element in a chain of extensions. In our reconstruction, however, it may become a primary topic.

4.4.1 Any word or connotation in a text may become thematized in this form in an interpretation and may attain a higher or lower place in an interpretive hierarchy.

4.4.2 A further example: the word *new* is introduced in the same sentence at an even lower level of thematic subordination: as an adjective in *the new red houses*.

The next sentence, however, does not develop the theme of Eveline's fatigue or of the evening nor of its subtheme, the passing man. It rather picks up the sub-subordinated word *new*, by way of semiotic opposition: 'one time there used to be a field there'. The word *new*, implying 'a shift from past to present', is decomposed into its components (past--present), presented in a reverse order. Thus, we moved from an FR in the present to an FR in the past through the semantic structure of a syntactically subordinated word.

4.4.3 To be sure, the leap from present to past based on an association from a secondary word is motivated in this text by Eveline's point of view. (We shall not go into an analysis here of how this point of view is constructed.) Eveline's being tired, her inward look (when the outside grew dark) and her stocktaking before leaving her home for good--all motivate the associative composition of this text, moving from present to past, from description to evaluation and vice-versa.

It must be noted that these qualities of Eveline are obtained by the reader as constructs except for the one direct observation, 'she was tired'.

4.4.4 Another telling example of the associative composition can be found in the transition from the second to the third paragraph of the story. After listing a number of people who had left her world since childhood (either dead or returned to England), the story tells us that 'now she was going to go away like the others, to leave her home'. *Home* is introduced as the necessary object of the verb *to leave*. The theme was 'leaving' rather than 'home'. But since all this is presented from within Eveline's consciousness, she responds with an association to the verbal element *home*; the next paragraph begins: 'Home! She looked round the room, reviewing all its familiar objects'.

From a paragraph centering in the past, we have shifted to a description of the interior of the house in the present. The shift occurred through one word, *home*, used in two different senses: the family framework and the physical house.

4.4.5 As we see, the Level of the Text Continuum is organized differently from the Reconstructed Level. The text continuum must provide ways of introducing new sentences and paragraphs, either through syntactic or semantic links. Eventually, all the material necessary for the Reconstructed Level will be provided (and the state of affairs conveyed), but only part of it is given explicitly in direct statements.

4.5 The semantic organization of the text continuum is a highly complex matter, which we cannot discuss here. Many semantic constructs from the reconstructed level are used for linking in the text continuum. A few examples are given here.

4.5.1 The first sentence is linked by the pronoun *she* to the title 'Eveline'. (It is also linked to the title by the sound cluster: EVEline--EVENINg--INVade--AVENue.)

The second sentence is linked to the first by the pronoun *her* but also by a double G:D relationship (Generalization: Detail): her leaning head is a detail (D_1) of Eveline's sitting and watching (G_1); the nostrils (D_2) a detail of her head (G_2).

The third sentence, *She was tired*, is linked through the pronoun and anaphora. It is also a generalization (G_3) of the previous sentence, though abstracting a different quality (from 'the leaning head') than the generalization which preceded the same sentence (*she sat at the window*). An interpretation may further generalize from the same second sentence as presenting Eveline in a sensuous rather than a rational mood (G_4).

In a simplified manner, we may represent it thus:

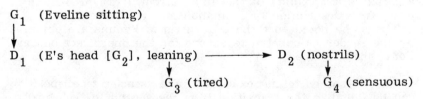

G_1 (Eveline sitting)

D_1 (E's head [G_2], leaning) $\longrightarrow$ D_2 (nostrils)

G_3 (tired) G_4 (sensuous)

4.5.2 The next sentence, however, *Few people passed*, has no direct link to the sentence preceding it. A reader must construct a link within the given FR to connect it with discontinuous elements in the preceding text. Indeed, it is both an example of the evening and the object of Eveline's 'watching'.

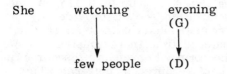

She   watching   evening
(G)

few people   (D)

4.5.3 Here is a schematized diagram of the major links in the text continuum of the whole passage.

Concatenation in text continuum:

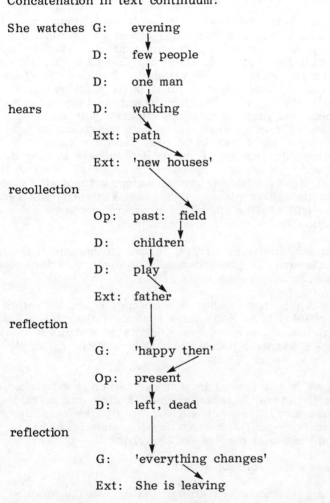

She watches   G: evening

D: few people

D: one man

hears   D: walking

Ext: path

Ext: 'new houses'

recollection

Op: past: field

D: children

D: play

Ext: father

reflection

G: 'happy then'

Op: present

D: left, dead

reflection

G: 'everything changes'

Ext: She is leaving

Ext: extension   Slanted arrows represent shifts to
D: detail   other FRs
G: generalization
Op: opposition

4.5.4 Though it would seem that the chain of linking in the text continuum is the primary level--indeed, it provides the 'floor' from which the FR is reconstructed--it in itself cannot be constituted without some material from those constructs. We cannot possibly account for the composition of any discourse on the Text Continuum Level without recourse to patterns which this level uses from the Reconstructed Level. Such are divisions of texts into thematic subunits, speakers, summary and details, etc. In short, the patterning on both levels must go hand in hand.

4.6 As we see from the 'Eveline' example, a sentence cannot be identified with one unit of meaning; almost every word or connotation may be linked with pertinent semantic material elsewhere in the text into patterns, which may then be summarized in sentences on the level of interpretation. Furthermore, texts intend to convey not one theme or idea, but multidimensional states of affairs. We cannot possibly decompose them into separate aspects and present each one separately in a text (though we can do it in an analysis). It is impossible to describe an event without providing some semantic material about its participants; chains-of-events sentences are made up by narratologists and are not typical for real texts. And so it is impossible to describe a character in action without the space in which the action takes place. Thus, any sentence--and certainly any FR--will provide material for several semantic patterns, in addition to its direct predications.

4.6.1 Moreover, involving several themes in one sentence is a favorable technique, in journalism as in literature. Here, for example, is a sentence from a news article.

(9) Miss Schimpf, whose father is a butcher in an A&P store in Lima, Ohio, is in many ways typical of the 12,300,000 undergraduates and graduate students on campuses today. ('College Students Squeezed into Career Paths', *The New York Times*, March 7, 1982)

Clearly, Miss S. is not typical in that her father is a butcher. The syntactic structure, if taken as one meaning-unit, would provide an absurdity. To understand properly, we must decompose the sentence and link each thematic element with further relevant material dispersed throughout the article.

5. The three dimensions of a text

5.0 Meanings are conveyed through texts. As I mentioned earlier (2.0.1), the structure of meanings is not identical with the structure of texts.

I use a three-dimensional model for the description of texts.
Since this part of the theory has been explained elsewhere
(Hrushovski 1979), I merely outline it briefly here.

5.1 As we saw in the 'Eveline' example, the perception of a
text involves patterning on two levels: the text continuum and
the reconstructed level. The patterns on both levels may be
separated into three dimensions, three complex constructs abstracted from the same text.

(A) The Dimension of Speech and Position
(B) The Dimension of Meaning and Reference
(C) The Dimension of the Organized Text

The dimensions are intertwined in a text and interdependent;
nevertheless they require separate construction and separate
methods for their description.

5.1.1 The Dimension of Meaning and Reference is constructed
along the lines I have discussed. It is important to note that
we do not necessarily have in a text an exhaustive list of
definite meanings and references. Even a literary text does
not provide a fixed 'possible world'. We have rather FiRs and
FRs (some--uncertain) in which there is a number of potentially possible and interpretation-dependent references, descriptions, and meanings.

5.2 There is, however, no information about real or fictional
FRs which is neutrally given. All information that we have
(perhaps with the exception of some immediate sense-data) is
mediated through various sources: speakers, creators of texts,
ideological or emotive positions, cultural attitudes. This spans
all we have absorbed about the world--from our mother to the
latest news report. In literary texts, our information about the
'fictional world' (in the IFiR) is mediated through the nature of
the narrator and the positions of various characters, and is
often not resolvable in one definite 'meaning'. This phenomenon
was discussed especially by M. Bakhtin, though his concept of
'polyphony' should not be restricted to Dostoevsky.

5.2.1 The mediation of information through sources is typical
of news reports as well. An example can be cited from a news
article in *The New York Times* (Oct. 23, 1977) about the SALT
negotiations between the United States and the Soviet Union.
At first glance, the reader gets an optimistic view. The
three stages of the title, however, contradict each other in
turn. The reader gets a long series of summarizing remarks
and direct quotes in a wavering pattern of optimistic and qualifying or detracting views. These views are further qualified
by such expressions as: *a breakthrough was apparently
achieved, an accord was probably unlikely before early next
year, but ... it was virtually certain.* The most optimistic

direct quote is from President Carter's speech in Des Moines, predicting *that within a few weeks we will have a SALT agreement that will be the pride of this country*; but, as the article tells us, Mr. Carter later qualified his remarks saying that *I don't know how many weeks it will take ... I think we've got a good prospect, but it's not firmed up yet. That's all I can say.*

5.2.2 The reader got a variety of sources: quotes from Carter's and Brezhnev's statements (however, selected by the author of the article); various sources close to the negotiations, described as *reports of major progress, details have been circulating in Washington*, or, more directly: *high-ranking administration officials* who held a special briefing for reporters. On the other hand, *one official* contradicted the reports.

We have direct quotes and specific details as well as summarizing generalizations such as the author's own statements about *optimistic remarks by President Carter* and *reports of major progress.*

The reader will further qualify Carter's remarks by the circumstances in which they were made: in a political speech in a remote place.

5.2.3 All this contradictory network of concrete details and assumptions is mediated again through three additional positions: that of the journalist, Bernard Gwertzman; the genre of a summarizing news article; *The New York Times.* Readers may be used to this newspaper and accept its reports as the truth, thereby neutralizing the three framing positions; but a comparison with other sources of information may show discrepancies.

5.2.4 This is by no means an unusual way of telling about a state of affairs. A person describing his or her mother may provide the listener with a similar medley of details, anecdotes, and generalizations; understanding involves not taking any single generalization about the mother's character or relationship separately from the other materials relating to the same FR. Many things that we want to say we are simply not capable of saying in one, definite statement.

5.3 The truth-value, weight of evidence, irony, exaggerations, circumstantial limitations, ideological bias, etc., of statements must be adjudged by the understander from what he knows about the speaker, the producer of a text or its genre.

The speaker's position, however, is not always given explicitly. Quite often, it must be reconstructed by the understander (using the understander's own limitations of knowledge and ideological bias) from the material at hand as well as from external information. Thus, in the journalist's remarks about the Administration's opinion, the reader has to sort out what elements reflect the journalist's position and which ones reflect the Administration. A sentence may be judged ironic when compared to external knowledge about the same FR or when the speaker's attitude is assessed (e.g. if he is Art Buchwald).

5.4 The meaning of an utterance ('speaker's meaning') is thus a result of processing the level of sense in relation to the FR, on the one hand, and to the constructed speaker's position, on the other.

5.4.1 The speaker himself, however, is a construct from the FR in which he is embedded. This is clear especially in fiction. It is not true, as some narratological models would have it, that there is a separate story and a separate narrator outside of it, presenting it. Actually, information about the world of a story is processed not only through a narrator (if he exists) but through the speech and consciousness of all characters and observers in the text. They, in turn, are themselves constructs built from the FRs in which they emerge.

Thus, a 'circularity' or interdependence occurs: we believe a character's words if he himself is believable; if the words, however, turn out to be partial or manipulative, we are forced to revise our image of the character himself.

5.4.2 This interdependence can be schematically represented in the following diagram (where S is a speaker and the text may start either with a speaker/narrator or with an 'objective' presentation of an FR).

Dimension A		S_1		S_2		S_3		S_4	
Dimension B	(FR)		FR		FR		FR		FR

5.5 Of special interest are dialogues or 'talk', in literature as well as in life. The interlocutors talk about things in an external FR_1 (or leap from one FR to another). At the same time, the speech situation itself constitutes an FR_2 which may be different from FR_1. The interlocutors may switch from their topic (FR_1) directly to their speech situation (FR_2). Moreover, their expressions about FR_1 reflect back on their positions within FR_2.

Thus, two Americans arguing in the sixties about the war in Vietnam refer directly to Vietnam but their words 'boomerang' and characterize at the same time the speakers themselves, their political and emotional attitudes.

5.5.1 Indeed, quite often talk 'about' things contributes less to those things than to the characterization and expression of the speakers themselves. This is certainly true for 'small talk'.

FR_2 ('talk') S_1 S_2

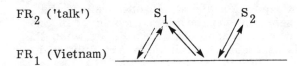

FR_1 (Vietnam) _____

This double structure is further complicated by the reflections of talk on the speakers' personalities beyond the given speech situation (S_1 = FR_3; S_2 = FR_4, with extensions in time beyond the speech situation).

5.5.2 The uses of the double level structure of talk are many. One most important use is for the composition of texts. A speaker may leap--in his words, in his consciousness, or in his analogies and generalizations--from one FR in time and space to another, thus spanning a vast field of experience.

5.6 I do not discuss here the third dimension, the Organi- zation of the Text. The order, rhythm, symmetries, and over- all structure of any text are of great importance, especially in their rhetorical and aesthetic functions. Sound patterns, repetition, segmentation, breaking up the information in stages, manipulations of the reader's attention, etc., are pertinent to literary and nonliterary texts (though essential to and often formalized in the former). Since no complex of meanings can be presented at once, the ordering of information, the shifts in attitude, and the detailing may affect the perception and the meaning of the text itself.

5.7 The organization of the text, in turn, employs patterns from the other two dimensions. Thus, along with such formal segmentation as divisions into strophes, chapters, paragraphs, or the use of titles and subtitles, the segmentation of texts may be based on thematic (sub-) divisions, distinctions between speakers (e.g. this is the normal technique for separating scenes in a drama), and an editor's (or narrator's) logical or rhetorical structuring of a text (e.g. summarizing an article in the first paragraph or bringing an effective anecdote up front).

6. Summary. We may now recapitulate the general frame- work for integrational semantics.
A text (as any other semiotic object) is patterned in three dimensions. Though autonomous, they are interlaced in the text; and they interact in such a way that patterns of one dimension may be used by the other or 'translated' onto it.
The second Dimension, of Meaning and Reference, is in turn constituted as a three-story construct. The elements of each story rely on outside authorities: the story of Regulating Principles is constructed from the Dimension of Speakers and Positions; the story of sense--from the 'language'; the story of FiR and FRs--from the 'World'.

The two schemes are analogous. The third levels, however, are not related to each other. In the domain of Meaning it is a 'map' of (a segment from) the 'World'; in the domain of the Text it is the structure of the autonomous textual object, on which the whole complex is based.

Text   Meaning

Dimension
  A: Speaker & Position
                        RP

  B: Meaning & Reference — sense ←——— language

                      FiR (FR) ←——— World

  C: Organized Text

NOTES

This paper was written at the National Humanities Center in North Carolina. My thanks are due to the Center for enabling me to follow such theoretical pursuits and, in particular, to Karen Carroll for her help in bringing the manuscript to its proper shape.

1. The ideas outlined in this theory were developed in the 1960s. At that time formal linguists would hardly listen to theories involving interpretation, considering interaction and understanding, and responding to the complexities of literary texts. Weinreich tried to implement some of my ideas, e.g. his 'transfer features', to the extent that they were 'formalizable' (see note 3).

2. See, for example, Reinhart (1980) and the excellent survey by de Beaugrand (1980).

3. Weinreich wrote in 1966: 'The fresh turn which this work has taken was due, above all, to three stimuli. The first was a realization, stemming from conversations with Benjamin Hrushovski, that a semantic theory is of marginal interest if it is incapable of dealing with poetic uses of language, and more generally, with interpretable deviance' (Weinreich 1980:188-189).

4. I mentioned this example in 1979 (also discussed by Reinhart), but only here is a full analysis given.

5. For a more detailed discussion, cf. Hrushovski (forthcoming b).

6. From 'Eveline' from *Dubliners* by James Joyce. Originally published in 1916 by B. W. Huebsch. Definitive text copyright © 1967 by the estate of James Joyce. Reprinted by permission of Viking Penguin Inc.

REFERENCES

Caton, Charles E. 1971. Overview: Philosophy. In: Semantics. Edited by Danny D. Steinberg and Leon A. Jakobovits. London, New York: Cambridge University Press.

De Beaugrand, Robert. 1980. Text, discourse and process. Norwood, N.J.: Ablex.

Hrushovski, Benjamin. 1976. Segmentation and motivation in the text continuum of literary prose, = Papers on Poetics and Semiotics, No. 5. Tel-Aviv: Tel-Aviv University.

Hrushovski, Benjamin. 1979. The structure of semiotic objects: A three-dimensional model. Poetics Today 1.1-2: 365-376. Also in The sign in music and literature. Edited by Wendy Steiner. Austin: University of Texas Press, 1981.

Hrushovski, Benjamin. 1980. The meaning of sound patterns in poetry: An interaction theory. Poetics Today 2.1a:39-56.

Hrushovski, Benjamin. (forthcoming a) Poetic metaphor and frames of reference. Poetics Today.

Hrushovski, Benjamin. (forthcoming b) Fictionality and fields of reference. Harvard Symposium.

Hrushovski, Benjamin, and Ziva Ben-Porath. 1974. Principles of a unified theory of the literary text. In: Structuralist poetics in Israel, = Papers on Poetics and Semiotics No. 1. Tel-Aviv: Tel-Aviv University.

Katz, Jerrold J. 1972. Semantic theory. New York: Harper and Row.

Reinhart, Tanya. 1980. Conditions for text coherence. Poetics Today 1.4:161-180.

Weinreich, Uriel. 1980. Explorations in semantic theory. In: On Semantics. Philadelphia: University of Pennsylvania Press.

THE LANGUAGE APRIORI:
A CONTRIBUTION OF HUMBOLDTIAN LINGUISTICS
TO THE THEORY OF COGNITION

Helmut Gipper
University of Münster

In the 1920s Bloomfield presented a new program for linguistics as a science. He sought to liberate linguistics from the domination of other disciplines such as psychology and anthropology, and to make it an autonomous science. His aim was to attain the exactness of physics and to replace all mentalistic concepts by physical terms.

His philosophical background was a behavioristic and neopositivistic one. His authorities were Albert Paul Weiss, Max F. Meyer, and J. P. Pavlov. On the grounds of their scientific convictions, Bloomfield made the following prediction (1935:89):

> The terminology in which at present we try to speak of
> human affairs--the terminology of 'consciousness', 'mind',
> 'perception', 'ideas', and so on--in sum, the terminology
> of mentalism and animism--will be discarded, much as we
> have discarded Ptolemaic astronomy and will be replaced
> in minor part by physiological terms and in major part by
> terms of linguistics.

His main model for linguistic description was that of stimulus-response. Linguistic analysis had to be concentrated on the phonological and morphological aspect of language, that is, on the outward form, the noises uttered by speakers and the responses that followed these stimuli. The existence of meaning was not denied but it was not thought of as a main subject of linguistics. Through the influence of Bloomfield's proposals, American linguistics developed a theory and a corresponding method of description called taxonomic structuralism. This kind of linguistic science can be characterized as behavioristic and antimentalistic in its theoretical and philosophical essence.

191

The success of Bloomfieldian structuralism is well known, and its limitations have become evident in recent years. The consequent neglect of the meaning problem proved pernicious. Central problems of linguistics and of human behavior and conduct, such as the interrelationship between thinking and speaking, between language and knowledge, could not be solved under these conditions. This failure was predictable. Jakobson's dictum has proved correct: linguistics without meaning is meaningless.

At the same time, another famous American linguist proposed a rather different program. Sapir (1929) stated that linguistics cannot be considered as an autonomous discipline but that it is deeply interrelated with neighboring sciences such as anthropology, ethnology, psychology, and sociology. For Sapir, linguistics is a symbolic guide to culture and to the interpretation of human conduct in general.

The following passage is of utmost importance for my main topic and for the proposals I want to make here. Sapir says (1929:209):

Language is a guide to 'social reality'. Though language is not ordinarily thought of as of essential interest to the students of social science, it powerfully conditions all our thinking about social problems and processes. Human beings do not live in the objective world alone, nor alone in the world of social activity as ordinarily understood, but are very much at the mercy of the particular language which has become the medium of expression for their society. It is quite an illusion to imagine that one adjusts to reality essentially without the use of language and that language is merely an incidental means of solving specific problems of communication or reflection. The fact of the matter is that the 'real world' is to a large extent unconsciously built up on the language habits of the group. No two languages are ever sufficiently similar to be considered as representing the same social reality. The worlds in which different societies live are distinct worlds, not merely the same world with different labels attached.

Everyone who is at all familiar with the European history of the philosophy of language recognizes immediately that these ideas very much resemble those which were expressed by Wilhelm von Humboldt a hundred years earlier.

Sapir's problem was followed and in some respect realized by his disciple Whorf, whose studies in the Hopi language greatly influenced his theory of knowledge. In 1940, Whorf declared that human thinking depends on the grammar or structure of the natural languages. People with different mother tongues think in different ways. He stated that there is a linguistic relativity principle.[1] But this idea was not a completely new one, either. Humboldt had expressed exactly the same thought in different words.

In the last 25 years, I have tried to verify Whorf's statements and postulates concerning the conception of space and time in Hopi. Gipper (1972) presents my findings.[2]

With Sapir and Whorf, semantics and the meaning problem were reintroduced into linguistics. In Germany, the so-called Sprachinhaltsforschung follows the road opened by Humboldt, with Weisgerber as its leading proponent.[3]

It is the direction of Sprachinhaltsforschung that I want to take here. Before doing so, I ought to refer--although very briefly--to Chomsky, who made another turn from antimentalistic structuralism to mentalistic generative grammar. Chomsky's decisive premise was the indisputable fact that every 'competent' speaker of a language, that is, everyone who has learned a language as his native tongue, is able to create--that is, to generate--an unlimited number of sentences he has never uttered before; likewise, as a listener, he can understand an unlimited number of sentences he has never heard before. In order to explain this astounding fact, one must answer the question of how the faculty of language, including the accomplishments just mentioned, is acquired. It is therefore necessary to refer to the process of language acquisition. Chomsky, in attempting to lay the philosophical and linguistic foundations of his theory, referred to the maxims of Cartesian philosophy (Chomsky 1977), especially the concept proposed by Leibniz, of 'idées innées', that is, the innate 'eingeborenen' ideas, although in fact, both these philosophers meant something quite different from Chomsky. In order to verify or disprove Chomsky's theory, we need a systematic comparative linguistic analysis of the process of language acquisition in the child. But this has not yet been accomplished.

But what about the 'innate ideas' in Chomsky's theory? It is his conviction that learning a language is not possible without innate faculties which enable the infant to acquire the language and to become a competent speaker. What is--exactly and precisely--'innate'? Saussure introduced the expression 'faculté du langage', that is to say, the faculty of language is innate; the concrete language, 'la langue', has to be learned completely. Chomsky (1967) goes further than that: for him, not only is the faculty of language learning inborn but linguistic universals, even a universal linguistic structure, are given before the processes of language acquisition start.

It is not yet possible to verify this very bold hypothesis. We do not even know the languages of the world well enough to be able to say what they really have in common. We can postulate universal traits on a fundamental, basic level, and we can state that all languages are sound languages, systems of signs for expressing and communicating meanings. And we can postulate universals on a very high level of abstraction and say that in each given language something can be predicated of something by means of certain categories. 'Speaking' means speaking about something to someone, and so on. But in real life, the linguist is confronted with an enormous variety of living linguistic structures between the basic and the abstract level just mentioned which are little known, even superficially. A child without a speaking environment of competent speakers of one of these natural languages will never develop such categories of its own: it will instead starve and die, as was demonstrated in the Middle Ages by the famous experiment of King Frederic II, of the Staufer dynasty. At any rate, Chomsky's innate linguistic universals cannot be proved in the near future.

Now let us delve somewhat more deeply into the central problem of cognition and let us ask what role language is supposed to play in it.

To make cognition--that is, man's knowledge of the world--possible, we have to imagine a model with at least two poles: the subjective pole of the human observer and the objective pole of the external world, in the broadest sense of the term.

Furthermore, we need a community of other observers linked together by the same means of communication and able to exchange their observations and to check them in mutual discourse and reflection. But the central position in our model must be assigned to the subjective pole, the human observer. Is he only a mirror of the external world, which is given to him via the senses, or does he take an active role in the play? We now know that Locke's position is untenable. Man's mind is not, as he supposed, a tabula rasa on which experience writes its data in the form of sensual impressions. The fact that the mind is able to do something with these first sensual impressions or simple ideas, as Locke calls them, contradicts his own premises. [4] At least the faculty of making complex ideas out of simple ideas and thus arriving at knowledge and cognition must be given, must be 'innate'.

We know that Kant proposed another solution of the problem: he made the subjective pole of cognition the master of the scene and endowed man's mind with faculties which not only enable him to have experiences and to know the outward world, but which determine the kind of experiences he will be able to have.

Here Kant's concept of a priori must be taken into account. For the sake of a better understanding of his position, I quote a decisive passage from the introduction of his *Critique of Pure Reason*: [5]

Although all our knowledge begins with experience, it does not follow that it arises entirely from experience. For it is quite possible that our empirical knowledge is a compound of that which we receive through impressions and that which our own faculty of knowing (incited by impressions) supplies from itself--a supplement to impressions which we do not distinguish from that raw material (i.e. impressions) until

long practice has roused our attention and rendered us
capable of separating one from the other. Hitherto it has
been supposed that all our knowledge must conform to the
objects, but, under that supposition, all attempts to establish any knowledge about them *a priori*, have come to
nothing. The experiment therefore ought to be made,
whether we should not succeed better by assuming that
objects must conform to our forms of knowledge. For this
would agree better with the required possibility of an
a priori knowledge of objects; that is, with the possibility
of settling something about those objects before they are
given us in experience.

We realize, then, the forms of possible knowledge are given.
These forms are the forms of perception, space and time, the
categories of understanding (quantity, quality, relation, and
modality), and the ideas of reason (self, universe, and God).
Language is not mentioned by Kant. We may ask: are categories and ideas possible without language? The answer is:
definitely not. We cannot think of concepts, categories, and
ideas in the proper sense of these words, but only in and with
language. Therefore language is to be considered as another
fundamental precondition for the human way of abstracting and
generalizing thinking, of knowledge and cognition. For this
reason I propose the postulation of a 'language apriori' in
order to give epistemology a sound base and foundation. In
doing so, I realize the difficulties which arise immediately.
Language has to be learned after man's birth and it is learned
by experience and in contact with the speaking community.
And in this case, Kant's apriori is not applicable.
But what about the status of Kant's conditions? Where and
when are they given? The only possibility of maintaining his
position would be to add expressly: these conditions are given
by birth, they are inborn or innate. But in this case, the
following difficulty arises: we all know that man is born in an
immature, fragile state. Physiologically speaking, he is a pre-
mature being. His brain is by no means fully developed. The
number of neurons is almost complete, but the important net of
dendrites, axons, and synapses which makes the whole a functioning system is still missing. In the first two years, the
weight of the brain increases by 350 percent.[6] During this time
the neuronal network is built up. The infant becomes capable
of using his senses; he acquires the forms of sensibility which
constitute the essence of Kant's apriori. But this phase of postnatal evolution is, of course, intimately linked with experience;
therefore Kant's apriori are not 'pure' in the sense he postulates in the *Critique of Pure Reason*. In his standard work,
Kant does not use the expression 'angeboren', innate or inborn,
and the interpreters of his philosophy even denied that he had
this concept in mind. But in 1790, nine years after the first

edition of the *Critique*, Kant had to defend his theory against
a colleague from Halle, Professor Eberhard, and then he stated
expressly: at least the faculty (of the apriori!) must be
'angeboren' (innate).[7] We now must add: this applies to the
faculty (in a nutshell!), but not to the functioning form! The
latter grows up and emerges in a postnatal phase of development: that is, it is dyed and tinged with experience. Even
more: without experience it does not develop at all, it
perishes.

Consequently, we can say: Kant's other apriori are not
'pure', either. Nevertheless, we are fully entitled to postulate:
they are and remain the preconditions of that special kind of
experience mankind is able to have. And the same is valid for
language. Though it is only the faculty of language which is
inborn, that is, given by birth, and though the concrete language has to be in toto learned afterward, the fact remains
undeniable: it is the fundamental precondition, the 'condition
of possibility' of human thinking and knowledge. It is in that
sense that I want to preserve the proposed concept 'language
apriori'.

At this point the central question arises: how does the language apriori come about? How does a human being acquire
his mother tongue and become a competent speaker of that language? The answer to the fundamental question of how a child
acquires his native language and thus acquires the capacity to
conquer, conceptually and mentally, his world of experience, is
of interest not only to linguists but to all human sciences.
Neo-Humboldtian linguistics, which is based on Humboldt's concept of language, regards this question as central to its research. That is why I have been working for about 12 years
on a plan for an 'evolutive grammar'. I presented it for the
first time at the German Philosophy Congress at Düsseldorf
in 1969 and also lectured on the subject at the University of
London in 1977.[8]

By 'evolutive grammar' I mean a global description of the
process of language learning encompassing all aspects and levels
of language. A global view means that, in addition to the phonetic, morphological, and syntactic level, the total vocabulary
must be included. I have chosen the expression 'evolutive' for
this kind of grammar because it also allows for the accompanying
biological--or more specifically, neurophysiological--processes.
This neurophysiological aspect must be taken into consideration
since it can give important insights into the possibilities and
limitations of language acquisition at various levels.

As I have mentioned, the enormous postnatal development of
the human brain is very important for the different stages of
language acquisition. More precisely, we now can say that
'evolutive grammar' means the exhaustive description of the
process of child language acquisition based on generalizable
aspects of empirical data. We are looking for a common denominator extractable from many individual cases, a denominator

which can be considered as representative of a particular language--in this case, the German language.

The next problem that presents itself is the method to be utilized. By what method can one adequately describe a learning process that lasts at least 14 to 16 years? We are confronted here with the old question of how one can describe changes in time which take place within complex structures. How can the sequence be appropriately accounted for?

Here I would like to follow the path already taken by Trier (1931), the founder of the study of semantic fields, 'Wortfeld-Forschung'. He researched the sphere of German vocabulary concerned with knowledge, skill, and understanding, and at the same time he showed how a linguistic field changes. Trier chose several historical states of the language, analyzed each synchronically, and then compared them with one another. Evolutive grammar should be dealt with in precisely this manner. From the beginning of vocalization--that is, from birth--synchronic cuts should be made during different phases of the child's sound and language development. These various stages should be described by means of what we might call 'cross-sectional' grammars. Now the question arises as to how many cross-sections are necessary and at what time intervals they must be made in order to provide real insight into language processes. The insights of linguistics, developmental psychology, and neurophysiology must all be taken into consideration.

Language development is certainly not even and continuous, but rather occurs in spurts that alternate with periods of bodily development. Therefore the stages of development that are characteristic for language acquisition must first of all be determined. Lenneberg, after an extensive survey of the literature on the subject, suggests that (1) actual language development begins at age two; (2) the most effective period of learning lies between the second and third year of life; (3) the child has mastered the underlying principles of its native language by age four and that, (4) after the twelfth or thirteenth year, that is, after puberty, usually no advancement in language acquisition can be noted (Lenneberg 1967:59-67). We can accept these statements only with great skepticism.

We may assume that the first stages are fundamental and therefore demand our special attention. This certainly applies to the first three years of life. We must pay precise attention not only to the phenomenon of crying, in which one can soon recognize emotional, expressive, and communicative intentions. We must also consider the so-called babbling phase, which is generally regarded as merely a phase during which various possible types of vocalization are tried out and playfully practiced without the intention of communicating. Here one should already be on the lookout for the beginnings of linguistic structure. The first connections between sound and meaning are of decisive importance, and I mean not just onomatopoetic constructions but also the association of semantic contents with spontaneous intentional utterances in general.

We are dealing with the conception and creation of that which we generally understand as the linguistic sign. We should devote special attention to the intentional use of such utterances which have the potential of soon developing into meaningful utterances, because these are the beginnings of language acquisition. Sounds used for survival, spontaneous expression, and contact with the language-speaking environment become linguistically meaningful and enable the child to make utterances of various kinds. This process must be registered in minute detail. Quite a few cross-sections would be necessary for the first three years of life, during which the transition from one-word to two-word and multiple-word utterances should be carefully noted. Subsequent cuts could probably be spaced further apart in time. Conceivably, we would have to make at least 10 to 15 cross-sections before the end of puberty at the age of 14 to 16. However, we are limited by the difference between what is desirable and what can be accomplished in practice. As things stand, only a limited research project is possible for our small team, partly because of the lack of adequate funding, and compromise will be unavoidable for certain technical reasons.

Thus far, the research project is completed for the first three years of life. More than 100 children have been observed by their parents with the guidance and assistance of my students. The parents kept a record of all that happened with their child linguistically during that time. Particular attention was paid to the occurrence of the first meaningful sounds or words and the special situation in which these first speech acts took place. The appearance of the first 'sentences', one word, two words, and so on, was noted, as well as the intention with which they were uttered (appeal, expression, question, etc.).

What we wanted to find out was how a linguistic view of the world ('sprachliche Weltansicht'), in Humboldt's sense of the term, is acquired. By 'linguistic view of the world' I mean the organization of the meanings of words in order to verbalize the phenomena of the external world of experience as well as the internal world of feelings and sensations (Gipper 1978).

Each language is supposed to transform the views and experiences of the language community into mental or conceptual fields of lexemes or words. Here I refer to the theory of linguistic fields set up by Trier and Weisgerber in the thirties. Examples of such fields are the fields of words for plants, for animals, for kinship terms, for color terms, for abstract terms in the area of moral and ethical thinking, etc.

The vocabulary has to be learned, of course, step by step. One starting-point may be some sound sequence uttered by the child spontaneously and without any specific intention. Jakobson (1968) stated that the first syllables generated by infants always have the structure consonant plus vowel, and those consonants and vowels occur first which are produced with the

greatest ease, for example: *b, p, m, n, d, t, g, k,* and
a, e, i, o, u.

I want to profit from Jakobson's considerations and to extend
his phonological data into the domain of semantics. The first
human sound sequences produced by the child, such as
mamama, papapa, etc. which are initially meaningless, attract
and acquire the meaning which is given to them by adults.
So the first, still meaningless *mamama* receives the meaning that
the speech community has already attached to this utterance.
In German, and in English, too, this is 'mother', although in
other languages it may have other meanings; but all of these
have close ties with an infant's world of experience, for instance, Latin *mamma* 'mother's breast', Spanish *mamar* 'to breast
feed', Japanese *mama* 'to eat', etc. As soon as the child's
spontaneous utterance produces the first practical results (for
example, causing the mother to appear), the already existing
bodily and emotional contact with the mother is effectively com-
plemented in a specific human way through the contact of language. When the association of sound and meaning first becomes
firmly fixed, the first linguistic sign, in Saussure's sense of
the term, becomes established. This is the first word and it
already has the character of a sentence or predication.

It is to be expected that there might also be languages in
which the first *mama* attracts the meaning of father, if the
speech community wants it this way. I had been looking for
such a language for several years and was very happy when a
Georgian linguist, G. Ramishwili, told me that in Georgian *mama*
means father, whereas *deda* is the word for mother. Intonation
can provide these signs with an expressive significance which
can be imperative, contact-seeking, interrogative, or summoning,
depending on the meaning the partner gives it. Using an expression of the psychologist Spitz (1973), one can talk about a
'global word', which still contains several linguistic functions
together in a nutshell. In this way, the word and the sentence
are shown to evolve from a common root. If shortly thereafter
papa, which is phonetically different, is learned and becomes
specialized to the meaning of 'father', this indicates the formation of a first linguistic field, the field of kinship terminology.

In this way, about 24 fields are built up in the first three
years (Gipper 1979). As a rule, a child learns to apply a certain vocalization to a particular extralinguistic phenomenon (for
example, the vocalization *bow wow* is used to refer to a dog)
and it seems convenient to use this vocalization for creatures
that are or seem similar to a dog. In this way, the utterance
bow wow can take on the meaning of 'a four-legged animal of a
certain size', and so a class is formed, to which cats and other
animals also belong. This oversized category is then divided
into smaller classes by the acquisition of new terms, such as
meow for cats, etc., in such a way that the valid rules of
usage and the limitations of the adult language are gradually
learned. The acquisition of generic terms frequently precedes

the acquisition of the more specific 'names' of species, for
example, *flower* is acquired before *rose, carnation,* etc.

We can now demonstrate the evolution of every lexical field
in the form of diagrams which clearly show the special starting-
point, the subsequent splitting up of concepts, and the process
of differentiation up to the point where the final structure of
the field is nearly completed.

In Münster there is a plexiglass model which gives an excellent picture of the whole process.[9] Imagine a soap bubble or
balloon. Before we fill it with air or gas, we are, analogically,
at the starting-point zero, the day of the child's birth. The
child grows up, the bubble or balloon grows larger. Through
experience and contact with the speaking environment, the
infant's bubble or balloon world grows steadily in all directions.
At the end of the first year, the first meaningful sounds and
words emerge. Now the globe has reached a certain circum-
ference. We can register the acquired words on the surface
area of the one-year globe, and by doing this we obtain a
survey and synopsis of the vocabulary reached at this stage.
Development continues: our globe enlarges, and at the end
of the second year the radius of the sphere has doubled in
size. On the surface of the two-year globe about 16 lexical
fields are recognized. Continuing in this fashion, we find
about 24 fields on the surface of the three-year globe, a vocabulary which enables the child to speak about all things of interest to him and which makes possible extensive communication
with the language community.

The child now has acquired the fundamental structure of his
mother tongue's view of the world. No essential area is missing;
all that will follow during the coming years is extension, ampli-
fication, and completion of this nucleus. The basic structure
of the house is given.

If we divide this globe into two halves at any point and look
at one of the circles now visible, we see the corresponding
diagram of that part of the vocabulary which has been cut open.
For the problem of cognition, the parts of vocabulary growth
that are of special interest are those which demonstrate the
emergence of concepts that are essentials of knowledge. I
mention only the emergence of the concept 'I', which is at the
basis of self-knowledge and consciousness of self, and the verb
to be, which is necessary for certain fundamental forms of
predication in Indo-European languages.

Descartes' *je pense donc je suis*, which has been translated by
Etienne de Courcelles into the famous *ego cogito ergo sum* (a
translation which is, by the way, somewhat unusual Classical
Latin!) is a maxim which cannot be thought of before the corresponding words and sentence structure are available. The diagram of our evolutive grammar shows how the *ich* comes up, and
it is quite interesting and far from self-evident how this is
accomplished. By no means does the infant begin with 'I'. At
first he refers to himself, perchance, with 'you' because he is

addressed in this way, or he uses his Christian name or the
term his parents prefer when speaking to him (*baby*, etc.).
Only with considerable effort does the child acquire the ability
to differentiate between *you* and *I*, and to refer to himself in
the way so natural to all of us. The same applies to all other
concepts which are indispensable for human knowledge and
cognition. Only when these preconditions are fulfilled is the
human being endowed with reason and logical thinking--the
ζῶον λόγον ἔχον--which is capable of scientific and philosophical
thinking (cf. Gipper 1977). Without the language apriori, this
decisive state can never be reached.

Thus linguistic research in this domain must be considered to
represent a main task to be completed in order to give epistemology a sound base and foundation.

NOTES

1. Cf. B. L. Whorf. Language, thought, and reality:
Selected writings. Edited by J. B. Carroll. New York: Wiley;
London: Chapman and Hall. 1956. Cf. especially pp. 207-219
and 220-232.

2. Two of my students, Ekkehart Malotki and Andrea
Stahlschmidt, have contributed to the solution of this problem.
Cf. E. Malotki. Hopi Raum. Eine sprachwissenschaftliche
Analyse der Raumvorstellung in der Hopi-Sprache. Tübingen:
Narr, 1979; A. Stahlschmidt. Das Verbalsystem des Hopi. Eine
semantische Strukturenanalyse der Hopi-Grammatik unter besonderer
Berücksichtigung von B. L. Whorfs Thesen zur Zeitauffassung
der Hopi-Indianer. Doctoral dissertation, University of Münster,
1982.

3. For further references, cf. H. Gipper and H. Schwarz,
Bibliographisches Handbuch der Sprachinhaltsforschung. Köln/
Opladen: Westdeutscher Verlag, 1962ff.

4. Cf. J. Locke. An essay concerning human understanding.
Vol. 2, Book III: Of words. London: Dent; New York:
Dutton. 1968.

5. Cf. A. Castell. An introduction to modern philosophy.
n.p.: Macmillan. 1943. 226-227.

6. Cf. E. Lenneberg. Biological foundations of language.
New York/London/Sydney: Wiley. 1967. Chapter 4, iv:
'Concomitants of physical maturation', 158-170; and B. Marquardt.
Die Sprache des Menschen und ihre biologischen Voraussetzungen.
Doctoral dissertation, University of Münster, 1980.

7. Cf. I. Kant. Ueber eine Entdeckung, nach der alle neue
Critik der reinen Vernunft durch eine ältere entbehrlich gemacht
werden soll. 1790,[2] 1791. In: Kants Werke. Vol. 5. Edited
by W. Weischedel. Darmstadt: Wissenschaftliche Buchgesellschaft.
1959. 293-373.

8. Cf. H. Gipper. Die genetische Interpretation der Sprache.
9. Kongreß für Philosophie. Düsseldorf, 1969. Edited by L.
Landgrebe. Meisenheim/Glan: Hain. 1972. 270-284. H. Gipper.

Evolutive grammar or how to become a competent speaker of a language. Special university lecture in linguistics at the University of London, May 2, 1977. Wege zur Universalienforschung. Festschrift H. Seiler. Edited by G. Bretschneider, Chr. Lehmann. Tübingen: Narr. 1980. 541-548.

9. A reproduction of this model is to be found in Gipper (1979:179).

REFERENCES

Bloomfield, L. 1935. Language or ideas. Lg. 11.89-95.
Chomsky, N. 1966. Cartesian linguistics: A chapter in the history of rationalist thought. New York/London: Harper and Row.
Chomsky, N. 1967. The general properties of language. In: Brain mechanisms underlying speech and language. Edited by F. L. Daley. New York/London: Gruner and Stratton. 73-88.
Gipper, H. 1972. Gibt es ein sprachliches Relativitätsprinzip? Untersuchungen zur Sapir-Whorf Hypothese. Frankfurt/M.: S. Fischer.
Gipper, H. 1977. Die Sonderstellung der menschlichen Sprache gegenüber den Verständigungsmitteln der Tiere. Mitteilungen der Berliner Gesellschaft für Anthropologie, Ethnologie und Urgeschichte 5.26-67.
Gipper, H. 1978. Sprachliches Weltbild, wissenschaftliches Weltbild und ideologische Weltanschauung. Sprache und Welterfahrung. Edited by J. Zimmermann. Munich: Fink. 160-176.
Gipper, H. 1979. Vom Aufbau des sprachlichen Weltbildes im Prozeß der Spracherlernung in den ersten drei Lebensjahren. Wirkendes Wort 29.165-180.
Jakobson, R. 1968. Child language, aphasia and phonological universals. The Hague: Mouton.
Lenneberg, E. 1967. The biological foundations of language. Hospital Practice, December. 59-67.
Sapir, E. 1929. The status of linguistics as a science. Lg. 5.207-214.
Spitz, R. [3]1973. Die Entstehung der ersten Objektbeziehungen. Direkte Beobachtungen an Säuglingen während des ersten Lebensjahres. Stuttgart: Klett. 7 os.
Trier, J. 1931, 1973. Der deutsche Wortschatz im Sinnbezirk des Verstandes. Von den Anfängen bis zum Beginn des 13. Jahrhunderts. Heidelberg: Winter.

THE BRAIN BASES FOR LANGUAGE FUNCTIONING: NEW INSIGHTS FROM PENETRATING HEAD INJURIES

Christy L. Ludlow
National Institute of Neurological and
Communicative Disorders and Stroke

Aphasia is a pervasive language loss following brain injury usually to the left side (hemisphere) of the brain. This was first described by Broca in 1861 (Schuell, Jenkins, and Jimenez-Pabon 1964). He described a patient following a stroke with slow halting speech, telegraphic in form, who had better language comprehension than expression. In post-mortem autopsy of the brain, Broca identified the third convolution of the left frontal lobe as the damaged region responsible for his patient's language disorder. Thirteen years later, Wernicke observed patients with fluent speech following a stroke but with limited comprehension of speech. These patients' lesions were in the temporo-parietal region, including the supramarginal and angular gyri surrounding the sylvian fissure of the left hemisphere. Such were the beginnings of the study of language breakdown following brain injury.

Today, neurolinguists study how language behavior is impaired following brain injury. By studying the dimensions of language breakdown following brain injury, it is expected that the inherent structure of language can be ascertained. If certain dimensions of language are affected independently by brain injury, those dimensions may thus be independent components of language functioning. For example, if syntactic structure were altered in some forms of aphasia without disturbance in semantic reference, these two dimensions of linguistic functioning may be separate in language behavior.

Computerized tomography (Hayward et al. 1977, Kertesz et al. 1979), referred to as CT scanning, has been available since 1973. This is an x-ray technique which provides a representation of the density of different brain structures in small sections referred to as pixels (1 mm^2), at several levels in the brain (Peterson and Kieffer 1976). Since bone, water, air, tissue, and blood have different densities, these can be differentiated on CT scans. Tumors, regions of cell loss, and calcification can thus be identified by the neuroradiologist when determining which brain regions have been damaged by stroke, disease, or injury.

The use of CT scanning results is of particular importance for neurolinguists who want to determine whether lesions in particular brain regions are associated with independent break-downs of different language dimensions. Figure 1 is the CT scan of an aphasic adult who sustained a head injury in the left hemisphere. The region of brain loss is indicated by the arrow, and involves all of the left temporal lobe. This region on the CT scan indicates a fluid-filled cavity following the excavation of debris and damaged tissue from the wound by the neurosurgeon.

Figure 1.   CT scan of a head-injured male with chronic aphasia associated with total destruction of temporal lobe brain tissue in the left hemisphere.

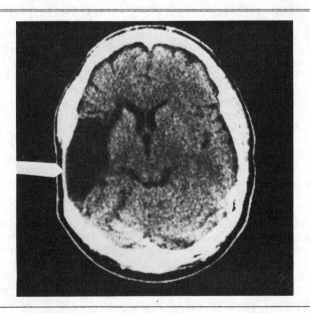

In this paper, I discuss some preliminary results of an investigation of head-injured men. The Vietnam Head Injury Study (VHIS) is currently examining veterans who sustained head injuries in Vietnam. Between 1967 and 1970, the neurosurgeons in the field maintained records on over 1100 veterans who received surgical treatment for head injury. Over 700 of these men have agreed to participate in an intensive multidisciplinary examination of their status 12 to 15 years following injury. Each participant receives a CT scan and extensive neurological, physical, motor, neuropsychological, audiological, speech and language, and behavioral examinations. The preliminary speech and language test results of some of the first 89 cases are discussed in this paper.

In this sample, only those with penetrating head injuries have been included. Such injuries are due to entry by a missile, such as a bullet or shrapnel fragment, into the brain. In all cases, neurosurgery was performed within 24 hours, with thorough debridement of the wound.

The speech and language assessment battery. The study of the extent and location of the brain injury and behavior of men 11 to 15 years following brain injury provided an opportunity to examine the pattern of language breakdown associated with lesions in particular locations of the brain following maximum recovery. In such a study, several questions can be addressed simultaneously: (1) whether different degrees of impairment are found in the various language modalities such as speech comprehension, speech and language expression, reading, and writing, dependent upon the location of brain injury; (2) whether different language systems can be independently impaired following brain injury or whether the degree of language breakdown is similar in each of the linguistic systems such as syntax, semantics, phonology, and phonetics; and (3) whether various levels of verbal information processing are impaired to different degrees following brain injury.

Thus the battery of speech and language tests being used is arranged to allow for comparison of behaviors on three dimensions: by language modality, by linguistic system, and by information processing demands. Each of these will be discussed in greater detail.

Language modalities. The different aphasia syndromes can be identified by the different degrees of impairment found in various language modalities. Weisenberg and McBride (1935) described expressive and receptive aphasia, based on the marked expressive language impairments and relatively good comprehension found in some Broca's aphasics in contrast with the fluent speech of Wernicke's aphasics with relatively poor understanding. Geschwind (1965, 1972) proposed a brain organization underlying several syndromes, and Goodglass and Kaplan (1972) developed the Boston Diagnostic Aphasia Examination according to his typology, and provided excellent clinical descriptions of each type. The distinguishing feature for each syndrome is the language modality which is most impaired. It is not the absolute amount of impairment on a particular test that is crucial for distinguishing between syndromes, but rather the pattern of different degrees of impairment across language modalities. There are two views regarding the conceptualization of language breakdown in aphasia. On the one hand, neurologists and neurolinguists describe all aphasic patients by syndrome and maintain that there are distinct differences between syndromes when described across language modalities and linguistic systems. On the other hand, speech-language pathologists have long conceived of aphasia as a unitary disorder, with a patient's overall severity of functioning being related to the degree of impairment in each language modality (Schuell, Jenkins, and Jimenez-Pabon 1964).

To determine whether patients are more impaired in one modality than another, patients must be tested on equivalent subtests in different modalities. In Table 1, a two-dimensional model is provided to allow comparison of patients functioning in different modalities when the linguistic materials are the same. Five different language modalities which have been reported in the aphasia literature (Ludlow 1981) as critical in syndrome classification are: auditory comprehension of language; speech repetition (imitation); speech expression; reading comprehension; and written expression. In the other direction, five different types of linguistic knowledge are identified: phonetic, phonologic, lexical, semantic, and syntactic.

If separate tests are used for each cell in this table, the patients' abilities to process the same linguistic material for speech expression, repetition, comprehension, reading, and writing can be compared.

Linguistic systems. The organization presented in Table 1 also illustrates how functioning within the same language modality but using different types of linguistic information can be assessed to determine whether patients have specific impairments in the use of a particular type of linguistic information. This approach will allow for determining whether, for example, some aphasic patients are particularly impaired in their comprehension and use of syntactic information, or whether they are impaired to a similar degree in their use of all types of linguistic information. This issue has importance for linguistic theory since it bears on the degree of interdependence between various linguistic systems. Further, issues regarding which types of linguistic knowledge might provide the main reference or framework for linguistic descriptions of language can be determined if one aspect of linguistic knowledge is found to be commonly affected in all cases of language breakdown.

Information processing. Cognitive psychologists have found that different levels of information processing have relevance to the breakdown of memory skills in various dementias (Caine et al. 1977; Weingartner et al. 1979a, 1979b). Since language is information and is stored in the brain in a similar fashion as other information we acquire, it is likely that different levels

Table 1. Schema for the analysis of language performance breakdown in aphasia being employed in the Vietnam Head Injury Study.

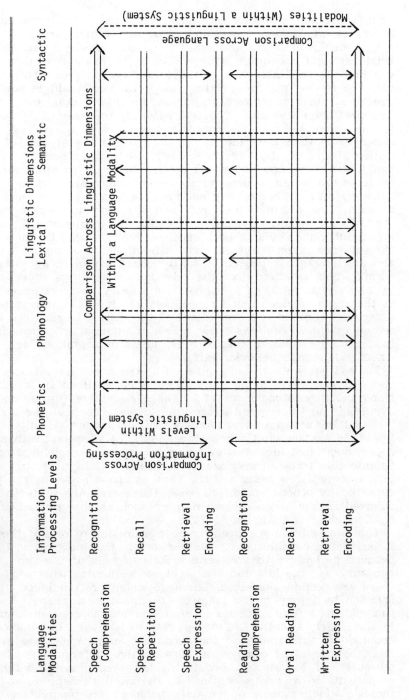

of information processing may have relevance to the breakdown of verbal information processing following brain injury.

Four different levels are being examined: recognition, recall, retrieval, and encoding. Our ability to understand road signs can provide an illustration of these four levels. We all recognize the road signs for parking, stop, turn left, single lane overtake, etc., and based on our stored information, we can interpret their meaning. To test recall of these signs, a subject is shown a sign and after it is taken away, the subject is asked to draw or describe it. If the subject has stored information of that symbol, his/her recall will be more accurate and rapid than if he/she had never seen it before. In retrieval, subjects are asked to draw signs from memory for parking, no passing, etc. Subjects may not remember some details and, overall, their production on retrieval is slower and less accurate than for recall. Symbol complexity and frequency of use affect subjects' skills in both recall and retrieval. In encoding, subjects are given a set of verbal directions or a map of a trip and are asked to represent them by drawing a sequence of road signs. This task requires the selection of meanings represented by signs, the retrieval of signs from memory, correct ordering of the signs, and accurate reproduction. It is of interest to determine whether the breakdown of the use of linguistic information in aphasia follows these levels of information processing in a manner similar to that of other areas of cognition, or whether language behavior differs.

Table 1 presents the organization of the experimental speech and language tests being used in the Vietnam Head Injury Study along the three dimensions of language modalities, linguistic systems, and information processing levels. Each of the tests is listed in the Appendix, along with its language modality, linguistic system, and processing level. In all cases, either a particular test already developed by others was adapted to fit into this framework or we developed a test to meet our needs; only a few tests are the same as those previously reported by others and in all cases these are only subtests selected from a large aphasia battery such as that published by Goodglass and Kaplan (1972).

This paper is only a preliminary examination of one of the issues being considered in this research. Our purpose is to examine patients with unilateral lesions to each of the two hemispheres, the left and the right, to determine whether there are certain aspects of language which are particularly affected by injury to the language dominant hemisphere, that is, the left hemisphere in right-handed males brain injured in their early twenties. Since pervasive language breakdown occurs only with injury to the dominant (left) hemisphere in right-handers, the comparison between the performance of patients with lesions confined to the left hemisphere and that of patients with lesions confined to the right hemisphere will indicate which aspects of language behavior are particularly impaired by injury to the left hemisphere, the hemisphere dominant for language, and might thus be of greater significance to linguistic behavior.

Subjects. Of the first 85 head-injured men seen by the VHIS, only 43 were confirmed to have brain lesions confined to one of the two hemispheres on CT scanning, and were right-handed both for sports and writing activities prior to brain injury. Twenty-one had lesions confined to the left hemisphere, 22 had lesions confined to the right hemisphere. The remaining 42 subjects either had invalid CT scans (2), had been left-handed prior to injury (7), or their lesions involved both the right and left hemispheres of their brain (33); none of these subjects were included in this report.

Based on the results of the extensive battery of speech and language tests (see Appendix), speech-language pathologists determined whether or not patients had aphasia (a pervasive language disorder), anomia (a naming disorder), dyslexia (marked reading difficulties), and/or dysgraphia (marked writing difficulties). The results are presented in Table 2. Overall, 23.8 percent of the left hemisphere damaged patients had some type of speech and/or language impairment, while only 9 percent of the right hemisphere damaged patients had a noticeable speech and/or language disorder. Only 14.1 percent of the unilateral left hemisphere damaged patients continued to exhibit aphasia 11 to 14 years following injury. Anomia, however--a specific naming disorder--was found in a slightly greater proportion of the left hemisphere damaged groups when the criterion of 40 percent or more errors on naming was used. Similarly, reading disorders were also slightly more frequent in the left hemisphere group. However, writing disorders (dysgraphia), were more frequent in the right hemisphere damaged group; almost three-quarters had marked difficulties in writing names and/or sentences.

The percentage of subjects performing at 100 percent correct on the two speech perception tasks is presented in Table 3. The percentages did not differ significantly between the two groups. Only a slightly higher percentage of the left hemisphere lesioned than right hemisphere lesioned patients performed correctly on both the temporal resolution (gap detection) task and the temporal order perception task. A further analysis of the location of patients' lesions within each hemisphere in relation with their performance of these tasks is needed to determine whether damage to the auditory association areas in either hemisphere is related to poor performance on either or both of these tasks.

For all of the remaining subsequent speech and language tests, a criterion score for designating a level below which performance was impaired was established by examining the frequency distribution of all 85 subjects' scores on each test and identifying the level below which 20 percent of the subjects scored.

Table 2. Percentage of right-handed head-injured men with unilateral lesions confined to the left and right hemispheres with various speech and language syndromes.

	% Patients with left hemisphere damaged subjects (N = 21)	% Patients with right hemisphere damaged subjects (N = 22)
Speech and language impaired	23.8	4.8
Aphasic	14.2	0.0
Dysnomic	57.1	38.0
Dyslexic	33.3	19.0
Dysgraphic	57.1	71.4

Table 3. Percentage right and left hemisphere damaged men performing correctly on phonetic perception tasks.

	% Subjects with correct performance	
	Left hemisphere damage	Right hemisphere damage
Discrimination of /sa/ from /sta/ at 70 msec. gap	61.1	35.7
Identification of /sa/ at inter-stimulus initiation interval of 60 msec.	26.3	17.6

No significant differences were found between the two groups on the Chi-Square Contingency Test.

Subsequently, the number of subjects falling at or below the twentieth percentile score on each test was determined within the group of subjects with lesions confined to the right hemisphere and within the group with lesions confined to the left hemisphere. Thus, the percentage of subjects scoring below the twentieth percentile level on each speech and language test within the right and left hemisphere damaged groups was compared statistically by computation of a chi-square, using the Chi-Square Contingency Test.

In Table 4, the percentage of subjects in the two groups falling in the impaired range on adapted versions of the Selnes-Rubens CVC Speech Discrimination and Production tests did not differ. The production task required CVC syllable recall following auditory presentation. There was no tendency for a greater number of the left hemisphere damaged patients to be impaired on CVC discrimination but there was a nonsignificant tendency for more left hemisphere patients to be impaired on production.

Table 4. Percentage of right and left hemisphere damaged men with scores below the 20th percentile on adapted Selnes-Rubens CVC Speech Discrimination and Production Tests.

	% of subjects scoring below 20th percentile	
	Left hemisphere damage	Right hemisphere damage
Discrimination of meaningful CVC words	9.5	10.5
Discrimination of nonsense CVC syllables	19.0	26.3
Production of meaningful CVC words	14.3	0.0
Production of nonsense CVC syllables	9.52	5.3

No significant differences were found between the two groups on the Chi-Square Contingency Test.

Table 5 presents the percentage of patients in each group impaired (with scores below the twentieth percentile) on our oral lexical retrieval test, an adapted version of the Boston Naming Test (Kaplan, Goodglass, and Weintraub 1978). In the same table, the percentage of subjects with more than 11 semantic errors and the percentage with more than one phonologic error are also presented. No significant differences were found between the two groups on these measures, although there was a slight tendency for more left than right hemisphere damaged patients to be impaired on this test.

Recall of lexical and semantic information on word and sentence repetition was tested, using the Repetition of Words and Repeating Phrases, High Probability and Low Probability Subtests from the Boston Diagnostic Aphasia Examination (Goodglass and Kaplan 1972). The percentage of subjects with left hemisphere lesions who scored below seven in recall of low probability semantic information was significantly greater than in the right hemisphere group (p = .027). No significant differences between the two groups were found on recall of single words or high probability phrases.

The Oral Reading Section of the Gates-McKillop Reading Diagnostic Tests (Gates and McKillop 1962) was used to assess oral recall of phonologic and semantic information from written material. Using the criterion for number of errors expected at an eighth grade reading level, a high proportion of both groups was impaired. The distribution of types of errors tended to differ between the left and right hemisphere damaged groups. The Chi-Square Contingency Test yielded a value of 2.58, with a nonsignificant probability of .10; a greater percentage of left hemisphere lesioned patients had more than four semantic errors than right hemisphere lesioned patients. On the percentage of subjects with phonologic errors, however, the two groups were similar.

Table 5. Percentage of right and left hemisphere damaged men with scores below the 20th percentile on an adaptation of the Boston Naming Test.

	Left hemisphere damaged subjects	Right hemisphere damaged subjects
% with scores below 25	18.2	5.0
% with greater than 11 semantic errors	13.6	5.0
% with more than 1 phonologic error	9.1	5.0

No significant differences were found between the two groups on the Chi-Square Contingency Test.

Table 6. Percentage of right and left hemisphere lesioned men impaired on repeating words and phrases of high and low probability.

	% of left hemisphere damaged subjects	% of right hemisphere damaged subjects
Scores less than 9 on word repetition	9.1	5.0
Scores less than 8 on high probability phrases	13.6	5.0
Scores less than 7 on low probability phrases	63.6*	25.0*

*χ^2 (observed) corrected for continuity = 4.85; p value of χ^2 = 0.027.

Table 7. Percentage right and left hemisphere lesioned men impaired on Oral Reading Subtest of Gates-McKillop.

	Left hemisphere damaged subjects	Right hemisphere damaged subjects
% with > 4 errors	59.0	76.2
% with > 4 semantic errors	40.9	14.3
% with > 1 phonologic error	22.7	19.0

No significant differences were found between the two groups on the Chi-Square Contingency Test.

In Table 8, the percentages of subjects impaired in each group on semantic and syntactic speech recognition and reading recognition tasks are presented.

Table 8. Percentage of left and right hemisphere lesioned men impaired on speech and reading semantic and syntactic recognition tasks.

	Left hemisphere damaged subjects	Right hemisphere damaged subjects
% with scores less than 97 on Spoken Adapted Token Test	27.3	5.0
% with scores less than 95 on Reading Adapted Token Test	28.6	4.80
% with scores less than 38 on Spoken Adapted Selnes Receptive Syntax Test	19.0	5.0
% with scores less than 38 on Reading Adapted Selnes Receptive Syntax Test	14.3	19.0

No significant differences were found between the two groups on the Chi-Square Contingency Test.

Adaptations of the Token Test, the Identification by Sentence Subtest from the Neurosensory Center Comprehensive Examination for Aphasia (Spreen and Benton 1969) were used to assess semantic comprehension from spoken and written material. On both tasks, there was a tendency for the left hemisphere group to have a higher percentage of subjects impaired than in the right hemisphere group, although neither differences were statistically significant.

On adaptations of the Selnes Receptive Syntax Test (1980) for speech comprehension and reading comprehension, only the speech comprehension task showed a slight tendency toward a greater proportion of left hemisphere patients being impaired. On reading recognition of syntactic structure, however, the proportion of right hemisphere patients with impaired performance was slightly higher than in the left hemisphere group, although this was nonsignificant.

Table 9. Percentage of left and right hemisphere damaged men impaired in speech and written semantic and syntactic expression.

	Left hemisphere damaged subjects	Right hemisphere damaged subjects
Adapted Selnes Speech Expressive Syntax Test:		
% < 15 sentences correct	27.3	9.5
% > 1 word omitted	18.2	4.8
% > 1 semantic error	18.2	14.3
% > 1 phonologic error	0.0	0.0
% > 1 function word error	13.6	0.0
Adapted Selnes Written Expressive Syntax Test:		
% < 15 sentences correct	38.1	15.8
% > 1 word omitted	9.5	15.8
% > 1 semantic error	23.8	0.0
% > 1 phonologic error	38.1	10.5
% > 1 function word error	14.3	21.0

No significant differences were found between the two groups on the Chi-Square Contingency Test.

Finally, the results of testing syntactic retrieval in both speech and writing are presented in Table 9. The Selnes Tests of Expressive Syntax were adapted to provide two similar tests of expressive syntax, one for writing, the other for speaking. There were similarities and differences in the two groups' performances in speech and written production of syntactic structures. Although none of the group differences was significant, a greater proportion of left hemisphere patients tended to make semantic errors in sentence production in both speaking and written expression. Different tendencies appear in the two groups in speaking and writing on the percentage of patients with word omissions, phonologic errors, and function word errors. In speech, a greater proportion of left hemisphere damaged patients tended to omit words or make errors on function words, while in writing there was a nonsignificant tendency for a greater proportion of right hemisphere damaged patients to omit words or make function word errors. Phonologic speech errors were not produced in either group, while a greater proportion of left hemisphere damaged patients tended to produce these in writing.

Table 10 summarizes the preliminary findings thus far, when examining in which linguistic areas and in which language modalities the left hemisphere damaged patients had deficits to a greater degree than the right hemisphere damaged patients.

Since this is a preliminary investigation with just over 20 subjects in each group, I have included both nonsignificant trends as well as statistically significant differences. On examining Table 10, the semantic column is the only linguistic system consistently affected in the left hemisphere damaged patients to a greater degree than in the right hemisphere lesioned group. The speech repetition and speech expression language modalities also tend to be more impaired in left hemisphere lesioned subjects; in the other language modalities, the percentage of right hemisphere lesioned subjects impaired showed a tendency to be greater than in the left hemisphere lesioned group in at least one linguistic system.

Discussion. Only one statistically significant difference was found between right and left hemisphere damaged patients: the frequency of deficits in the recall of semantic information with a low probability of occurrence was greater in the left hemisphere lesioned group. A similar tendency for a greater proportion of the left hemisphere damaged patients to be impaired was found on other tests of semantic information. This was the only linguistic dimension to have a consistent pattern of greater impairment in the left hemisphere patients than in the right hemisphere patients.

Examination of the results by language modality and level of information processing indicated few consistent trends. First, when examined by level of information across the speech and written modalities, there are differences between the information processing levels in the two avenues of language reception and expression. Only some of the speech and reading recognition tasks had a tendency toward a greater proportion of left hemisphere damaged patients being impaired than right hemisphere damaged patients. Further, the various linguistic types of tasks which evidenced left hemisphere impairment for reading and speech recognition differed. Thus, reading and speech recognition were not specifically impaired by damage to the left hemisphere and were not similar in their pattern of linguistic disturbances. The speech recall and oral reading tasks also did not show a consistent pattern across various types of linguistic information. Finally, the speech and written retrieval tasks differed in their pattern, demonstrating an independence in the pattern of breakdown in these two areas of language coding.

Table 10. Summary of results comparing left and right hemisphere lesioned men on language performance tasks.

Language Modalities	Processing Levels	Phonetic	Phonological	Lexical	Semantic	Syntax
					Linguistic Systems	
Speech Comprehension	Recognition	≥Left	≥Right		≥Left	≥Left
Speech Repetition	Recall		≥Left	≥Left	>Left*	≥Left
Speech Expression	Retrieval		≥Left	≥Left	≥Left	≥Left
Reading Comprehension	Recognition		Equal	≥Left	≥Left	≥Right
Oral Reading	Recall		Equal	≥Left	≥Left	≥Right
Written	Retrieval		≥Left	≥Right	≥Left	≥Left

*p < .025

≥| indicates data shows a nonsignificant trend for the group identified to have a greater proportion of patients impaired on that task.

[ ] Linguistic system with deficits found in a greater proportion of left hemisphere lesioned subjects.

In speech repetition, retrieval, and recall, a tendency for a greater proportion of left hemisphere damaged patients to be impaired was found on all tasks in each linguistic system. On oral reading and written retrieval tasks, however, the pattern was quite different, with the proportion of right hemisphere damaged patients being similar to that of the left hemisphere damaged patients on some tasks. And on two tasks of syntactic recall and lexical retrieval, the proportion of right hemisphere damaged patients being impaired tended to be greater.

This dissimilarity in performance on speech retrieval and written retrieval is similar to the results reported by Friederici et al. (1981), who found that naming disorders of aphasic patients differed for oral naming and written naming. Further, the equivalent impairments on some writing tasks in the left and right hemisphere lesioned groups are similar to the results of Kertesz et al. (1982), who found a high proportion of right hemisphere post-CVA patients had residual deficits on writing tasks.

Based on these preliminary results, then, the representation of semantic information seems to be primarily a capacity of the left hemisphere. Although the right hemisphere may have a role in processing semantic information, this capacity is less than that of the left hemisphere. No other aspect of linguistic information was so clearly affected to a greater degree by left hemisphere damage than semantic information.

With regard to language modality, speech expression was the only language function which was consistently affected to a greater degree by left hemisphere damage. This would be expected, given the previous findings that speech expression is found only in the left hemisphere following sectioning of the corpus callosum (Zaidel 1979). Speech recognition did not evidence a marked tendency to have greater breakdown in the left hemisphere, indicating some bilateral representation of language particularly for recognition. This finding is also in agreement with previous research by Zaidel (1979), who reported word and phrase recognition capabilities in the right hemispheres in patients following sectioning of the corpus callosum.

Similar patterns of breakdown were found following right and left hemisphere lesions for written retrieval. In fact, on the oral reading, reading receptive syntax, and written expression tests, a greater proportion of patients with right hemisphere damage tended to have deficits. Thus written language, and graphic lexical representation in particular, may require both right and left hemisphere functioning. However, these results cannot be interpreted as indicating that written language is bilaterally represented; otherwise, deficits in written language comprehension would not have occurred following unilateral damage in either group. Rather, both right and left hemisphere functioning may be involved in processing written language for recognition and particularly for retrieval. These preliminary findings might indicate a different brain basis for oral language processing than for written language processing. The two language functions did not break down in a parallel fashion following left and right brain injury, indicating that written language is not an exact replication of oral language. Also, a greater frequency of both recognition disorders (dyslexia) and retrieval disorders (dysgraphia) were found in both right and left brain injury. This could be due to written language processing being more of a whole brain activity. An alternate possibility would be that perceptual problems occurred in both groups, which could account for more difficulties being found in written language processing.

I would now like to return to the major finding that the only significant difference between the two groups was the greater frequency in breakdown in recall of low probability phrases in the left hemisphere damaged patients. Possibly, lexical re-trieval and recall is primarily based in the left hemisphere and this is the basis for the greater language faculties of the left hemisphere. Further, a disturbance of lexical retrieval may be the basis for aphasia, the language disorder which affects all avenues of language functioning. In right hemi-sphere injury, when the lexical store of the left hemisphere is not damaged and damage occurs elsewhere in the brain, lan-guage efficiency can be reduced somewhat but all areas of language functioning are not affected. We know that lexical retrieval, or anomia, is common to all types of aphasia to vary-ing degrees (Goodglass 1980) and that the residual of recovery from aphasia is anomia, that is, lexical retrieval is the last aspect of language to return to normal functioning levels (Kertesz 1979).

However, two issues seem more difficult to explain if we argue that lexical retrieval deficits are the basis for language disorders. First, the description of Broca's aphasia as a dis-order of syntactic expression would seem difficult to explain with this hypothesis. These patients are known for their telegraphic speech and their omission of function or closed class words. It has also been found that these patients have language recognition difficulties for syntactic structure similar to those in their spoken language (Zurif et al. 1972, Zurif and Caramazza 1976). Zurif (1980) reviewed the results of several studies he and his co-workers conducted on the lexical recognition and retrieval of open and closed class words by Broca's aphasics. They found that the Broca's aphasics were similarly impaired in their recognition of closed class words as in their recognition of open class words. Zurif (1980: 310) proposed that 'the relative inability of Broca's aphasics either to produce closed class items in speech or make use of them in comprehension is tied to a disruption of the specialised mechan-ism for retrieving closed class items, foreclosing the ability to use these items as syntactic placeholders'. Thus, a specific lexical retrieval deficit for function words could explain the syntactic deficits in Broca's aphasia.

The second issue that would seem difficult to explain concerns the observed language processing deficits found following right hemisphere lesions, leading us to assume some language role of the right hemisphere in language function. However, since equal deficits occur following left hemisphere damage, these right hemisphere functions must not be able to substitute entirely for what is lost in the left hemisphere even 11 to 14 years after brain injury.

One could propose that in normal language functioning, both right and left hemisphere functioning are involved in cerebral activation for language. Lassen and Larsen (1980) have reported studies of blood flow patterns during listening and during speech in normal adults and have found that both hemispheres show activation to an equal degree. Thus, there may be bilateral brain involvement during language functioning but the control areas are based in the left hemisphere. The control center may contain the lexical knowledge while the other brain regions provide the stimulus input, activation, and arousal functions required for language functioning. Thus, arousal provided by stimulus input and activation of language retrieval may be contributed in part at least by right hemisphere functioning. If right hemisphere functioning is impaired by brain lesion, then these functions may become less efficient even though the lexical knowledge remains intact in the left hemisphere. Thus, only the activation and accessibility of lexical knowledge becomes less efficient. Those aspects of language information which are bilaterally represented, as evidenced by the work of Zaidel (1979), are able to recover to as efficient a performance as prior to brain injury. It is only when highly specific lexical knowledge which is contained only in the left hemisphere is interfered with that there is generalized language disorder, aphasia. Thus, recovery from aphasia following left hemisphere damage will occur to varying degrees except for those aspects specific to the left hemisphere language base, that is, highly discrete lexical semantic fields-- which contain lower frequency items in the lexicon.

This is, of course, all highly speculative, but it seems to be the best explanation of the data currently available. We hope that through further more detailed study of patients with penetrating head injuries, our understanding of the brain bases for language functioning can develop beyond its present state.

APPENDIX

Listing of speech and language tests
developed, selected, or adapted
for use in the Vietnam Head Injury Study

Test		Language modality	Linguistic system	Processing level
(1)	Speech Perception /sa/-/sta/ /sa/-/as/	Speech comprehension	Phonetic	Recognition
(2)	Adapted Selnes-Reubens Auditory Discrimination			
	Meaningful words	Speech comprehension	Phonologic	Recognition
	Nonsense words	Speech comprehension	Phonetic	Recognition
(3)	GFW Auditory Discrimination*	Speech comprehension	Phonologic	Recognition
(4)	Adapted Token Test	Speech comprehension	Semantic Lexical	Recognition
(5)	Adapted Selnes-Receptive Syntax	Speech comprehension	Syntactic	Recognition
(6)	ACTS (Shewan)*	Speech comprehension	Syntactic	Recognition
(7)	Word and Phrase Repetition			
	Word Low and high probability (from BDAE)	Speech repetition	Lexical Semantic	Recall
(8)	Repetition of Oral Movements and Syllables (from BDAE)	Speech repetition	Phonetic	Recall
(9)	Speech Repetition of ACTS*	Speech repetition	Syntactic	Recall
(10)	Adapted Selnes-Rubens Speech Articulation Test			
	Nonsense syllables	Speech repetition	Phonetic	Recall
	Meaningful words		Phonologic	Recall
(11)	Automatic Speech (from BDAE)	Speech expression	Lexical	Recall
(12)	Boston Naming Test	Speech expression	Lexical	Retrieval
(13)	Word Fluency			
	Animal categories (from BDAE)	Speech expression	Lexical	Retrieval
	FAS (from NCCEA)	Speech expression	Phonologic Lexical	Retrieval
(14)	Adapted Selnes Oral Expressive Syntax	Speech expression	Syntactic	Retrieval
(15)	Williams Visual vs. Tactile Naming*	Speech expression	Lexical	Retrieval
(16)	Aphasia Severity Rating Scale (from BDAE)	Speech expression	Phonologic Lexical Semantic Syntactic	Encoding
(17)	Description of Use* (from NCCEA)	Speech expression	Semantic	Encoding
(18)	Adapted Reporters' Test	Speech expression	Syntactic	Encoding
(19)	Oral Spelling Comprehension (from BDAE)	Reading comprehension	Phonologic	Recognition

Test	Language modality	Linguistic system	Processing level
(20) Reading Token Test	Reading comprehension	Semantic	Recognition
(21) Adapted Selnes Receptive Syntax- Reading Comprehension	Reading comprehension	Syntactic Lexical	Recognition
(22) Gates-McKillop Reading Test	Oral reading	Phonologic Lexical Semantic Syntactic	Recall
(23) Adapted Boston Naming-Writing	Written expression	Lexical	Retrieval
(24) Adapted Selnes Expressive Syntax- Writing	Written expression	Syntactic	Retrieval
(25) Communicative Abilities in Daily Living (Holland 1981) Overall communication measure			

Control tests:
For Dysarthria and Dyspraxia:
  Oral Peripheral Testing
  Volitional Oral Movements
Motor Imitation Token Test (Limb Apraxia)
*These tests are administered only to patients with aphasia.

NOTE

Appreciation for assistance with data collection is expressed to Christine Fair, Jeanette Rosenberg, and Betsy Sauder. James D. Dillon, M.D., LTC/MC/USAR, is responsible for overall direction of the Vietnam Head Injury Project. This study is under the auspices of the Veterans Administration (VA Contract No. IGA V101 (91)M-79031-2), with the cooperation and support of the United States Army, Navy, and Air Force.

REFERENCES

Caine, E. D., M. H. Ebert, and H. Weingartner. 1977. An outline for the analysis of dementia: The memory disorder of Huntington's disease. Neurology (Minneapolis) 27.1087-1092.

Friederici, A. D., P. W. Schoenle, and H. Goodglass. 1981. Mechanisms underlying writing and speech in aphasia. Brain and Language 13.212-222.

Gates, A. I., and A. S. McKillop. 1961. Gates-McKillop Reading Diagnostic Tests. Los Angeles: Western Psychological Services.

Geschwind, N. 1965. Disconnexion syndromes in animals and man. Brain 88.237-294, 585-644.

Geschwind, N. 1972. Language and the brain. Scientific American 226.76-83.

Goodglass, H. 1980. Disorders of naming following brain injury. American Scientist 68.647-655.

Goodglass, H., and E. Kaplan. 1972. Assessment of aphasia and related disorders. Philadelphia: Lea and Febiger.

Hayward, R. W., M. A. Naeser, and L. M. Zatz. 1977. Cranial computed tomography in aphasia. Radiology 123.653-660.

Kaplan, E., H. Goodglass, and S. Weintraub. 1978. The Boston Naming Test. Boston: E. Kaplan and H. Goodglass.

Kertesz, A. 1979. Aphasia and associated disorders: Taxonomy, localization and recovery. New York: Grune and Stratton.

Kertesz, A., W. Harlock, and R. Coates. 1979. Computer tomographic localization, lesion size and prognosis in aphasia and nonverbal impairment. Brain and Language 8.34-50.

Kertesz, A. 1982. Right-hemisphere deficits, lesion size and location. Journal of Clinical Neuropsychology 4.283-299.

Lassen, N. A., and B. Larsen. 1980. Cortical activity in the left and right hemisphere during language-related brain functions. Phonetica 37.27-37.

Ludlow, C. L. 1981. Recovery and rehabilitation of adult aphasic patients: Relevant research advances. In: Communication disorders. Edited by R. W. Rieber. New York: Plenum. 149-177.

Peterson, H. O., and S. A. Kieffer. 1976. Computed tomography of the head (addendum to chapter on neuroradiology). In: Clinical neurology, Vol. 1. Edited by A. B. Baker and L. H. Baker. Hagerstown, N.Y.: Harper and Row. 257-290.

Selnes, Ola. 1980. Receptive Test of Syntax and Expressive Test of Syntax. Developed under NINCDS Contract #N01-NS-2378. Minneapolis: Hennepin County Medical Center.

Schuell, H., J. J. Jenkins, and E. Jimenez-Pabon. 1964. Aphasia in adults: Diagnosis, prognosis and treatment. New York: Hoeber Medical Division, Harper and Row.

Spreen, O., and A. L. Benton. 1969. Neurosensory center comprehensive examination for aphasia. Victoria, B.C.: University of Victoria Press.

Weingartner, H., E. D. Caine, and M. H. Ebert. 1979a. Imagery, encoding and the retrieval of information from memory: Some specific encoding retrieval changes in Huntington's disease. Journal of Abnormal Psychology 88.52-58.

Weingartner, H., E. D. Caine, and M. H. Ebert. 1979b. Encoding processes, learning and recall in Huntington's disease. Advances in Neurology 23.215-225.

Zaidel, E. 1979. The split and half brains as models of congenital language disability. In: The neurological bases of language disorders in children: Methods and directions for research. Edited by C. L. Ludlow and M. E.

Doran-Quine. Bethesda, Md.: U.S. Government Printing
Office, NIH Publication No. 79-440.

Zurif, E. B. 1980. Language mechanisms: A neuropsychological perspective. American Scientist 68.305-311.

Zurif, E. B., and A. Caramazza. 1976. Psycholinguistic
structures in aphasia: Studies in syntax and semantics.
In: Studies in neurolinguistics, Vol. 1. Edited by H.
Whitaker and H. A. Whitaker. New York: Academic Press.
261-292.

Zurif, E. B., A. Caramazza, and R. Myerson. 1972. Grammatical judgments of agrammatic aphasics. Neuropsychologia
10.405-417.

THE PERCEPTUAL ACQUISITION
OF ENGLISH PHONOLOGY BY JAPANESE STUDENTS

Felix Lobo, S.J. and Kensaku Yoshida
Sophia University, Tokyo

Introduction.   Language is said to be primarily speech.
However, in Japan, it is still taught primarily by means of
reading and writing.   A quick glance at English textbooks
used in Japanese junior and senior high schools reveals that
there are almost no chapters in which English phonology is
treated in a systematic manner.   Pronunciation is introduced
mainly for reinforcing new vocabulary items, or for reading
texts, but not as an independent system in itself.

Furthermore, even when pronunciation is taught, it usually
centers on production of difficult English sounds, and very
seldom on the perceptual discrimination of those sounds.
Therefore, many students experience great difficulties in
listening comprehension, even though their pronunciation
itself may not be so bad.

The purpose of our research was to identify the perceptual
difficulties in sound discrimination experienced by our students
as a preliminary to finding a remedy for them.

For our research we referred mainly to two areas of language
acquisition research.   The first was the field of error analysis
and the second was that of children's perceptual acquisition
of phonology.

Articles and books published in the last 15 years in the
field of error analysis assume an interlanguage stage (Selinker
1972) in the foreign learner's acquisition of the target language and various types of errors (Selinker 1972, Corder 1974,
Richards 1971) which cannot be explained by simply contrasting
the linguistic structures of the learner's native language with
those of the target language.   Whereas contrastive analysis
emphasizes linguistic structure alone in predicting the difficulties
the learner might encounter in learning the target language
(Lado 1957), error analysis also employs psycholinguistic factors

224

such as the student's learning strategies in trying to explain the errors made by the learner.

Of the many types of errors suggested by the proponents of error analysis, two basic types which are then further sub-divided stand out: transfer or interlingual errors, and over-generalization or intralingual errors. Transfer errors are those caused by some sort of interference from the native language structure of the learner, while overgeneralization errors are caused by overextending the target language structure to inappropriate situations.

Taylor (1975) showed that transfer errors occurred more frequently at the elementary stages of second language learning and overgeneralization errors more frequently at the intermediate stages. Yoshida (1981) observed a similar phenomenon in foreign language learning in an informal analysis of an English diary kept by a Japanese junior high school student. However, both studies dealt with the acquisition of English syntax.

The object of our research was to see whether this same tendency could also be noted in the Japanese learner's perceptual acquisition of English phonology.

We had frequently observed that students who were quite capable of discriminating English /r-l/ in known vocabulary items had great difficulty in discriminating the same pair of phonemes when confronted with unknown words. They would hear *Rebecca* as /lebeka/, or *rip-off* as /lipɔf/. We therefore turned to perception research to see whether knowledge of vocabulary actually influenced the perception of sounds. Barton (1976, 1978) had found that young children acquiring the sound system of their native language were influenced by knowledge of a word in their perception of individual phonemes. The children showed a tendency to hear sounds in terms of the word they knew when paired with a word they did not know. This, of course, was phonological and not precise phonetic analysis.

Since a number of studies in second language acquisition maintain that the processes of learning a second language are similar to those of first language acquisition (McLaughlin 1975, Dulay and Burt 1974, Corder 1981), we took Barton's results as a basis for hypothesizing a parallel tendency in Japanese students perceiving the English sound system.

On the basis of the foregoing considerations, our experiment was conducted with the position that transfer errors are more frequent in the beginning stages of language learning, whereas overgeneralization errors are more frequent at later stages of language learning, even in the case of the perceptual acquisition of English phonology. We hypothesized furthermore that knowledge of the word influences the subjects' performance in perceiving phonological contrasts.

Hypothesis. Implicit in the primary error categories transfer and overgeneralization is the assumption of a sequence of the acquisition of English phonology by Japanese students of English. Stage 1 is the stage where the learner does not yet know English very well and consequently tends to make transfer errors, that is, his perception is influenced by those sounds which exist in his native language, Japanese. During Stage 2 knowledge of words in English influences the perception of sounds. At Stage 3 the learner has acquired enough English to make more overgeneralization errors than transfer errors. And in the final stage, Stage 4, the English phonological system has been acquired to such an extent that it is referred to independently in judging English sounds, irrespective of knowledge of the words in which they appear. It is only at this stage that a learner can be said to have acquired perceptual mastery of the English phonological system resulting in error-free analysis.

Experiment

Subjects. A total of 47 male and 49 female subjects took part in this experiment, of whom 30 were students majoring in English, 10 in the sciences, and 5 in law. There were also 16 junior high school students and 20 college graduates, as well as 15 others on whom we do not have sufficient personal data. Of the 96 subjects, 25 had lived in a foreign country and had used English as the means of communication for over one year, 59 had never been abroad, and 12 gave no response. Only 19 answered that they had had any formal training in English pronunciation, while 57 had never received any formal training, and 21 did not respond to that question. Of the 19 positive replies, 16 said they had practiced /b-v/, 19 /r-l/, and 17 /s-θ/.

Material. For our experiment we took the following three pairs of English phonemes which are supposedly difficult for Japanese students from the viewpoint of contrastive analysis: /b-v/, /r-l/, and /s-θ/.

The material was based on the principle of minimal pairs. Eighteen pairs of words were prepared for each test, of which 6 pairs were actual (or sense) words, 6 were nonsense words, and 6 a combination of actual (or sense) and nonsense words. For the test, a recording was made of one member of each of the 18 pairs. In the case of sense word pairs and nonsense word pairs, 3 of each phoneme in the minimal pair (e.g. 3 /b/-initial words and 3 /v/-initial words) were recorded. In the case of the combination of sense/nonsense pairs, the nonsense words were recorded. However, even in this case, 3 instances of each phoneme were selected for the sense words. Altogether, therefore, 9 instances of each phoneme were recorded for each test, with only word-initial position being

contrasted in our experiment (cf. Appendix for the actual
material used).

The recording was made in an unechoic room (1000Hz/350dB)
and the interval between items was set at a relatively long
four seconds, since our experiment was in phonology and not
in phonetics or auditory perception, where the interval would
have to be much shorter. We wanted the subjects to have
enough time to refer to their long-term memory in making
their choices.

Procedure. The subjects were originally divided into two
groups. One group was tested in an ordinary classroom and
the other group was tested in a soundproof room (1000Hz/
120dB). All the subjects were given the test material, but
were told not to look at the test pairs until after they had
heard them over the speaker first. The following instructions
were given the subjects:

You will hear one word spoken over the speaker. After
you hear the word, refer to your test sheet and circle the
word you heard. Among the test material there will be
actual English words as well as nonsense words which do
not exist in English. However, the word you will hear
could be either. Do not look at the next pair until you
have heard the word for that pair over the speaker first.

After they had circled their choices for all 54 test items
(three tests), they were told to go back and mark any words
they knew to be actual English words. Then they were told to
fill out a questionnaire concerning their past exposure to English. (Unfortunately, not everyone was given the questionnaire in the beginning of the experiment).

Results. We first analyzed the results of the two groups of
students tested in different situations, one in an ordinary
classroom and the other in a soundproof laboratory, to see if
there would be any differences between the groups. However,
the main patterns of errors of the two groups turned out to
be quite similar, allowing us to combine their results for our
analysis. The greatest number of errors was seen in the
sense/nonsense word pairs, and the pattern of errors in the
sense/nonsense pairs was also very similar (a more detailed
discussion of the results is given further on in this paper).

We divided the subjects into six groups on the basis of
their error rates, assuming that there might be differences in
the results depending on the subjects' level of phonological
acquisition. The division was as follows: group 1 (G1) made
the fewest errors overall (0-10 percent error rate); group 2
(G2), 10.1-20 percent; group 3 (G3), 20.1-30 percent; group 4
(G4), 30.1-40 percent; group 5 (G5), 40.1-50 percent; and
group 6 (G6), an error rate of 50.1 percent or more. There

were 26 subjects in G1, 21 in G2, 21 in G3, 9 in G4, 11 in G5, and 8 in G6.

With the foregoing consideration in mind, let us first look at the overall error rates. The highest number of errors occurred in the /r-l/ pairs, whereas the fewest errors were in the /s-θ/ pairs. The difference between the error rates in the /b-v/ and /r-l/ pairs was not significant at the .05 level, but the pattern of errors (Figure 1) among the 6 groups suggests even now that the /r-l/ pairs were probably the most difficult.

We next looked at the error rates of the sense, nonsense, and sense/nonsense pairs to see how much knowledge of a word influenced the subjects' performance. It will be remembered that the basis of our analysis was the subjects' subjective judgments as to which words were actual English words and which were nonsense words.

Overall, the sense/nonsense pairs registered the greatest number of errors in all three phoneme pairs. This shows that knowledge of the word does affect the judgment of the subjects in their discrimination of word forms. In other words, the subjects in many cases based their judgments of the sound in a word on their knowledge of the language in question and not on its phonological representation. As a group, the G1 subjects registered more errors in the sense word pairs than in the sense/nonsense word pairs in /b-v/, G2 subjects registered more errors in both the sense and nonsense word pairs in /r-l/, and G5 subjects registered more errors in the sense word pairs in /b-v/. However, chi-squared analyses showed that none of the differences was significant at the .05 level.

By contrast, the least errors were made in the sense word pairs, although the difference was significant statistically only in the case of /b-v/. However, in cases where more errors were registered in the sense than in the other pairs, the differences were not significant. This seems to suggest, at least in the /b-v/ contrast, that with knowledge of the words, the subject makes fewer errors than otherwise, i.e. he seems to discriminate more on the basis of the phonological difference itself than on the knowledge of the words when he knows either both words or neither.

Next, we analyzed the types of errors made in the sense and nonsense pairs to see whether there was any difference in those pairs which were marked as known and those marked unknown by the subjects. We found that in the sense word pairs there was a significant tendency for subjects to perceive the sound which exists in the native language as the sound which does not; the subjects seemed to be making overgeneralization errors in the sense word pairs. On the other hand, in the case of the nonsense word pairs, a substantial increase could be noted in errors where the subjects perceived the 'foreign' sound in terms of their native sound. This seems to reflect an increased tendency for transfer errors and a decrease for overgeneralization errors, thus making the differences between error types insignificant.

We observed this tendency in the case of the /r-l/ pairs where neither /r/ nor /l/ actually exists in Japanese. The Japanese subjects seemed to be hearing the Japanese /r/ as being closer to the English /l/ than /r/. However, chi-squared analysis of the individual groups reveals that the spread in /r/ and /l/ errors was not as significant in the case of the /r-l/ pairs as in the other pairs, suggesting that there were students who tended to hear the Japanese /r/ as English /r/ as well.

The only exceptions in this analysis were that G1 subjects tended to make overgeneralization errors in both sense and nonsense pairs in the /b-v/ and /s-θ/ pairs, and that G6 subjects tended to make more errors in perceiving /r/ as /l/ in the sense pairs and /l/ as /r/ in the nonsense pairs. However, the differences in these cases were not significant. It might be suggested, nevertheless, that the G1 subjects have acquired the English phonological system to the extent that knowledge of vocabulary does not influence their perception of the sounds. In other words, they were able, at least in the case of the /b-v/ and /s-θ/ pairs, to discriminate the words solely on the basis of the phonology, regardless of knowledge they might have had of the vocabulary items themselves.

Let us summarize the results thus far. (1) The /r-l/ discrimination is most difficult; the /s-θ/ discrimination tends to be the easiest. (2) Knowledge of the vocabulary items affects phonological perception. Errors in the sense/nonsense pairs were the highest in almost all cases. (3) Overgeneralization errors occur more often when the subject has knowledge of both test words, while there is an increase in transfer errors when neither word is known to the subject. (4) The greater the subject's knowledge of English phonology, the more overgeneralization errors he makes.

Let us briefly go back to the problem of /b-v/. It is curious that there were so many errors in a phonological pair which should, theoretically, have been just as easy as /s-θ/--in both cases one member of the pair actually exists in the subjects' native language while the other does not. As was seen earlier, the error rate in /b-v/ turned out to be higher than in /s-θ/ and almost as high as in /r-l/.

It turns out that although we originally constructed the material so that one-third of the test pairs were sense word pairs, one-third nonsense word pairs, and one-third sense/nonsense word pairs, the subjects thought differently. Far fewer sense word pairs were selected in /b-v/ than in /r-l/, and fewer also than in /s-θ/ (significant at the .05 level).

As a correlate, more sense/nonsense pairs were selected in /b-v/ than in either /r-l/ or /s-θ/, if we consider the chi-squared analyses of the individual groups.

The foregoing results suggest that knowledge of the vocabulary items used in the test materials might have been one reason why there were so many errors in /b-v/. It will be remembered that the lowest error rates occurred in the sense pairs, and the highest error rates in the sense/nonsense pairs. Therefore, since the contrast /b-v/ had the fewest sense pairs and the most sense/nonsense pairs, the probability of overall errors was higher than in the other two cases. This also shows that some knowledge of the vocabulary item itself greatly influences the phonological perception of the word.

It seems, therefore, that the vocabulary items used in the /b-v/ test were more difficult than in the other tests, and this, rather than a difference in the phonological nature of the words in itself, could explain the many errors in the /b-v/ pairs.

This vocabulary difficulty was further confirmed when we compared our original material with the test persons' subjective judgments as to which words were actual English words. More errors were made in the items included in the /b-v/ test than in the other tests, and the errors in /b-v/ showed significant differences when compared with errors in the /r-l/ and /s-θ/ tests. The words used in the /b-v/ test, it seems, actually were more difficult.

Discussion. On the basis of these results let us now reconsider our original hypothesis.

We had hypothesized that there should be differences in the types of errors made by Japanese learners of English, depending on the learner's acquisition stage. The results confirmed this. When a subject knew the word used, his perception was based more on the sound existing in English but not in Japanese than when he did not know the word; whereas, when he did not know the word, his errors were influenced more by the sound existing in Japanese than when he did.

Taylor (1975) and Yoshida (1981) suggested that the first type of structural errors made in learning a second or foreign language would most probably be transfer errors because the learner can refer only to the structure of his native language at the beginning of learning. The same principle seems to apply in the case of perceptual acquisition of phonology as well. Although we could not definitely conclude that transfer errors occur before overgeneralization errors, the fact that overgeneralization errors occurred more often after the subject had learned the English word, while there was a rise in the incidence of transfer errors in cases where the words were unknown to the subjects, would suggest such a sequence.

Whether the influence of knowledge of vocabulary comes before overgeneralization errors can be assessed from the fact that G1 subjects made overgeneralization errors in both sense and nonsense pairs, whether they knew the words or not. That is, the perception of the phonological distinction was not

influenced by their knowledge of the words. Even the G1 subjects, however, showed transfer and overgeneralization tendencies in the /r-l/ pairs, although this was statistically insignificant, suggesting that in the more difficult pairs, their judgment
may somehow be influenced by whether or not they know the
words in question. It seems, then, that overgeneralization
errors occur at the phonological level where knowledge of
vocabulary and other considerations do not interfere with the
judgment of phonological discrimination.

The effect of knowledge of vocabulary on phonological discrimination was a very important factor in judging a learner's
stage of phonology acquisition. Our previous discussion of
the /b-v/ contrast suggested that the difficulty of vocabulary
could have been the most important factor in the differences
with the other tests. To confirm this, we checked a popular
English pocket dictionary prepared especially for high school
students studying for college entrance examinations[1] and found
that of the 18 actual English words which we had included in
the /b-v/ test, three words--*verb, ballad,* and *vest*--had no
dictionary entry. On the other hand, all the words used in
the /s-θ/ test were listed in the dictionary, as were all those
used in the /r-l/ test except *wrist*. We further examined the
Ministry of Education guidelines for junior high school textbooks and found that only three words--*very, village,* and
visit--were listed under *v* in the list of required vocabulary
items, while there were 46 under *b*, 17 under *r*, 26 under *l*,
75 under *s*, and 25 under *th* (of which 11 were /θ/).

This all seems to suggest that the vocabulary items in /b-v/
were, in fact, more difficult than those in the other pairs,
making it very plausible that the differences in errors between
/b-v/ and the other test pairs were due to knowledge of
vocabulary rather than to pure phonological factors.

This is not to exclude the possibility that for Japanese
speakers /b-v/ is in fact more difficult phonologically than
/s-θ/. Perhaps the results were influenced by our experimental procedure itself: had we changed the order of presentation or added a pretest practice session, the results might
have come out differently. However, since knowledge of
vocabulary influenced the perception of the phonemes in all
three tests, difficulty in vocabulary items can be considered
a major factor in explaining the significantly different test
results for /b-v/ word pairs over the other test pairs.

Conclusion. In our experiment we tested the hypothesis
that there are four stages through which a Japanese learner
of English has to pass in order to attain mastery in the perception of English phonology. In the first stage, transfer
errors were most frequent; in the second, knowledge of
vocabulary influenced the perception of phonology; in the
third stage, overgeneralization errors predominated; and by

the fourth and final stage, the phonological system was finally in place as an independent system in itself.

The results also showed that in sense word pairs, i.e. where some sort of knowledge of the vocabulary was available to the subjects, overgeneralization errors predominated. In the case of /r-l/, where neither the /r/ nor the /l/ actually exists in Japanese, the difference between the two was not as significant as in the other phoneme pairs. However, more /l/-initial words were mistaken as /r/ words than the other way round, suggesting that, to the Japanese, /r/ was closer in perception to the English /l/. In the case of the nonsense word pairs, transfer errors increased in almost all cases, supporting the hypothesis that when the words are unknown to the learner, he tends to make more transfer errors than at a later stage when he has better knowledge of the vocabulary of the language in question. Knowledge of vocabulary plays an important role in the perception of phonological differences. Before the subject is able to make judgments on purely phonological evidence, knowledge of vocabulary influences his perception of phonology.

Beyond these specific results, our experiment also supports Corder's (1981) view of the objective of error analysis as a way to assess a learner's state and strategies of second or foreign language acquisition.

To use Krashen's (1981) theory of the monitor, we can posit the following 'learning' stages for the Japanese students' perceptual acquisition of English phonology. The Japanese learner must first go through a stage of transfer; then, as he gradually comes to know the words in English, he associates the individual words with the sounds he hears. Only after he has had enough exposure to a number of English words with a certain phoneme does he begin to dissociate meaning from the sound of the word. This is when he begins to overgeneralize and hears everything on the basis of the foreign sound, even when the actual sound presented to him is a sound which exists in his native language. Only after this stage does the learner finally acquire English phonology as an independent system.

APPENDIX

The test pairs for /b-v/, /r-l/, and s-θ/.

/b-v/		/r-l/		/s-θ/	
1. boce	voce	rund	lund	sersday	Thursday
2. bigger	vigor	ruk	look	soob	thoob
3. baif	vaif	wrist	list	sing	thing
4. beng	veng	rayst	layst	soup	thoup
5. berb	verb	remp	lemp	some	thumb
6. ballad	valid	right	light	seed	theed
7. buff	vuff	runch	lunch	seem	theme
8. bizit	visit	runk	lunk	scissors	thizors
9. borry	vorry	read	lead	serm	therm
10. base	vase	rike	like	sick	thick
11. bean	vean	ripe	laip	sep	thep
12. bone	vone	ronn	lonn	saz	thaz
13. boosh	voosh	rock	lock	sout	thout
14. berry	very	run	lun	sank	thank
15. berse	verse	red	lead	seef	thief
16. back	vak	wrong	long	serd	third
17. best	vest	rouk	louk	sife	thaif
18. boat	vote	roast	loaste	sink	think

NOTES

This research was funded by a grant in aid for scientific research (project number 00445043) from the Japanese Ministry of Education.

For precise tabulations and figures supporting this research, contact the authors at Sophia University, Kioi-cho, Chiyoda-ku, Tokyo, Japan.
   1. Cf. Y. Akao, ed. (1975). Fundamental English words and phrases. Tokyo: Obunsha.

REFERENCES

Barton, David. 1976. Phonemic discrimination and the knowledge of words in children under three years. Papers and reports on child language development 11.61-68.
Barton, David. 1978. The discrimination of minimally different pairs of real words by children aged 2;3 to 2;11. In: The development of communication. Edited by N. Waterson and C. Snow. New York: John Wiley.
Corder, S. Pit. 1974. Error analysis. In: Techniques in applied linguistics. Edited by J. Allen and S. P. Corder. London: Oxford.

Corder, S. Pit. 1981. Error analysis and interlanguage. London: Oxford.

Dulay, Heidi, and Marina K. Burt. 1974. A new perspective on the creative construction process in child second language acquisition. Language Learning 24.2:253-278.

Krashen, Stephen D. 1981. Second language acquisition and second language learning. Oxford: Pergamon.

Lado, Robert. 1957. Linguistics across cultures. Ann Arbor: University of Michigan.

McLaughlin, Barry. 1978. Second language acquisition in childhood. Hillsdale, N.J.: Erlbaum.

Richards, Jack C. 1971. A non-contrastive approach to error analysis. English Language Teaching 25.3:204-219.

Selinker, Larry. 1972. Interlanguage. IRAL 10.2:209-232.

Taylor, Barry. 1975. The use of overgeneralization and transfer learning strategies by elementary and intermediate students in ESL. Language Learning 25.1:73-107.

Yoshida, Kensaku. 1981. The use of error analysis in the foreign language classroom. Bulletin of the faculty of foreign language and studies, Sophia University 17.111-127.

ASK AND IT SHALL BE GIVEN UNTO YOU: CHILDREN'S REQUESTS

Susan Ervin-Tripp
University of California, Berkeley

Introduction. 'Ask and it shall be given unto you'.
Infants start seeking help from others before they are a
year old. Like chimpanzees, they reach out to what they
want. Then they reach while looking at you. In this way
they point out two complements at once: the goal, and the
agent or instrument for achieving it.

How do children progress from primitive means to the diversity of adult speech? The children we have been studying are
successful about half the time in getting what they want. How
do they learn to succeed? If I say 'It's already noon', I can
get adults to go to lunch. If I say 'I'm not through yet', I
can stop you. Yet neither time am I talking about leaving or
not leaving. This subtlety is characteristic of adult speech.

To get a request across, one must be able to do five things:
(a) get attention; (b) express clearly what is wrong or what
is wanted; (c) keep on good terms with the addressee, to
get cooperation; (d) be persuasive; (e) remedy failures.

Attention. For children, the first problem is to get the
attention of others. It may not seem so, since they always
seem to be interrupting. But that very fact is a symptom of
the difficulty involved.

How does one know when it is appropriate to interrupt? One
must be able to recognize when the standing questions have
been answered, when the topic has been resolved. Since a
young child cannot do this, jumping into a conversation,
especially one among adults, is very difficult to do well.

For several years David Gordon and I have been studying
requests in naturalistic videotapes taken in four families. We
found that when other people were talking, 89 percent of the
time the two-year-olds simply blurted out requests. But only
31 percent of the school-age youngsters did that. The older

children not only tried to get attention more often, but they used more effective attention getters, e.g. calling out 'Hey Joe' instead of just 'hey'.

But the youngest children remained with an insurmountable problem of inferior status. At every level of relevance, their interruptions were more often ignored (Ervin-Tripp 1979).

Clarity. Even when one succeeds in getting attention, one needs to be clear about what is wanted. Children's first requests seem to express pretty directly when their attention is fixed, and they are clear because they are accompanied by gestures. These early requests include negatives or prohibitions, vocatives which foreground the agent, goal objects and states like *more juice* and *up*, problem statements like *it's stuck*, claims to possession like *that's mine*, and imperatives which focus on means. Ambiguity or lack of clarity becomes more of a problem as children begin to talk of absent objects, and as they become more devious in later years.

The delicate issue of balance between clarity and an ambiguity that leaves the listener options has not yet arisen. It is this problem that teenagers later solve by trying to have it both ways, as in (1).

(1) We haven't gotten our allowances yet. Hint hint.

Politeness. By the third year, differences that are socially based begin to emerge. First, the children recognize a right on their part to receive help. In the case of expectable rights, children do not provide politeness markings. When they expect cooperation, they use the normal form I have described.

Mothers (and later, nursery school teachers) are told about problems.

(2) (4.3 to mother:) This won't stick.
(3) (To nursery school teacher:) Jean, we didn't have a snack.
(4) (To teacher:) Jason's trying to take my stuff.

Mothers and teachers are told what the child wants or needs, and are given blunt imperatives. In our texts, 90 percent of the requests to the mothers by two- and three-year-olds had no polite markers of any sort.

Fathers are treated somewhat differently. They receive significantly fewer imperatives than mothers. We think this may be because they serve the children less often. In the following example (from Lawson 1967), the same request is made differently to mother and to father.

(5) (Child (2) to mother:)   'Mommy, I want milk'
    (Child (2) to father:)
    What's that?   'Milk'
    My milk, Daddy.   'Yes, it's your milk.'
    Daddy, yours. Yours   'OK, it's mine.'
      Daddy? Ok, yours.
    It's milk, Daddy.   'Yes, it is.'
    You want milk, Daddy? 'I have some, thank you.'
    Milk in there, Daddy? 'Yes.'
    Daddy, I want some, please?
    Please, Daddy, huh?

In this example, the politeness markers used are *please, OK*, and the repeated naming of the father. And, of course, there is the long, devious build-up.

In role play, Andersen (1977) found children represented the mothers as being given more imperatives both by their children and by their husbands. And Hollos and Beeman (1978), who studied elicited requests in Norway, commented that though Norwegian children generally favored indirectness, with the mothers they were not only direct but even rude. They pointed out that mother-child interaction is the wrong place in which to look for children's social discrimination.

Researchers in our data received 60 percent polite conventional requests from the two- and three-year-olds. This exemplifies the general pattern of treating outsiders differently. The simplest forms, such as *please*, are used by the two-year-olds. By nursery school much more complex imbedded polite forms appear, as shown in (6).

(6) (Nursery school child (5.5) to adult visitor:)
    Do you think you could put your foot right there?
      (B. A. O'Connell)

We believe one reason for the special treatment of 'visitors' is that one cannot assume their cooperation.

A second general case leading to use of conventional polite forms is the 'request for the goods of another'. The only instances of two- and three-year-olds' polite speech to the mother involved possessions. When two- or three-year-olds wanted a younger sibling's toys, they chose polite forms 44 percent of the time; in other cases, 9 percent of the time.

A common choice in this case is the permission request, as in the 'Can I' frame, shown in (7).

(7) (Nursery school child to peer:) Can I have one of the
    reds (wheedling tone)? (B. A. O'Connell)

A request that presumes on any territory of the addressee gets a conventional polite form, as example (8) illustrates.

(8) (Four-year-old to sister, age two and a half;)
Addie, why don't you show Gina what you **wore**. OK?

Telling his sister what to show another is presumably not his
right, but an adult's right.

Our argument here is that the simple polite markers we see
at first, such as *please, can you, can I,* and *d'you wanna,*
are not just markers of status of the addressee. Instead,
what they seem to indicate is that the child separates these
cases of presupposed, presumed cooperation from the cases
where compliance cannot be assumed.

Among the two-year-olds, the doubtful cases include fathers
who do not usually supply food, outsiders who do not attend
to one's needs, and owners who do not have to give up their
property. What we have seen, then, is that even at two years
of age, children have a sense of their rights. Often this is
articulated explicitly.

(9) (Brother to sister:)   Carrie, stop sucking your fingers.
    (Sister to brother:)   David, you're not the boss of me.
    (A. Rogers)

All of this seems very familiar. In a parallel case of adult
requests, it was found that in waitresses' speech *please* is more
often used in those requests to cooks which are beyond their
normal duties (Ervin-Tripp 1976).

It is commonly said that in adult speech imperatives are used
to inferiors. A better description is that imperatives and other
direct forms occur whenever cooperation can be assumed. This
includes joint tasks. It includes presumed rights, for instance,
the right to one's own property when it is taken by a peer or
subordinate.

Conversely, the special markings we call polite are brought
into play whenever cooperation cannot be assumed, be it because the other is more powerful or because the other has
rights over the goods involved.

I have called this issue 'keeping on good terms' because the
children seem to recognize the incursion that these demands
make in cases where cooperation cannot be assumed.

School-age children add some new dimensions to this sensitivity. They take into account the trajectory of action of the
addressee. For specially difficult tasks, or for disruption of
ongoing activity or conversations, they add polite features.

(10) To peer in nursery school:
     Kyle, would you tie this right here?

We found the youngest children were sensitive to addressee
status and possession rights. The last features to be learned
were just those that took the most imagination about the
perspective of the other. By five to eight years of age,

children were polite in only 12 percent of those cases where the listener was already cooperating; but in 54 percent of cases where the activity proposed would interrupt the listener. Imperatives decreased from 60 percent to 27 percent under these conditions of interruption. This seems to be a clear case of the growth of social perspective-taking.

Deference vs. persuasion. One could argue that the kinds of conventional politeness just cited are aspects of being persuasive. Yet the evidence on this point is ambiguous. For instance, on second tries after refusals, children become less polite. In one study in nursery schools by Wood and Gardner (1980), it was found that children used conventional politeness much more frequently to dominant partners. In pairings of equals, requests that were more polite were more successful. But in family data, where the speakers tend to differ in age and rank, our findings were quite different. We were surprised to see that the most polite requests were the least successful. And when the different levels of 'cost' were controlled according to rights, intrusion, and so on, no significant advantage to being polite was noted, except that adults ignored the children less. From the point of view of family experience, politeness is learned from modeling, not from the reinforcement of efficacy (Ervin-Tripp, O'Connor, and Rosenberg 1982).

Table 1. Adults' responses to polite and nonpolite control forms.

	Ignore	Refuse	Comply	N
Polite form	.04%*	.50%	.46%	80
Nonpolite form	120*	.43	.36	168

*Difference p   .001
Polite: Polite questions, permission forms, explanations or justifications, implicit questions or statements, or consequences.
Nonpolite: Imperatives, cries, gestures, ellipsis, *I want, I need*.

The role-playing data clearly show that children regard these formal contrasts as a way to identify social rights. They used both the frequency of directives and the percentage of direct blunt forms to identify superior status, e.g. parent vs. child, doctor vs. nurse, father vs. mother. This seems to show that, beyond any attempt to be persuasive, such forms may have acquired a symbolism of deference (Andersen 1977; Mitchell-Kernan and Kernan 1977).

Are these politeness forms merely arbitrary markers or do they have any semantic content? Clearly, some, such as *please,* are formal markers. Eventually, this becomes an urgency indicator when combined with aggravated voice.

(11) Give it to me please!

But many of the formal politeness markers are analyzable, and have to do with the reasons for refusals, as (12) through (14) show.

(12) I can't help, I'm busy.
vs. Can you help?

(13) I don't want to.
vs. Do you wanna?

(14) You can't go out, it's too cold.
vs. Can I go out?

Probably most of the cases of use of these forms are idiomatic routines. But their continued survival in unreduced forms suggests that sometimes speakers attend to their literal meanings. Garvey (1975) has shown that nursery school children's excuses have the same semantic range as their requests--dealing with features of willingness, ability or permission, and reasons and rights.

Indirectness. Eventually, speakers rely on shared knowledge for clarity. Consequently, this type of indirect request is most frequent with adults, particularly people who have worked or lived together for a long time, and are compatible. To be explicit in these situations, even when politely so, seems rude, since it could imply that the other person does not know what is going on. Typically, the content of these types of indirect requests can refer to an expected obstacle or provide a reminder, such as it's noon. In adult speech, they can even be couched as jokes about obstacles or inaction, as in (15) and (16).

(15) (To someone blocking passage through a door:)
You make a fine door, Sal.

(16) (To someone who has not passed the menus around the table:)
Are you collecting those?

We have seen that even two-year-olds speaking to adults often focus their attention on obstacles rather than specifying means. Thus their utterances may seem indirect. Later, we find them making corrections or calling attention to norm violations, as in (17) and (18), spoken by a four-year-old.

(17) No, I said THREE spoonfuls.
(18) That doesn't go there, it goes THERE.

Preschool children can do a great deal of effective organizing of each other's actions through structuring games. *Pretend that's our car* can accomplish a shift in rights, just as *I'm the mommy and you're the baby* can give the speaker prerogatives to order. Consequently, many of the control moves of children make use of the normal trajectory of this play and do not require explicit formulation. That is, the children draw on prior shared knowledge.

In school-age children, less explicitness occurs on the second or third round of requests when children expect the addressee to be awaiting a request. In these cases, inexplicitness or indirecteness is based on shared knowledge and seems a kind of economy.

We have found that, by the age of seven or eight, children resort to the indirectness of adults. This development seems to be social in origin. Requests are addressed to the partner's 'point of view' and leave him options. In one experiment children were asked to obtain marker pens or letters from adult strangers who were busy and give them to their parents. We meanwhile observed how the children who were either younger or older than seven years of age (that is, before or after second grade) framed their requests (Gordon, Budwig, Strage, and Carrell 1980).

The indirect speech of the younger children included the examples given in (19) through (21).

(19) I need a blue marker.
(20) Where's the marker?
(21) The marker's broken. I need a new one.

The older children focused on obstacles, as adults do. Theoretically, this focus allows the listener to deny the request gracefully. Or they displaced responsibility and hence did not seem to be demanding.

(22) Are there any more markers?
(23) Do you have a green marker I could use?
(24) She told me to get a letter for my parents.

By the time a child reaches teenage, these forms can be combined in complicated ways to deal with uncomfortable situations. In example (25), a 12-year-old was a guest in the household of friends of her parents.

(25) Do you have any water I could drink?

In this case, an explicitly polite permission request, *Can I drink water?* is embedded in an obstacle question which seems a little odd since it has no realistic foundation: *Do you have*

any water? By avoiding commitment for the person who will
get the water, and by displacing to the conditional, an even
more delicate politeness is achieved.

Thus, our data does not reveal such indirectness, which is
socially based on taking the perspective of the hearer, until
around the third grade. We may find, however, that there is
a good deal of cultural variation in encouraging children to
avoid explicitness. For instance, Hollos and Beeman (1978)
found that four- and five-year-old Norwegian children would
use their mothers as intermediaries to strangers, whereas the
nine- to ten-year-olds, like the older children in our own
study, could say to a store keeper *Have you chocolates?* or to
a neighbor *That cake is very good* when they wanted some.

Persuasion. To be persuasive is the fourth requirement.
We found that two- and three-year-olds give justifications for
the specific request in only 6 percent of their control moves.
The older children added them to 14 percent of theirs. For
the older children justifications, to some extent, seemed to replace the formal polite rituals since they decreased. In Garvey's study of requests between four- and five-year-olds,
justifications outnumbered polite forms almost two to one. This
change suggests that a justified specific request is believed to
be legitimate and its social cost goes down.

There is an important cognitive basis for this rise in justifications. Around the age of three, we see children begin to
'question' adult refusals and directives with *why?* (DeCastros
Campos and DeLemos 1979), and then supply explanations or
justifications for adult refusals and directives with *because*.
Eventually, the children justify their own moves. But this
history shows that justifying starts in the child's search for
rationality in the moves of others. This in turn may be derived from adult modeling of justifications. If so, a good deal
of social variation, depending on adult customs, would be expected.

The first cases of a high use of justification are in instances
when the child is trying to stop another's activity. Here, the
context does not supply a clear reason for compliance, and the
child may be asking for a favor. The kinds of explanations
may refer to rights, or to reasons. Reasons are intensified
on second tries, in order to persuade.

These justifications are reasonably oriented to the child's
view of social rights. For example, *I want it* or *I need it* are
common on second tries. They seem to be viewed by children
as self-contained and sufficient explanations, as are the wants
of others. Four-year-old Tommy loved to see the sprinklers
turned on and kept on trying to get everyone 'off camera' to
see them, as shown in (26).

(26) (Tommy to mother:) Well Gina wants to see the
sprinklers, don't you Gina?

Example (27) quotes another, older child's threat to his mother.

(27) If you don't give it to me now, I won't want it later.

Thus, the mother is seen as motivated to answer the child's wants.

The reasons supplied by the time the children are four are already oriented to the expected addressee roles. To an adult, the child would use supporting information that evoked the caregiver role as in (28) and (29).

(28) (Beth, 5, to mother:) Mommy, I want you to open all of them, the paint, so I won't have to have trouble.

(29) (Lisa, 4, to researcher:) OK, we don't know all these pages, so you read 'em.

The statement of contrast in abilities seemed enough of a justification to mitigate the request to adults.

For younger speakers, on the other hand, the emphasis was on rights, norms, or facts. The children seemed to socialize the younger partners.

(30) (Age 4 to age 2:) Get out of my space. This is my space.

(31) (Age 8 to age 4:) We only have a little more, OK? So don't use one on every Valentine.

Eventually, older speakers have learned to use the justifications or preconditions alone as requests.

Indirectness is part of the system of keeping on good terms, not part of the art of persuasion. Yet at the same time that questioning obstacles appears, we find the development of much more artful persuasion. By reframing activities the persuader accommodates to the purposes and viewpoint of the hearer. Examples (32) and (33) are paraphrases of events which were not tape-recorded, in which an eight-year-old seeks to influence her four-year-old brother:

(32) (Sister to brother:) D'ya wanna be Santa Claus? Here, take these toys to the basement. (She packs her laundry in her nightgown and he carries it downstairs.)

In example (33), the boy had been becoming increasingly whiny because he wanted his tricycle to be taken along in a station wagon overloaded with bicycles for a family bike trip. He was wearing a Batman cape.

(33) (Sister to brother:) Batman, you don't need a bike.
You can _fly_ over everyone faster than the bikes! (He
accepted.)

On both occasions, the request is disguised as a proposal
for play in which the boy has a desirable role. This method
both accommodates to his perspective and is drawn from
strategies normally used by children among themselves, such
as 'pretends'. Reframing is a method which makes cooperation
flow out of the natural trajectory of the new activity. It is
successful if one takes into account the recipient's motives
and if the recipient feels cooperative.

Summary. Our studies have shown that children can _appear_
indirect at any age. But at first the basis is attentional focus.
Only by mid childhood does deliberate deviousness come to the
fore.
We have found that by the age of two or three, children have
some sense of rights and obligations. They make direct and
simple requests when they have a right to cooperation. But
they make conventionally polite requests when they think they
do not have such a right.
By four years of age or a little earlier, we find children making this reasoning explicit. They call on rights, norms, and
reasons for action when trying to persuade. It is not until
age eight or older that we find children able to understand well
the perspective of the listener. They question the obstacles
to the listener as an available excuse, to save the listener's
face in refusing. Conventionally polite forms become relatively
less important then, being reserved for cases where explicitness is necessary. Their artful persuasion can reframe the
request in terms desirable to the hearer.
We have argued that persuasion to act and the control of
social relations are not identical. Persuasion has to do with
manipulating activity contexts or bringing to mind needs,
rights, norms, threats, and promises related to the desired
act. The control of social relations is done through two
mechanisms: at first, by the use of conventional polite forms,
and later, in mid childhood, going 'off record' and considering
the addressee's point of view. While the data base from which
we have worked is European and American, we suspect that
some of the developmental limitations will prove universal.

NOTE

Work on this project has been funded by Grants MH-26063
and NSF-BNS-7826539. The data collection and analysis owe
a great deal to David Paul Gordon, M. Catherine O'Connor,
Jarrett Rosenberg, Georgette Stratos, Ruth Bennett, Julie
Gerhardt, Miriam Petruck, and Iskander Savasir.

REFERENCES

Andersen, Elaine. 1977. Learning to speak with style. Unpublished doctoral dissertation. Stanford University.

DeCastro Campos, Maria F., and Claudia DeLemos. 1979. Pragmatic routes and the development of 'causal' expressions. Wassenaar, Netherlands, Child language seminar.

Ervin-Tripp, Susan. 1976. Is Sybil there? The structure of some American English directives. Language in Society 5.25-66.

Ervin-Tripp, Susan. 1979. Turn-taking in children's conversations. In: Developmental pragmatics. Edited by Elinor Ochs and Bambi Schieffelin. New York: Academic Press.

Ervin-Tripp, Susan, Mary Catherine O'Connor, and Jarrett Rosenberg. 1982. Language and power in the family. In: Language and power. Edited by Cheris Kramerae and Muriel Schulz. Urbana-Champaign: University of Illinois Press.

Ervin-Tripp, Susan, and David Paul Gordon. (in press) The development of requests. In: Communicative competence: Acquisition and intervention. Edited by R. E. Schiefelbusch. Baltimore: University Park Press.

Garvey, Catherine. 1975. Requests and responses in children's speech. Journal of Child Language 2.41-63.

Gordon, David, Nancy Budwig, Amy Strage, and Patricia Carrell. 1980. Children's requests to unfamiliar adults: Form, social functions, age variation. 1980 Boston Conference in Language Development, October.

Hollos, Marida, and William Beeman. 1978. The development of directives among Norwegian and Hungarian children: An example of communicative style in culture. Language in Society 7.345-356.

Lawson, Craig. 1967. Request patterns in a two-year-old. Unpublished MS. Berkeley, Calif.

Mitchell-Kernan, Claudia, and Keith Kernan. 1977. Pragmatics of directive choice among children. In: Child discourse. Edited by C. Mitchell-Kernan and S. M. Ervin-Tripp. New York: Academic Press.

Wood, Barbara, and Royce Gardner. 1980. How children 'get their way': Directives in communication. Communication Education 29.264-272.